Big Data for Chimps

Philip Kromer and Russell Jurney

Beijing · Boston · Farnham · Sebastopol · Tokyo

Big Data for Chimps

by Philip Kromer and Russell Jurney

Printed in the United States of America.

Published by O'Reilly Media, Inc., 1005 Gravenstein Highway North, Sebastopol, CA 95472.

O'Reilly books may be purchased for educational, business, or sales promotional use. Online editions are also available for most titles (*http://safaribooksonline.com*). For more information, contact our corporate/institutional sales department: 800-998-9938 or *corporate@oreilly.com*.

Acquisitions Editor: Mike Loukides	**Indexer:** Wendy Catalano
Editors: Meghan Blanchette and Amy Jollymore	**Interior Designer:** David Futato
Production Editor: Matthew Hacker	**Cover Designer:** Ellie Volckhausen
Copyeditor: Jasmine Kwityn	**Illustrator:** Rebecca Demarest
Proofreader: Rachel Monaghan	

October 2015:   First Edition

Revision History for the First Edition

2015-09-25:   First Release

See *http://oreilly.com/catalog/errata.csp?isbn=9781491923948* for release details.

978-1-491-92394-8

[LSI]

Table of Contents

Preface

Big Data for Chimps will explain a practical, actionable view of big data. This view will be centered on tested best practices as well as give readers street-fighting smarts with Hadoop.

Readers will come away with a useful, conceptual idea of big data. Insight is data in context. The key to understanding big data is scalability: infinite amounts of data can rest upon distinct pivot points. We will teach you how to manipulate data about these pivot points.

Finally, the book will contain examples with real data and real problems that will bring the concepts and applications for business to life.

What This Book Covers

Big Data for Chimps shows you how to solve important problems in large-scale data processing using simple, fun, and elegant tools.

Finding patterns in massive event streams is an important, hard problem. Most of the time, there aren't earthquakes—but the patterns that will let you predict one in advance lie within the data from those quiet periods. How do you compare the trillions of subsequences in billions of events, each to each other, to find the very few that matter? Once you have those patterns, how do you react to them in real time?

We've chosen case studies anyone can understand, and that are general enough to apply to whatever problems you're looking to solve. Our goal is to provide you with the following:

- The ability to think at scale--equipping you with a deep understanding of how to break a problem into efficient data transformations, and of how data must flow through the cluster to effect those transformations

- Detailed example programs applying Hadoop to interesting problems in context
- Advice and best practices for efficient software development

All of the examples use real data, and describe patterns found in many problem domains, as you:

- Create statistical summaries
- Identify patterns and groups in the data
- Search, filter, and herd records in bulk

The emphasis on simplicity and fun should make this book especially appealing to beginners, but this is not an approach you'll outgrow. We've found it's the most powerful and valuable approach for creative analytics. One of our maxims is "robots are cheap, humans are important": write readable, scalable code now and find out later whether you want a smaller cluster. The code you see is adapted from programs we write at Infochimps and Data Syndrome to solve enterprise-scale business problems, and these simple high-level transformations meet our needs.

Many of the chapters include exercises. If you're a beginning user, we highly recommend you work through at least one exercise from each chapter. Deep learning will come less from having the book in front of you as you *read* it than from having the book next to you while you *write* code inspired by it. There are sample solutions and result datasets on the book's website.

Who This Book Is For

We'd like for you to be familiar with at least one programming language, but it doesn't have to be Python or Pig. Familiarity with SQL will help a bit, but isn't essential. Some exposure to working with data in a business intelligence or analysis background will be helpful.

Most importantly, you should have an actual project in mind that requires a big-data toolkit to solve—a problem that requires scaling out across multiple machines. If you don't already have a project in mind but really want to learn about the big-data toolkit, take a look at Chapter 3, which uses baseball data. It makes a great dataset for fun exploration.

Who This Book Is Not For

This is not *Hadoop: The Definitive Guide* (that's already been written, and well); this is more like *Hadoop: A Highly Opinionated Guide*. The only coverage of how to use the bare Hadoop API is to say, "in most cases, don't." We recommend storing your data in one of several highly space-inefficient formats and in many other ways encourage you to willingly trade a small performance hit for a large increase in programmer joy. The book has a relentless emphasis on writing scalable code, but no content on writing performant code beyond the advice that the best path to a 2x speedup is to launch twice as many machines.

That is because for almost everyone, the cost of the cluster is far less than the opportunity cost of the data scientists using it. If you have not just big data but huge data (let's say somewhere north of 100 terabytes), then you will need to make different trade-offs for jobs that you expect to run repeatedly in production. However, even at petabyte scale, you will still develop in the manner we outline.

The book does include some information on provisioning and deploying Hadoop, and on a few important settings. But it does not cover advanced algorithms, operations, or tuning in any real depth.

What This Book Does Not Cover

We are not currently planning to cover Hive. The Pig scripts will translate naturally for folks who are already familiar with it.

This book picks up where the Internet leaves off. We're not going to spend any real time on information well covered by basic tutorials and core documentation. Other things we do not plan to include:

- Installing or maintaining Hadoop.
- Other MapReduce-like platforms (Disco, Spark, etc.) or other frameworks (Wukong, Scalding, Cascading).
- At a few points, we'll use Unix text utils (cut/wc/etc.), but only as tools for an immediate purpose. We can't justify going deep into any of them; there are whole O'Reilly books covering these utilities.

Theory: Chimpanzee and Elephant

Starting with Chapter 2, you'll meet the zealous members of the Chimpanzee and Elephant Company. Elephants have prodigious memories and move large, heavy volumes with ease. They'll give you a physical analogue for using relationships to assemble data into context, and help you understand what's easy and what's hard in moving around massive amounts of data. Chimpanzees are clever but can only think about one thing at a time. They'll show you how to write simple transformations with a single concern and how to analyze petabytes of data with no more than megabytes of working space.

Together, they'll equip you with a physical metaphor for how to work with data at scale.

Practice: Hadoop

In Doug Cutting's words, Hadoop is the "kernel of the big-data operating system." It is the dominant batch-processing solution, has both commercial enterprise support and a huge open source community, and runs on every platform and cloud—and there are no signs any of that will change in the near term.

The code in this book will run unmodified on your laptop computer or on an industrial-strength Hadoop cluster. We'll provide you with a virtual Hadoop cluster using a docker that will run on your own laptop.

Example Code

You can check out the source code for the book (*https://github.com/bd4c/big_data_for_chimps-code*) using Git:

```
git clone https://github.com/bd4c/big_data_for_chimps-code
```

Once you've run this command, you'll find the code examples in the examples/ch_XX directories.

A Note on Python and MrJob

We've chosen Python for two reasons. First, it's one of several high-level languages (along with Python, Scala, R, and others) that have both excellent Hadoop frameworks and widespread support. More importantly, Python is a very readable language. The code samples provided should map cleanly to other high-level languages, and the approach we recommend is available in any language.

In particular, we've chosen the Python-language MrJob framework. It is open source and widely used.

Helpful Reading

- *Programming Pig* by Alan Gates is a more comprehensive introduction to the Pig Latin language and Pig tools. It is highly recommended.

- *Hadoop: The Definitive Guide* by Tom White is a must-have. Don't try to absorb it whole—the most powerful parts of Hadoop are its simplest parts—but you'll refer to it often as your applications reach production.

- *Hadoop Operations* by Eric Sammer—hopefully you can hand this to someone else, but the person who runs your Hadoop cluster will eventually need this guide to configuring and hardening a large production cluster.

Feedback

Contact us! If you have questions, comments, or complaints, the issue tracker (*http://bit.ly/bd4c_issues*) is the best forum for sharing those. If you'd like something more direct, email *flip@infochimps.com* and *russell.jurney@gmail.com* (your eager authors) —and you can feel free to cc: *meghan@oreilly.com* (our ever-patient editor). We're also available via Twitter:

- Flip Kromer (@mrflip)
- Russell Jurney (@rjurney)

Conventions Used in This Book

The following typographical conventions are used in this book:

Italic
> Indicates new terms, URLs, email addresses, filenames, and file extensions.

`Constant width`
> Used for program listings, as well as within paragraphs to refer to program elements such as variable or function names, databases, datatypes, environment variables, statements, and keywords.

`Constant width bold`
> Shows commands or other text that should be typed literally by the user.

`Constant width italic`
> Shows text that should be replaced with user-supplied values or by values determined by context.

 This element signifies a tip or suggestion.

 This element signifies a general note.

This element indicates a warning or caution.

Using Code Examples

Supplemental material (code examples, exercises, etc.) is available for download at *https://github.com/bd4c/big_data_for_chimps-code*.

This book is here to help you get your job done. In general, if example code is offered with this book, you may use it in your programs and documentation. You do not need to contact us for permission unless you're reproducing a significant portion of the code. For example, writing a program that uses several chunks of code from this book does not require permission. Selling or distributing a CD-ROM of examples from O'Reilly books does require permission. Answering a question by citing this book and quoting example code does not require permission. Incorporating a significant amount of example code from this book into your product's documentation does require permission.

We appreciate, but do not require, attribution. An attribution usually includes the title, author, publisher, and ISBN. For example: "*Big Data for Chimps* by Philip Kromer and Russell Jurney (O'Reilly). Copyright 2015 Philip Kromer and Russell Jurney, 978-1-491-92394-8."

If you feel your use of code examples falls outside fair use or the permission given here, feel free to contact us at *permissions@oreilly.com*.

Safari® Books Online

 *Safari Books Online* is an on-demand digital library that delivers expert content in both book and video form from the world's leading authors in technology and business.

Technology professionals, software developers, web designers, and business and creative professionals use Safari Books Online as their primary resource for research, problem solving, learning, and certification training.

Safari Books Online offers a range of plans and pricing for enterprise, government, education, and individuals.

Members have access to thousands of books, training videos, and prepublication manuscripts in one fully searchable database from publishers like O'Reilly Media, Prentice Hall Professional, Addison-Wesley Professional, Microsoft Press, Sams, Que,

Peachpit Press, Focal Press, Cisco Press, John Wiley & Sons, Syngress, Morgan Kaufmann, IBM Redbooks, Packt, Adobe Press, FT Press, Apress, Manning, New Riders, McGraw-Hill, Jones & Bartlett, Course Technology, and hundreds more. For more information about Safari Books Online, please visit us online.

How to Contact Us

Please address comments and questions concerning this book to the publisher:

O'Reilly Media, Inc.
1005 Gravenstein Highway North
Sebastopol, CA 95472
800-998-9938 (in the United States or Canada)
707-829-0515 (international or local)
707-829-0104 (fax)

We have a web page for this book, where we list errata, examples, and any additional information. You can access this page at *http://bit.ly/big_data_4_chimps*.

To comment or ask technical questions about this book, send email to *bookquestions@oreilly.com*.

For more information about our books, courses, conferences, and news, see our website at *http://www.oreilly.com*.

Find us on Facebook: *http://facebook.com/oreilly*

Follow us on Twitter: *http://twitter.com/oreillymedia*

Watch us on YouTube: *http://www.youtube.com/oreillymedia*

## PART I

Introduction: Theory and Tools

In Chapters 1–4, we'll introduce you to the basics about Hadoop and MapReduce, and to the tools you'll be using to process data at scale using Hadoop.

We'll start with an introduction to Hadoop and MapReduce, and then we'll dive into MapReduce and explain how it works. Next, we'll introduce you to our primary dataset: baseball statistics. Finally, we'll introduce you to Apache Pig, the tool we use to process data in the rest of the book.

In Part II, we'll move on to cover different analytic patterns that you can employ to process any data in any way needed.

## CHAPTER 1

Hadoop Basics

Hadoop is a large and complex beast. It can be bewildering to even begin to use the system, and so in this chapter we're going to purposefully charge through the minimum requirements for getting started with launching jobs and managing data. In this book, we will try to keep things as simple as possible. For every one of Hadoop's many modes, options, and configurations that is essential, there are many more that are distracting or even dangerous. The most important optimizations you can make come from designing efficient workflows, and even more so from knowing when to spend highly valuable programmer time to reduce compute time.

In this chapter, we will equip you with two things: the necessary mechanics of working with Hadoop, and a physical intuition for how data and computation move around the cluster during a job.

The key to mastering Hadoop is an intuitive, physical understanding of how data moves around a Hadoop cluster. Shipping data from one machine to another—even from one location on disk to another—is outrageously costly, and in the vast majority of cases, dominates the cost of your job. We'll describe at a high level how Hadoop organizes data and assigns tasks across compute nodes so that as little data as possible is set in motion; we'll accomplish this by telling a story that features a physical analogy and by following an example job through its full lifecycle. More importantly, we'll show you how to read a job's Hadoop dashboard to understand how much it cost and why. Your goal for this chapter is to take away a basic understanding of how Hadoop distributes tasks and data, and the ability to run a job and see what's going on with it. As you run more and more jobs through the remaining course of the book, it is the latter ability that will cement your intuition.

What does Hadoop do, and why should we learn about it? Hadoop enables the storage and processing of large amounts of data. Indeed, it is Apache Hadoop that stands at the middle of the big data trend. The Hadoop Distributed File System (HDFS) is the platform that enabled cheap storage of vast amounts of data (up to petabytes and beyond) using affordable, commodity machines. Before Hadoop, there simply wasn't a place to store terabytes and petabytes of data in a way that it could be easily accessed for processing. Hadoop changed everything.

Throughout this book, we will teach you the mechanics of operating Hadoop, but first you need to understand the basics of how the Hadoop filesystem and MapReduce work together to create a computing platform. Along these lines, let's kick things off by making friends with the good folks at Chimpanzee and Elephant, Inc. Their story should give you an essential physical understanding for the problems Hadoop addresses and how it solves them.

Chimpanzee and Elephant Start a Business

A few years back, two friends—JT, a gruff chimpanzee, and Nanette, a meticulous matriarch elephant—decided to start a business. As you know, chimpanzees love nothing more than sitting at keyboards processing and generating text. Elephants have a prodigious ability to store and recall information, and will carry huge amounts of cargo with great determination. This combination of skills impressed a local publishing company enough to earn their first contract, so Chimpanzee and Elephant, Incorporated (C&E for short) was born.

The publishing firm's project was to translate the works of Shakespeare into every language known to man, so JT and Nanette devised the following scheme. Their crew set up a large number of cubicles, each with one elephant-sized desk and several chimp-sized desks, and a command center where JT and Nanette could coordinate the action.

As with any high-scale system, each member of the team has a single responsibility to perform. The task of each chimpanzee is simply to read a set of passages and type out the corresponding text in a new language. JT, their foreman, efficiently assigns passages to chimpanzees, deals with absentee workers and sick days, and reports progress back to the customer. The task of each librarian elephant is to maintain a neat set of scrolls, holding either a passage to translate or some passage's translated result. Nanette serves as chief librarian. She keeps a card catalog listing, for every book, the location and essential characteristics of the various scrolls that maintain its contents.

When workers clock in for the day, they check with JT, who hands off the day's translation manual and the name of a passage to translate. Throughout the day, the chimps radio progress reports in to JT; if their assigned passage is complete, JT will specify the next passage to translate.

If you were to walk by a cubicle mid-workday, you would see a highly efficient interplay between chimpanzee and elephant, ensuring the expert translators rarely had a wasted moment. As soon as JT radios back what passage to translate next, the elephant hands it across. The chimpanzee types up the translation on a new scroll, hands it back to its librarian partner, and radios for the next passage. The librarian runs the scroll through a fax machine to send it to two of its counterparts at other cubicles, producing the redundant, triplicate copies Nanette's scheme requires.

The librarians in turn notify Nanette which copies of which translations they hold, which helps Nanette maintain her card catalog. Whenever a customer comes calling for a translated passage, Nanette fetches all three copies and ensures they are consistent. This way, the work of each monkey can be compared to ensure its integrity, and documents can still be retrieved even if a cubicle radio fails.

The fact that each chimpanzee's work is independent of any other's—no interoffice memos, no meetings, no requests for documents from other departments—made this the perfect first contract for the C&E crew. JT and Nanette, however, were cooking up a new way to put their million-chimp army to work, one that could radically streamline the processes of any modern paperful office.[1] JT and Nanette would soon have the chance of a lifetime to try it out for a customer in the far north with a big, big problem (we'll continue their story in "Chimpanzee and Elephant Save Christmas" on page 17).

Map-Only Jobs: Process Records Individually

As you'd guess, the way Chimpanzee and Elephant organize their files and workflow corresponds directly with how Hadoop handles data and computation under the hood. We can now use it to walk you through an example in detail.

The bags on trees scheme represents transactional relational database systems. These are often the systems that Hadoop data processing can augment or replace. The "NoSQL" (Not Only SQL) movement of which Hadoop is a part is about going beyond the relational database as a one-size-fits-all tool, and using different distributed systems that better suit a given problem.

Nanette is the Hadoop NameNode (*http://bit.ly/namenode*). The NameNode manages the HDFS. It stores the directory tree structure of the filesystem (the card catalog), and references to the data nodes for each file (the librarians). You'll note that Nanette worked with data stored in triplicate. Data on HDFS is duplicated three times to ensure reliability. In a large enough system (thousands of nodes in a petabyte Hadoop cluster), individual nodes fail every day. In that case, HDFS automatically creates a new duplicate for all the files that were on the failed node.

---

1 Some chimpanzee philosophers have put forth the fanciful conceit of a "paperless" office, requiring impossibilities like a sea of electrons that do the work of a chimpanzee, and disks of magnetized iron that would serve as scrolls. These ideas are, of course, pure lunacy!

JT is the JobTracker (*http://bit.ly/hadoop_jt*). He coordinates the work of individual MapReduce tasks into a cohesive system. The JobTracker is responsible for launching and monitoring the individual tasks of a MapReduce job, which run on the nodes that contain the data a particular job reads. MapReduce jobs are divided into a map phase, in which data is read, and a reduce phase, in which data is aggregated by key and processed again. For now, we'll cover map-only jobs (we'll introduce reduce in Chapter 2).

Note that in YARN (Hadoop 2.0), the terminology changed. The JobTracker is called the ResourceManager, and nodes are managed by NodeManagers. They run arbitrary apps via containers. In YARN, MapReduce is just one kind of computing framework. Hadoop has become an application platform. Confused? So are we. YARN's terminology is something of a disaster, so we'll stick with Hadoop 1.0 terminology.

Pig Latin Map-Only Job

To illustrate how Hadoop works, let's dive into some code with the simplest example possible. We may not be as clever as JT's multilingual chimpanzees, but even we can translate text into a language we'll call *Igpay Atinlay*.[2] For the unfamiliar, here's how to translate standard English into Igpay Atinlay (*http://bit.ly/pig_latin*):

- If the word begins with a consonant-sounding letter or letters, move them to the end of the word and then add "ay": "happy" becomes "appy-hay," "chimp" becomes "imp-chay," and "yes" becomes "es-yay."
- In words that begin with a vowel, just append the syllable "way": "another" becomes "another-way," "elephant" becomes "elephant-way."

Example 1-1 is our first Hadoop job, a program that translates plain-text files into Igpay Atinlay. This is a Hadoop job stripped to its barest minimum, one that does just enough to each record that you believe it happened but with no distractions. That makes it convenient to learn how to launch a job, how to follow its progress, and where Hadoop reports performance metrics (e.g., for runtime and amount of data moved). What's more, the very fact that it's trivial makes it one of the most important examples to run. For comparable input and output size, no regular Hadoop job can outperform this one in practice, so it's a key reference point to carry in mind.

We've written this example in Python, a language that has become the lingua franca of data science. You can run it over a text file from the command line—or run it over petabytes on a cluster (should you for whatever reason have a petabyte of text crying out for pig-latinizing).

---

2 Sharp-eyed readers will note that this language is really called *Pig Latin*. That term has another name in the Hadoop universe, though, so we've chosen to call it Igpay Atinlay—Pig Latin for "Pig Latin."

Example 1-1. Igpay Atinlay translator, pseudocode

```
for each line,
  recognize each word in the line
  and change it as follows:
    separate the head consonants (if any) from the tail of the word
    if there were no initial consonants, use 'w' as the head
    give the tail the same capitalization as the word
    thus changing the word to "tail-head-ay"
  end
  having changed all the words, emit the latinized version of the line
end
```

```python
#!/usr/bin/python

import sys, re

WORD_RE = re.compile(r"\b([bcdfghjklmnpqrstvwxz]*)([\w\']+)")
CAPITAL_RE = re.compile(r"[A-Z]")

def mapper(line):
  words = WORD_RE.findall(line)
  pig_latin_words = []
  for word in words:
    original word = '' join(word)
    head, tail = word
    head = 'w' if not head else head
    pig_latin_word = tail + head + 'ay'
    if CAPITAL_RE.match(pig_latin_word):
      pig_latin_word = pig_latin_word.lower().capitalize()
    else:
      pig_latin_word = pig_latin_word.lower()
    pig_latin_words append(pig_latin_word)
  return " ".join(pig_latin_words)

if __name__ == '__main__':
  for line in sys.stdin:
    print mapper(line)
```

It's best to begin developing jobs locally on a subset of data, because they are faster and cheaper to run. To run the Python script locally, enter this into your terminal's command line:

```
cat /data/gold/text/gift_of_the_magi.txt|python examples/ch_01/pig_latin.py
```

The output should look like this:

Theway agimay asway youway owknay ereway iseway enmay onderfullyway iseway enmay
owhay oughtbray iftsgay otay ethay Babeway inway ethay angermay Theyway
inventedway ethay artway ofway ivinggay Christmasway esentspray Beingway iseway
eirthay iftsgay ereway onay oubtday iseway onesway ossiblypay earingbay ethay
ivilegepray ofway exchangeway inway asecay ofway uplicationday Andway erehay
Iway avehay amelylay elatedray otay youway ethay uneventfulway oniclechray ofway
otway oolishfay ildrenchay inway away atflay owhay ostmay unwiselyway
acrificedsay orfay eachway otherway ethay eatestgray easurestray ofway eirthay
ousehay Butway inway away astlay ordway otay ethay iseway ofway esethay aysday
etlay itway ebay aidsay atthay ofway allway owhay ivegay iftsgay esethay otway
ereway ethay isestway Ofway allway owhay ivegay andway eceiveray iftsgay uchsay
asway eythay areway isestway Everywhereway eythay areway isestway Theyway areway
ethay agimay

That's what it looks like when run locally. Let's run it on a real Hadoop cluster to see how it works when an elephant is in charge.

 Besides being faster and cheaper, there are additional reasons for why it's best to begin developing jobs locally on a subset of data: extracting a meaningful subset of tables also forces you to get to know your data and its relationships. And because all the data is local, you're forced into the good practice of first addressing "what would I like to do with this data?" and only then considering "how shall I do so efficiently?" Beginners often want to believe the opposite, but experience has taught us that it's nearly always worth the upfront investment to prepare a subset, and not to think about efficiency from the beginning.

Setting Up a Docker Hadoop Cluster

We've prepared a docker image you can use to create a Hadoop environment with Pig and Python already installed, and with the example data already mounted on a drive. You can begin by checking out the code. If you aren't familiar with Git, check out the Git home page (*http://git-scm.com/*) and install it. Then proceed to clone the example code Git repository (*https://github.com/bd4c/big_data_for_chimps-code*), which includes the docker setup:

```
git clone --recursive http://github.com/bd4c/big_data_for_chimps-code.git \
  bd4c-code
cd bd4c-code
ls
```

You should see:

```
Gemfile README.md cluster docker examples junk notes numbers10k.txt vendor
```

Now you will need to install VirtualBox (*https://www.virtualbox.org/*) for your platform, which you can download from the VirtualBox website (*http://bit.ly/dl_virtual box*). Next, you will need to install Boot2Docker, which you can find from *https://*

docs.docker.com/installation/. Run Boot2Docker from your OS menu, which (on OS X or Linux) will bring up a shell, as shown in Figure 1-1.

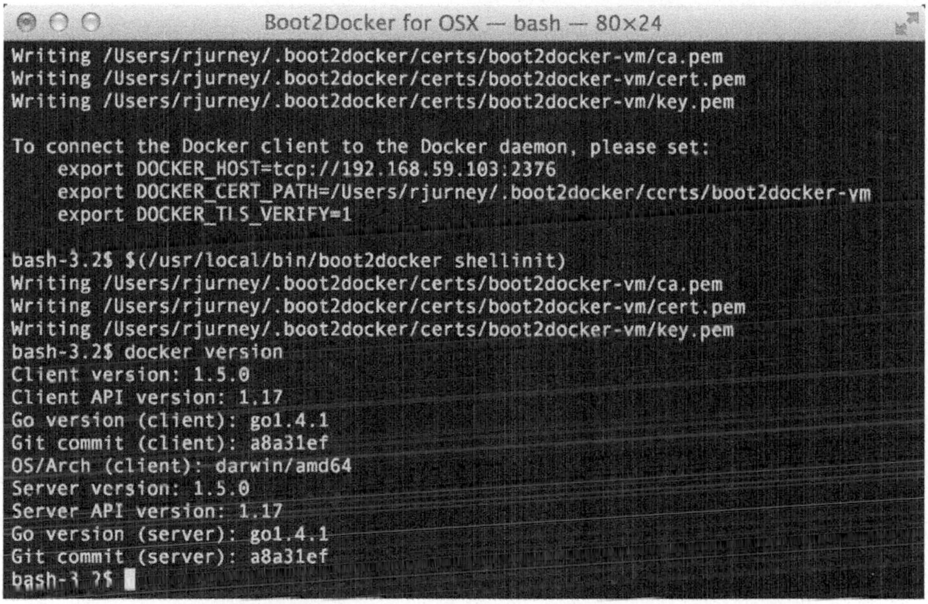

Figure 1-1. Boot2Docker for OS X

We use Ruby scripts to set up our docker environment, so you will need Ruby v. >1.9.2 or >2.0. Returning to your original command prompt, from inside the bd4c-code directory, let's install the Ruby libraries needed to set up our docker images:

```
gem install bundler # you may need to sudo
bundle install
```

Next, change into the `cluster` directory, and repeat `bundle install`:

```
cd cluster
bundle install
```

You can now run docker commands against this VirtualBox virtual machine (VM) running the docker daemon. Let's start by setting up port forwarding from localhost to our docker VM. From the `cluster` directory:

```
boot2docker down
bundle exec rake docker:open_ports
```

While we have the docker VM down, we're going to need to make an adjustment in VirtualBox. We need to increase the amount of RAM given to the VM to at least 4 GB. Run VirtualBox from your OS's GUI, and you should see something like Figure 1-2.

Figure 1-2. Boot2Docker VM inside VirtualBox

Select the Boot2Docker VM, and then click Settings. As shown in Figure 1-3, you should now select the System tab, and adjust the RAM slider right until it reads at least 4096 MB. Click OK.

Now you can close VirtualBox, and bring Boot2Docker back up:

```
boot2docker up
boot2docker shellinit
```

This command will print something like the following:

```
Writing /Users/rjurney/.boot2docker/certs/boot2docker-vm/ca.pem
Writing /Users/rjurney/.boot2docker/certs/boot2docker-vm/cert.pem
Writing /Users/rjurney/.boot2docker/certs/boot2docker-vm/key.pem
    export DOCKER_TLS_VERIFY=1
    export DOCKER_HOST=tcp://192.168.59.103:2376
    export DOCKER_CERT_PATH=/Users/rjurney/.boot2docker/certs/boot2docker-vm
```

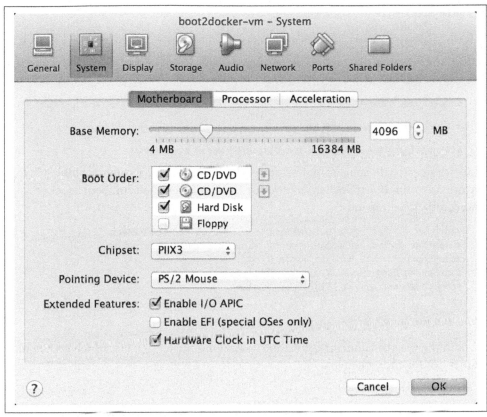

Figure 1-3. VirtualBox interface

Now is a good time to put these lines in your ~/.bashrc file (make sure to substitute your home directory for <home_directory>):

```
export DOCKER_TLS_VERIFY=1
export DOCKER_IP=192.168.59.103
export DOCKER_HOST=tcp://$DOCKER_IP:2376
export DOCKER_CERT_PATH=/<home_directory>/.boot2docker/certs/boot2docker-vm
```

You can achieve that, and update your current environment, via:

```
echo 'export DOCKER_TLS_VERIFY=1' >> ~/.bashrc
echo 'export DOCKER_IP=192.168.59.103' >> ~/.bashrc
echo 'export DOCKER_HOST=tcp://$DOCKER_IP:2376' >> ~/.bashrc
echo 'export DOCKER_CERT_PATH=/<home_dir>/.boot2docker/certs/boot2docker-vm' \
  >> ~/.bashrc
source ~/.bashrc
```

Check that these environment variables are set, and that the docker client can connect, via:

```
echo $DOCKER_IP
echo $DOCKER_HOST
bundle exec rake ps
```

Now you're ready to set up the docker images. This can take a while, so brew a cup of tea after running:

```
bundle exec rake images:pull
```

Once that's done, you should see:

```
Status: Image is up to date for blalor/docker-hosts:latest
```

Now we need to do some minor setup on the Boot2Docker virtual machine. Change terminals to the Boot2Docker window, or from another shell run boot2docker ssh, and run these commands:

```
mkdir -p          /tmp/bulk/hadoop      # view all logs there
# so that docker-hosts can make container hostnames resolvable
sudo touch        /var/lib/docker/hosts
sudo chmod 0644   /var/lib/docker/hosts
sudo chown nobody /var/lib/docker/hosts
exit
```

Now exit the Boot2Docker shell.

Back in the cluster directory, it is time to start the cluster helpers, which set up hostnames among the containers:

```
bundle exec rake helpers:run
```

If everything worked, you can now run cat /var/lib/docker/hosts on the Boot2Docker host, and it should be filled with information. Running bundle exec rake ps should show containers for host_filer and nothing else.

Next, let's set up our example data. Run the following:

```
bundle exec rake data:create show_output=true
```

At this point, you can run bundle exec rake ps and you should see five containers, all stopped. Start these containers using:

```
bundle exec rake hadoop:run
```

This will start the Hadoop containers. You can stop/start them with:

```
bundle exec rake hadoop:stop
bundle exec rake hadoop:start
```

Now ssh to your new Hadoop cluster:

```
ssh -i insecure_key.pem chimpy@$DOCKER_IP -p 9022 # Password chimpy
```

You can see that the example data is available on the local filesystem:

```
chimpy@lounge:~$ ls /data/gold/
airline_flights/  demographic/  geo/  graph/  helpers/  serverlogs/  sports/
text/  twitter/  wikipedia/  CREDITS.md  README-archiver.md  README.md
```

Now you can run Pig, in local mode:

```
pig -l /tmp -x local
```

And we're off!

Run the Job

First, let's test on the same tiny little file we used before. The following command
does not process any data but instead instructs Hadoop to process the data. The command will generate output that contains information about how the job is
progressing:

```
hadoop jar /usr/lib/hadoop-mapreduce/hadoop-streaming.jar \
  -Dmapreduce.cluster.local.dir=/home/chimpy/code -fs local -jt local \
  -file ./examples/ch_01/pig_latin.py -mapper ./examples/ch_01/pig_latin.py \
  -input /data/gold/text/gift_of_the_magi.txt -output ./translation.out
```

You should see something like this:

```
WARN fs.FileSystem: "local" is a deprecated filesystem name. Use "file:///"...
WARN streaming.StreamJob: -file option is deprecated, please use generic...
packageJobJar: [./examples/ch_01/pig_latin.py] [] /tmp/...
INFO Configuration.deprecation: session.id is deprecated. Instead, use...
INFO jvm.JvmMetrics: Initializing JVM Metrics with processName=JobTracker...
INFO jvm.JvmMetrics: Cannot initialize JVM Metrics with...
INFO mapred.FileInputFormat: Total input paths to process : 1
INFO mapreduce.JobSubmitter: number of splits:1
INFO mapreduce.JobSubmitter: Submitting tokens for job: job_local292160259_0001
WARN conf.Configuration: file:/tmp/hadoop-chimpy/mapred/staging/...
WARN conf.Configuration: file:/tmp/hadoop-chimpy/mapred/staging/...
INFO mapred.LocalDistributedCacheManager: Localized file:/home/chimpy/...
WARN conf.Configuration: file:/home/chimpy/code/localRunner/chimpy/...
WARN conf.Configuration: file:/home/chimpy/code/localRunner/chimpy/...
INFO mapreduce.Job: The url to track the job: http://localhost:8080/
INFO mapred.LocalJobRunner: OutputCommitter set in config null
INFO mapreduce.Job: Running job: job_local292160259_0001
INFO mapred.LocalJobRunner: OutputCommitter is...
INFO mapred.LocalJobRunner: Waiting for map tasks
INFO mapred.LocalJobRunner: Starting task:...
INFO mapred.Task:  Using ResourceCalculatorProcessTree : [ ]
INFO mapred.MapTask: Processing split: file:/data/gold/text/...
INFO mapred.MapTask: numReduceTasks: 1
INFO mapred.MapTask: (EQUATOR) 0 kvi 26214396(104857584)
INFO mapred.MapTask: mapreduce.task.io.sort.mb: 100
INFO mapred.MapTask: soft limit at 83886080
INFO mapred.MapTask: bufstart = 0; bufvoid = 104857600
INFO mapred.MapTask: kvstart = 26214396; length = 6553600
INFO mapred.MapTask: Map output collector class =...
```

```
INFO streaming.PipeMapRed: PipeMapRed exec [/home/chimpy/code/./pig_latin.py]
INFO streaming.PipeMapRed: R/W/S=1/0/0 in:NA [rec/s] out:NA [rec/s]
INFO streaming.PipeMapRed: R/W/S=10/0/0 in:NA [rec/s] out:NA [rec/s]
INFO streaming.PipeMapRed: R/W/S=100/0/0 in:NA [rec/s] out:NA [rec/s]
INFO streaming.PipeMapRed: Records R/W=225/1
INFO streaming.PipeMapRed: MRErrorThread done
INFO streaming.PipeMapRed: mapRedFinished
INFO mapred.LocalJobRunner:
INFO mapred.MapTask: Starting flush of map output
INFO mapred.MapTask: Spilling map output
INFO mapred.MapTask: bufstart = 0; bufend = 16039; bufvoid = 104857600
INFO mapred.MapTask: kvstart = 26214396(104857584); kvend =...
INFO mapred.MapTask: Finished spill 0
INFO mapred.Task: Task:attempt_local292160259_0001_m_000000_0 is done. And is...
INFO mapred.LocalJobRunner: Records R/W=225/1
INFO mapred.Task: Task 'attempt_local292160259_0001_m_000000_0' done.
INFO mapred.LocalJobRunner: Finishing task:...
INFO mapred.LocalJobRunner: map task executor complete.
INFO mapred.LocalJobRunner: Waiting for reduce tasks
INFO mapred.LocalJobRunner: Starting task:...
INFO mapred.Task:  Using ResourceCalculatorProcessTree : [ ]
INFO mapred.ReduceTask: Using ShuffleConsumerPlugin:...
INFO mapreduce.Job: Job job_local292160259_0001 running in uber mode : false
INFO mapreduce.Job:  map 100% reduce 0%
INFO reduce.MergeManagerImpl: MergerManager: memoryLimit=652528832...
INFO reduce.EventFetcher: attempt_local292160259_0001_r_000000_0 Thread...
INFO reduce.LocalFetcher: localfetcher#1 about to shuffle output of map...
INFO reduce.InMemoryMapOutput: Read 16491 bytes from map-output for...
INFO reduce.MergeManagerImpl: closeInMemoryFile -> map-output of size: 16491...
INFO reduce.EventFetcher: EventFetcher is interrupted.. Returning
INFO mapred.LocalJobRunner: 1 / 1 copied.
INFO reduce.MergeManagerImpl: finalMerge called with 1 in-memory map-outputs...
INFO mapred.Merger: Merging 1 sorted segments
INFO mapred.Merger: Down to the last merge-pass, with 1 segments left of...
INFO reduce.MergeManagerImpl: Merged 1 segments, 16491 bytes to disk to...
INFO reduce.MergeManagerImpl: Merging 1 files, 16495 bytes from disk
INFO reduce.MergeManagerImpl: Merging 0 segments, 0 bytes from memory into...
INFO mapred.Merger: Merging 1 sorted segments
INFO mapred.Merger: Down to the last merge-pass, with 1 segments left of...
INFO mapred.LocalJobRunner: 1 / 1 copied.
INFO mapred.Task: Task:attempt_local292160259_0001_r_000000_0 is done. And is...
INFO mapred.LocalJobRunner: 1 / 1 copied.
INFO mapred.Task: Task attempt_local292160259_0001_r_000000_0 is allowed to...
INFO output.FileOutputCommitter: Saved output of task...
INFO mapred.LocalJobRunner: reduce > reduce
INFO mapred.Task: Task 'attempt_local292160259_0001_r_000000_0' done.
INFO mapred.LocalJobRunner: Finishing task:...
INFO mapred.LocalJobRunner: reduce task executor complete.
INFO mapreduce.Job:  map 100% reduce 100%
INFO mapreduce.Job: Job job_local292160259_0001 completed successfully
INFO mapreduce.Job: Counters: 33
  File System Counters
```

```
          FILE: Number of bytes read=58158
          FILE: Number of bytes written=581912
          FILE: Number of read operations=0
          FILE: Number of large read operations=0
          FILE: Number of write operations=0
     Map-Reduce Framework
          Map input records=225
          Map output records=225
          Map output bytes=16039
          Map output materialized bytes=16495
          Input split bytes=93
          Combine input records=0
          Combine output records=0
          Reduce input groups=180
          Reduce shuffle bytes=16495
          Reduce input records=225
          Reduce output records=225
          Spilled Records=450
          Shuffled Maps =1
          Failed Shuffles=0
          Merged Map outputs=1
          GC time elapsed (ms)=11
          CPU time spent (ms)=0
          Physical memory (bytes) snapshot=0
          Virtual memory (bytes) snapshot=0
          Total committed heap usage (bytes)=441450496
     Shuffle Errors
          BAD_ID=0
          CONNECTION=0
          IO_ERROR=0
          WRONG_LENGTH=0
          WRONG_MAP=0
          WRONG_REDUCE=0
     File Input Format Counters
          Bytes Read=11224
     File Output Format Counters
          Bytes Written=16175
     INFO streaming.StreamJob: Output directory: ./translation.out
```

This is the output of the Hadoop streaming JAR as it transmits your files and runs them on the cluster.

Wrapping Up

In this chapter, we've equipped you with two things: the necessary mechanics of working with Hadoop, and a physical intuition for how data and computation move around the cluster during a job. We started with a story about JT and Nanette, and learned about the Hadoop JobTracker, NameNode, and filesystem. We proceeded with a Pig Latin example, and ran it on a real Hadoop cluster.

We've covered the mechanics of the Hadoop Distributed File System (HDFS) and the map-only portion of MapReduce, and we've set up a virtual Hadoop cluster and run a single job on it. Although we are just beginning, we're already in good shape to learn more about Hadoop.

In the next chapter, you'll learn about MapReduce jobs—the full power of Hadoop's processing paradigm. We'll start by continuing the story of JT and Nannette, and learning more about their next client.

## CHAPTER 2

MapReduce

In this chapter, we're going to build on what we learned about HDFS and the map-only portion of MapReduce and introduce a full MapReduce job and its mechanics. This time, we'll include both the shuffle/sort phase and the reduce phase. Once again, we begin with a physical metaphor in the form of a story. After that, we'll walk you through building our first full-blown MapReduce job in Python. At the end of this chapter, you should have an intuitive understanding of how MapReduce works, including its map, shuffle/sort, and reduce phases.

First, we begin with a metaphoric story…about how Chimpanzee and Elephant saved Christmas.

Chimpanzee and Elephant Save Christmas

It was holiday time at the North Pole, and letters from little boys and little girls all over the world flooded in as they always do. But this year, the world had grown just a bit too much. The elves just could not keep up with the scale of requests—Christmas was in danger! Luckily, their friends at Chimpanzee and Elephant, Inc., were available to help. Packing their typewriters and good winter coats, JT, Nanette, and the crew headed to the Santaplex at the North Pole. Here's what they found.

Trouble in Toyland

As you know, each year children from every corner of the earth write to Santa to request toys, and Santa—knowing who's been naughty and who's been nice—strives to meet the wishes of every good little boy and girl who writes him. He employs a regular army of toymaker elves, each of whom specializes in certain kinds of toys: some elves make action figures and dolls, while others make xylophones and yo-yos (see Figure 2-1).

Figure 2-1. The elves' workbenches are meticulous and neat

Under the elves' old system, as bags of mail arrived, they were examined by an elven postal clerk and then hung from the branches of the Big Tree at the center of the Santaplex. Letters were organized on the tree according to the child's town, as the shipping department has a critical need to organize toys by their final delivery schedule. But the toymaker elves must know what toys to make as well, and so for each letter, a postal clerk recorded its Big Tree coordinates in a ledger that was organized by type of toy.

So to retrieve a letter, a doll-making elf would look under "Doll" in the ledger to find the next letter's coordinates, then wait as teamster elves swung a big claw arm to retrieve it from the Big Tree (see Figure 2-2). As JT readily observed, the mail couldn't be organized both by toy type and also by delivery location, and so this ledger system was a "necessary evil." The next request for Lego is as likely to be from Cucamonga as from Novosibirsk, and letters can't be pulled from the tree any faster than the crane arm can move!

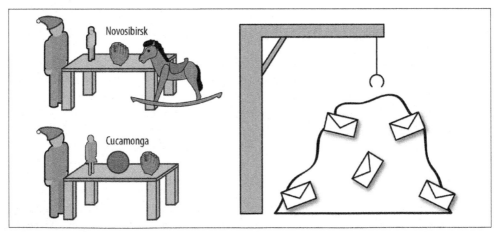

Figure 2-2. Little boys' and girls' mail is less so

What's worse, the size of Santa's operation meant that the workbenches were very far from where letters came in. The hallways were clogged with frazzled elves running from Big Tree to workbench and back, spending as much effort requesting and retrieving letters as they did making toys. This complex transactional system was a bottleneck in toy making, and mechanic elves were constantly scheming ways to make the claw arm cope with increased load. "Throughput, not latency!" trumpeted Nanette. "For hauling heavy loads, you need a stately elephant parade, not a swarm of frazzled elves!"

Chimpanzees Process Letters into Labeled Toy Forms

In marched Chimpanzee and Elephant, Inc. JT and Nanette set up a finite number of chimpanzees at a finite number of typewriters, each with an elephant deskmate. Strangely, the C&E solution to the too-many-letters problem involved producing *more* paper. The problem wasn't in the amount of paper, it was in all the work being done to service the paper. In the new world, all the rules for handling documents are simple, uniform, and local.

Postal clerks still stored each letter on the Big Tree (allowing the legacy shipping system to continue unchanged), but now also handed off bags holding copies of the mail. As she did with the translation passages, Nanette distributed these mailbags across the desks just as they arrived. The overhead of recording each letter in the much-hated ledger was no more, and the hallways were no longer clogged with elves racing to and fro.

The chimps' job was to take letters one after another from a mailbag, and fill out a toy form for each request. A toy form has a prominent label showing the type of toy, and a body with all the information you'd expect: name, nice/naughty status, location, and so forth. You can see some examples here:

```
Deer SANTA

I wood like a doll for me and
and an optimus prime robot for my
brother joe

I have been good this year

love julia

# Good kids, generates a toy for Julia and a toy for her brother
# Toy Forms:
#    doll  | type="green hair"  recipient="Joe's sister Julia"
#    robot | type="optimus prime" recipient="Joe"

Greetings to you Mr Claus, I came to know of you in my search for a reliable
and reputable person to handle a very confidential business transaction,
which involves the transfer of a large sum of money...

# Spam
```

```
# (no toy forms)

HEY SANTA I WANT A YANKEES HAT AND NOT
ANY DUMB BOOKS THIS YEAR

FRANK

# Frank is a jerk. He will get a lump of coal.
# Toy Forms:
#   coal | type="anthracite" recipient="Frank" reason="doesn't like to read"
```

The first note, from a very good girl who is thoughtful of her brother, creates two toy forms: one for Joe's robot and one for Julia's doll. The second note is spam, so it creates no toy forms. The third one yields a toy form directing Santa to put coal in Frank's stocking (Figure 2-3).

Figure 2-3. A chimp mapping letters

Processing letters in this way represents the map phase of a MapReduce job. The work performed in a map phase could be anything: translation, letter processing, or any other operation. For each record read in the map phase, a mapper can produce zero, one, or more records. In this case, each letter produces one or more toy forms (Figure 2-4). This elf-driven letter operation turns unstructured data (a letter) into a structured record (toy form).

Figure 2-4. A chimp "mapping" letters, producing toy forms

Next, we move on to the shuffle/sort phase, which uses the letters as input.

Pygmy Elephants Carry Each Toy Form to the Appropriate Workbench

Here's the new wrinkle on top of the system used in the translation project. Next to every desk now stood a line of pygmy elephants, each dressed in a cape listing the types of toy it would deliver. Each desk had a pygmy elephant for archery kits and dolls, another one for xylophones and yo-yos, and so forth—matching the different specialties of toymaker elves.

As the chimpanzees would work through a mailbag, they'd place each toy form into the basket on the back of the pygmy elephant that matched its type. At the completion of a bag (a map phase), the current line of elephants would *shuffle* off to the workbenches, and behind them a new line of elephants would trundle into place. What fun! (See Figure 2-5.)

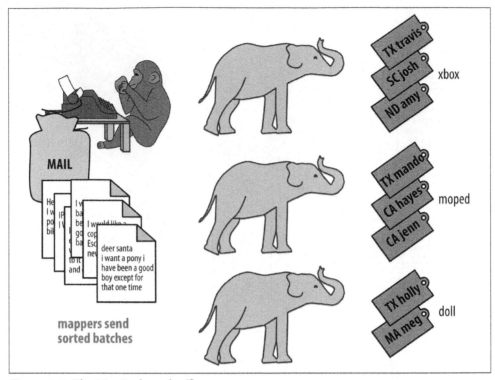

Figure 2-5. The MapReduce shuffle

Finally, the pygmy elephants would march through the now-quiet hallways to the toy shop floor, each reporting to the workbench that matched its toy types. All of the workbenches (the archery kit/doll workbench, the xylophone/yo-yo workbench, etc.) had a line of pygmy elephants, one for every C&E desk.

This activity by the pygmy elephants represents the shuffle/sort phase of a MapReduce job, in which records produced by mappers are grouped by their key (the toy type) and delivered to a reducer for that key (an elf!).

Now the reduce phase begins: toymaker elves begin producing a steady stream of toys, no longer constrained by the overhead of walking the hallway and waiting for Big Tree retrieval on every toy (Figure 2-6).

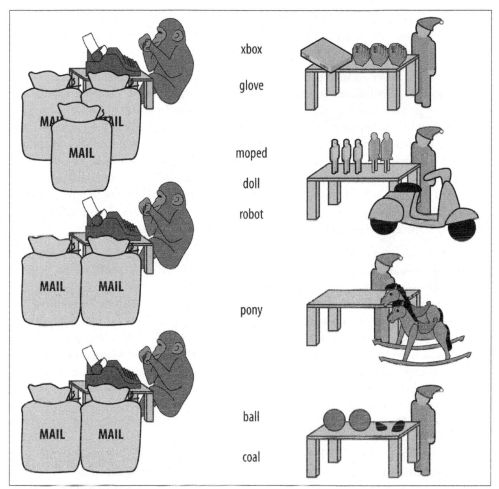

xbox

glove

moped

doll

robot

pony

ball

coal

Figure 2-6. The Reduce process

Our MapReduce job is complete, and toy making is back on track!

Having previously introduced map-only Hadoop in our first story, in this story we introduced the shuffle/sort and reduce operations of Hadoop MapReduce. The toymaker elves are the reducers—they receive all the mapped records (toy forms) corresponding to one or more group keys (the type of toy). The act of toy making is the reduce operation. The pygmy elephants represent the shuffle/sort—the movement of data from mappers to reducers. That is how the MapReduce paradigm works! This simple abstraction powers Hadoop MapReduce programs. It is the simplicity of the scheme that makes it so powerful.

In Chapter 1, you worked with a simple-as-possible Python script, which let you learn the mechanics of running Hadoop jobs and understand the essentials of the HDFS.

Document translation is an example of an "embarrassingly parallel" problem: each record could be processed individually, just as it was organized in the source files. This was a *map-only* job, an operation we'll discuss more in Part II.

Hadoop's real power comes from the ability to process data in context, using what's known as the MapReduce paradigm. Every MapReduce job is a program with the same three phases: map, shuffle/sort phase, and reduce. In the map phase, your program processes its input in any way you see fit, emitting labeled output records. Between map and reduce is the Hadoop shuffle/sort. In the shuffle/sort phase, Hadoop groups and sorts the mapped records according to their labels. Finally, in the reduce phase, your program processes each sorted, labeled group and Hadoop stores its output on HDFS. That shuffle, or *grouping-by-label*, part is where the magic lies: it ensures that no matter where the relevant records started, they arrive at the same place at a reducer in a predictable manner, ready to be synthesized.

If MapReduce is the core of Hadoop's operation, then getting to *think* in MapReduce terms is the key to effectively using Hadoop. In turn, thinking in MapReduce requires that you develop an innate, physical sense of how Hadoop moves data around. You can't understand the fundamental patterns of data analysis in Hadoop—grouping, filtering, joining records, and so forth—without knowing the basics. Having read the explanation offered in "Chimpanzee and Elephant Save Christmas" on page 17, you should now have an intuitive understanding of how Hadoop and MapReduce work. If you're still confused, reread the beginning of this chapter until you master the material on an intuitive level.

Example: Reindeer Games

Santa Claus and his elves are busy year-round, but Santa's flying reindeer do not have many responsibilities outside the holiday season. As flying objects themselves, they spend a good part of their multimonth break pursuing their favorite hobby: ufology (the study of unidentified flying objects and the search for extraterrestrial civilization). So you can imagine how excited they were to learn about the dataset of more than 60,000 documented UFO sightings we're going to work with here.

Of course, 60,000 sightings is much higher than a reindeer can count (only four hooves!), so JT and Nanette occasionally earn a little good favor from Santa Claus by helping the reindeer answer questions about the UFO data. We can do our part by helping our reindeer friends understand how long people wait to report UFOs.

UFO Data

The UFO data is located on the docker HDFS we set up in Chapter 1. Let's begin by checking our input data. First, ssh into the gateway node and run this command to see the top five lines of the UFO sightings sample:

```
cat /data/gold/geo/ufo_sightings/ufo_sightings-sample.tsv|head -5
```

Note that gold in this path stands for *gold standard data* (in other words, data that has been checked and validated to be correct).

The UFO data is in tab-separated values (TSV) format. It has been formatted to fit on the page:

```
1995-10-09T05:00:00Z    1995-10-09T05:00:00Z    Iowa City, IA
            Man repts. witnessing "flash, ...
1995-10-10T05:00:00Z    1995-10-11T05:00:00Z    Milwaukee, WI
    2 min.   Man  on Hwy 43 SW of Mil...
1995-01-01T06:00:00Z    1995-01-03T06:00:00Z    Shelton, WA
            Telephoned Report:CA woman visit...
1995-05-10T05:00:00Z    1995-05-10T05:00:00Z    Columbia, MO
    2 min.   Man repts. son's bizarre...
1995-06-11T05:00:00Z    1995-06-14T05:00:00Z    Seattle, WA
            Anonymous caller repts. sighting...
```

Group the UFO Sightings by Reporting Delay

In the Chimpanzee and Elephant, Inc., world, a chimp performs the following tasks:

1. Read and understand each letter.
2. Create a new intermediate item having a label (the type of toy, a key) and information about the toy (the work order, a value).
3. Hand it to the elephant who delivers to that toy's workbench.

We're going to write a Hadoop mapper that serves a similar purpose:

1. Read the raw data and parse it into a structured record.
2. Create a new intermediate item having a label (the number of days passed before reporting a UFO, a key) and a count (one sighting for each input record, a value).
3. Hand it to Hadoop for delivery to that label/group's reducer.

Mapper

In order to calculate the time delay in reporting UFOs, we've got to determine that delay by subtracting the time the UFO was sighted from the time the UFO was reported. As just outlined, this occurs in the map phase of our MapReduce job. The mapper emits the time delay in days, and a counter (which is always 1).

You may need to install the iso8601 library, via:

```
pip install iso8601
```

The mapper code in Python looks like this:

```
#!/usr/bin/python
# Example MapReduce job: count ufo sightings by location.

import sys, re, time, iso8601 # You can get iso8601 from https://pypi.python.org/
  pypi/iso8601

# Pull out city/state from ex: Town, ST
word_finder = re.compile("([\w\s]+),\s(\w+)")

# Loop through each line from standard input
for line in sys.stdin:
  # Remove the carriage return, and split on tabs - maximum of 3 fields
  fields = line.rstrip("\n").split("\t", 2)
  try:
    # Parse the two dates, then find the time between them
    sighted_at, reported_at, rest = fields
    sighted_dt = iso8601.parse_date(sighted_at)
    reported_dt = iso8601.parse_date(reported_at)
    diff = reported_dt - sighted_dt
  except:
    sys.stderr.write("Bad line: {}".format(line))
    continue
  # Emit the number of days and one
  print "\t".join((str(diff.days), "1"))
```

You can test the mapper like this:

```
cat /data/gold/geo/ufo_sightings/ufo_sightings-sample.tsv | python \
  examples/ch_02/ufo_mapper.py
```

The intermediate output looks like this:

```
0       1
889     1
346     1
1294    1
12      1
14689   1
12      1
...
```

These are the records our reducer will receive as input. Just as the pygmy elephants transported work orders to elves' workbenches, Hadoop delivers each mapped record to the reducer, the second stage of our job.

Reducer

In our previous example, the elf at each workbench saw a series of work orders, with the guarantee that (a) work orders for each toy type are delivered together and in order; and (b) this was the only workbench to receive work orders for that toy type. Similarly, in this job, the reducer receives a series of records (UFO reports, values), grouped by label (the number of days passed before reporting a UFO, a key), with a guarantee that it is the unique processor for such records.

Our reducer is tasked with creating a histogram. The reducer is thus concerned with grouping similar time delays together. The reduce key in this case is the number of days passed before reporting a UFO (e.g., 0, 1, 10, or 35 days). In the reducer, we're keeping count; the count for each element of the reduce key/group is incremented by the count (1) as each record is processed. Because Hadoop guarantees that all reduce keys of one value go to one reducer, we can extrapolate that if the reduce key changes, then we are done with the previous group and reduce key. Being done with the previous group, it is time to emit our record about that group: in this case, the reduce key itself and the sum of counts of values for that reduce key. And so our histogram is populated with *reduced* values.

Note that in this example (based on one by Michael Noll (*http://bit.ly/python_mapre duce*)), *to sort is to group*. Take a moment and reread the last paragraph, if necessary. This is the magic of MapReduce: when you perform a sort on a set of values, you are implicitly grouping like records together. MapReduce algorithms take advantage of this implicit grouping, making it explicit via APIs.

Moving on, our reducer looks like this:

```
#!/usr/bin/python
# Example MapReduce job: count ufo sightings by hour.
import sys, re

current_days = None
curreent_count = 0
days = None

# Loop through each line from standard input
for line in sys.stdin:
  # split the line into two values, using the tab character
  days, count = line.rstrip("\n").split("\t", 1)

  # Streaming always reads strings, so must convert to integer
  try:
    count = int(count)
  except:
    sys.stderr.write("Can't convert '{}' to integer\n".format(count))
    continue

  # If sorted input key is the same, increment counter
  if current_days == days:
    current_count += count
  # If the key has changed...
  else:
    # This is a new reduce key, so emit the total of the last key
    if current_days:
      print "{}\t{}".format(current_days, current_count)
```

```
    # And set the new key and count to the new reduce key/reset total
    current_count = count
    current_days = days

# Emit the last reduce key
if current_days == days:
  print "{}\t{}".format(current_days, current_count)
```

Always test locally on a sample of data, if at all possible:

```
cat /data/gold/geo/ufo_sightings/ufo_sightings-sample.tsv | python \
    examples/ch_02/ufo_mapper.py | \
sort | python examples/ch_02/ufo_reducer.py|sort -n
```

Note that we've added a sort -n to the end of the commands so that the lowest values will appear first. On Hadoop, this would take another MapReduce job.

The output looks like this:

```
-1  3
0 51
1 17
2 9
3 4
4 4
5 2
6 1
10  1
15  1
30  2
57  1
74  1
115 1
179 1
203 1
```

This command demonstrates an execution pattern for testing MapReduce code, and it goes like this:

```
cat /path/to/data/file | mapper | sort | reducer
```

Being able to test MapReduce code locally is important because Hadoop is a batch system. In other words, Hadoop is *slow*. That's a relative term, because a large Hadoop cluster is blazingly fast at processing terabytes and even petabytes of data. However, the shortest Hadoop job on a loaded cluster can take a few minutes, which can make debugging a slow and cumbersome process. The ability to bypass this several-minute wait by running locally on a sample of data is essential to being productive as a Hadoop developer or analyst.

Now that we've tested locally, we're ready to execute our MapReduce job on Hadoop using Hadoop Streaming (*http://bit.ly/hadoopstreaming*), which is a utility that lets users run jobs with any executable program as the mapper and/or the reducer. You can use Python scripts, or even simple shell commands like wc or others. If you're writing a dynamic language script (e.g., a Python, Ruby, or Perl script) as a mapper or reducer, be sure to make the script executable, or the Hadoop job will fail.

The streaming command to run our Python mapper and reducer looks like this:

```
hadoop jar /usr/lib/hadoop-mapreduce/hadoop-streaming.jar \
    -Dmapreduce.cluster.local.dir=/home/chimpy/code -fs local \
    -jt local -files examples/ch_02/ufo_mapper.py,examples/ch_02/ufo_reducer.py \
    -mapper ufo_mapper.py -reducer ufo_reducer.py -input \
    /data/gold/geo/ufo_sightings/ufo_sightings-sample.tsv -output ./ufo.out
```

You'll see output similar to what you saw at the end of Chapter 1. When the job is complete, view the results:

```
cat ./ufo.out/* | sort -n
```

The results should be identical to the output of the local execution:

```
-1   3
0  51
1  17
2   9
3   4
4   4
5   2
6   1
10   1
15   1
30   2
57   1
74   1
115 1
179 1
203 1
```

While the results are identical, the potentials vary—the difference between the local and Hadoop runs being that the Hadoop execution on a large cluster could scale to petabytes of UFO sightings! Note that there are some negative values—imperfections in our data that we may need to filter out before visualizing our results. Big data often contains such surprises.

Plot the Data

When people (or reindeer) work with data, their end goal is to uncover some answer or pattern. They most often employ Hadoop to turn big data into small data, then use traditional analytics techniques to turn small data into answers and insights. One such technique is to *plot* the information. If a picture is worth 1,000 words, then even a basic data plot is worth reams of statistical analysis.

That's because the human eye often gets a rough idea of a pattern faster than people can write code to divine the proper mathematical result. A few lines of Python can create a histogram to present to our reindeer pals, to give a gestalt sense of UFO reporting delays.

To create a histogram chart, we'll run a Python script on our docker gateway:

```python
#!/usr/bin/python
# Example histogram: UFO reporting delay by day

import numpy as np
import matplotlib.pyplot as plt

day_labels = []
counts = []

file = open("ufo_hist.tsv")
for line in file:
  fields = line.rstrip("\n").split("\t", 1)
  days, count = fields
  day_labels.append(int(days))
  counts.append(int(count))

plt.title("UFO Reporting Delays")
plt.bar(day_labels, counts)
plt.savefig("UFO_Reporting_Delays.png")
```

To view the chart, we need to get the image back on your local machine, and then open it:

```
# Enter password 'chimpy'
scp -i insecure_key.pem -P 9022 chimpy@$DOCKER_IP:UFO_Reporting_Delays.png .
open UFO_Reporting_Delays.png
```

The chart looks like Figure 2-7.

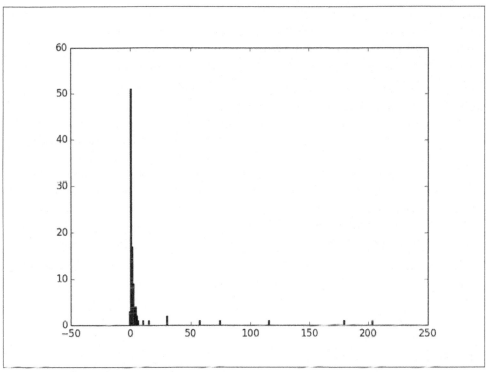

Figure 2-7. UFO reporting delays

Reindeer Conclusion

We've now taken a Python streaming Hadoop job from map, through shuffle/sort, and into reduce. In addition, we have subsequently converted this reduced output into a histogram chart. This workflow is typical, as we'll see throughout the book.

Hadoop Versus Traditional Databases

We've covered the basic operation of Hadoop MapReduce jobs on a Hadoop cluster, but it is worth taking a moment to reflect on how operating Hadoop differs from operating a traditional relational database. *Hadoop is not a database.*

Fundamentally, the storage engine at the heart of a traditional relational database does two things: it holds all the records, and it maintains a set of indexes for lookups and other operations (the crane arm in Santa's legacy system). To retrieve a record, it must consult the appropriate index to find the location of the record, then load it from the disk. This is very fast for record-by-record retrieval, but becomes cripplingly inefficient for general high-throughput access. If the records are stored by location and arrival time (as the mailbags were on the Big Tree), then there is no "locality of access" for records retrieved by, say, type of toy—records for Lego will be spread all across the disk. With traditional drives, the disk's read head has to physically swing back and forth in a frenzy across the drive platter, and though the newer flash drives have smaller retrieval latency, it's still far too high for bulk operations.

What's more, traditional database applications lend themselves very well to low-latency operations (such as rendering a web page showing the toys you requested), but very poorly to high-throughput operations (such as requesting every single doll order in sequence). Unless you invest specific expertise and effort, you have little ability to organize requests for efficient retrieval. You either suffer a variety of nonlocality-and-congestion-based inefficiencies, or wind up with an application that caters to the database more than to its users. You can to a certain extent use the laws of economics to bend the laws of physics (as the commercial success of Oracle and Netezza shows), but the finiteness of time, space, and memory presents an insoluble scaling problem for traditional databases.

Hadoop solves the scaling problem by not solving the data organization problem. Rather than insist that the data be organized and indexed as it's written to disk, catering to every context that could be requested, Hadoop instead focuses purely on the throughput case.

The MapReduce Haiku

The bargain that MapReduce proposes is that you agree to only write programs fitting this haiku:

```
data flutters by
    elephants make sturdy piles
  context yields insight
```

More prosaically, we might explain MapReduce in three phases.

Phase	Description	Explanation
Map	Process and label	Turn each input record into any number of labeled records
Group-sort	Sorted context groups	Hadoop groups those records uniquely under each label, in a sorted order (you'll see this also called the shuffle/sort phase)
Reduce	Synthesize (process context groups)	For each group, process its records in order; emit anything you want

The trick lies in the group-sort (or shuffle/sort) phase: assigning the same label to two records in the map phase ensures that they will become local in the reduce phase.

The records in phase 1 (map) are out of context. The mappers see each record exactly once, but with no promises as to order, and no promises as to which mapper sees which record. We've *moved the compute to the data*, allowing each process to work quietly on the data in its workspace. Over at C&E, Inc., letters and translation passages aren't preorganized and they don't have to be; JT and Nanette care about keeping all the chimps working steadily and keeping the hallways clear of interoffice document requests.

Once the map attempt finishes, each *partition* (the collection of records destined for a common reducer, with a common label, or key) is dispatched to the corresponding machine, and the mapper is free to start a new task. If you notice, the only time data moves from one machine to another is when the intermediate piles of data get shipped. Instead of an exhausted crane arm, we now have a dignified elephant parade, conducted in concert with the efforts of our diligent workers.

Map Phase, in Light Detail

Digging a little deeper into the mechanics of it all, a mapper receives one record at a time. By default, Hadoop works on text files, and a record is one line of text. However, there is a caveat: Hadoop actually supports other file formats and other types of storage beside files. But for the most part, the examples in this book will focus on processing files on disk in a readable text format. The whole point of the mapper is to "label" the record so that the shuffle/sort phase can track records with the same label.

Hadoop feeds the mapper that one record, and in turn, the mapper spits out one or more *labeled records*. Usually the values in each record's fields are some combination of the values in the input record and a simple transformation of those values. But the output is allowed to be anything (the entire record, some subset of fields, the phase of the moon, the contents of a web page, nothing…), and at times we'll solve important problems by pushing that point. The mapper can output those records in any order, at any time in its lifecycle, each with any label.

Group-Sort Phase, in Light Detail

In the group-sort (or shuffle/sort) phase, Hadoop transfers all the map output records in a partition to the corresponding reducer. That reducer merges the records it receives from all mappers, so that each group contains all records for its label regardless of what machine it came from. What's nice about the shuffle/sort phase is that you don't have to do anything for it. Hadoop takes care of moving the data around for you. What's less nice about the shuffle/sort phase is that it is typically the performance bottleneck. Later, we'll learn how to take care of Hadoop so that it can move the data around smartly.

Reduce Phase, in Light Detail

Whereas the mapper sees single records in isolation, a reducer receives one key (the label) and *all* records that match that key. In other words, a reducer operates on a group of related records. Just as with the mapper, as long as it keeps eating records and doesn't fail, the reducer can do anything with those records it pleases and emit anything it wants. It can emit nothing, it can contact a remote database, it can emit nothing until the very end and then emit one or a zillion records. The output can be text, it can be video files, it can be angry letters to the president. They don't have to be labeled, and they don't have to make sense. Having said all that, usually what a reducer emits are nice well-formed records resulting from sensible transformations of its input, like the count of records, the largest or smallest value from a field, or full records paired with other records. And though there's no explicit notion of a label attached to a reducer output record, it's pretty common that within the record's fields are values that future mappers will use to form labels.

Once you grasp the map-sort/shuffle-reduce data flow we've just introduced, you'll understand enough about MapReduce to reason about the large-scale motion of data and thus your job's performance.

Wrapping Up

You've just seen how records move through a MapReduce workflow, both in theory and in practice. This can be challenging material to grasp, so don't feel bad if you don't get all of it right away. While we did our best to simplify a complex phenomenon, we hope we've still communicated the essentials. We encourage you to reread this chapter until you get it straight. You may also try revisiting this chapter after you've read a bit further in the book. Once you've performed a few Pig GROUP BYs, this material may feel more natural.

You should now have an intuitive sense of the mechanics behind MapReduce Remember to come back to this chapter as you read the rest of the book. This will aide you in acquiring a deep understanding of the operations that make up the strategies and tactics of the analytic toolkit. By the end of the book, you'll be converting Pig syntax into MapReduce jobs in your head! You'll be able to reason about the cost of different operations and optimize your Pig scripts accordingly.

That covers MapReduce for now (don't worry, we'll revisit it in Chapter 7, which covers joins). Next, we'll introduce you to the dataset we'll be working on: baseball! Then we'll introduce Apache Pig, a high-level language and tool that will generate MapReduce jobs for you. Once we cover all that, we'll move on to learning analytic patterns in Pig in Part II of the book.

## CHAPTER 3

A Quick Look into Baseball

In this chapter, we will introduce the dataset we use throughout the book: baseball performance statistics. We will explain the various metrics used in baseball (and in this book), such that if you aren't a baseball fan you can still follow along.

Nate Silver (*http://bit.ly/nate_silver*) calls baseball the "perfect dataset." There are not many human-centered systems for which this comprehensive degree of detail is available, and no richer set of tables for truly demonstrating the full range of analytic patterns.

For readers who are not avid baseball fans, we provide a simple—some might say "oversimplified"—description of the sport and its key statistics. For more details, refer to Joseph Adler's *Baseball Hacks* (O'Reilly) or Max Marchi and Jim Albert's *Analyzing Baseball Data with R* (Chapman & Hall).

The Data

Our baseball statistics come in tables at multiple levels of detail.

Putting people first as we like to do, the people table lists each player's name and personal stats (height and weight, birth year, etc.). It has a primary key, the player_id, formed from the first five letters of the player's last name, first two letters of their first name, and a two-digit disambiguation slug. There are also primary tables for ballparks (parks, which lists information on every stadium that has ever hosted a game) and for teams (teams, which lists every Major League team back to the birth of the game).

The core statistics table is bat_seasons, which gives each player's batting stats by season (to simplify things, we only look at offensive performance). The player_id and year_id fields form a primary key, and the team_id foreign key represents the team that played the most games in a season. The `park_teams` table lists, for each team, all "home" parks in which a player played by season, along with the number of games and range of dates. We put "home" in quotes because technically it only signifies the team that bats last (a significant advantage), though teams nearly always play those home games at a single stadium in front of their fans. However, there are exceptions, as you'll see in Chapter 4. The `park_id`, `team_id`, and `year_id` fields form its primary key, so if a team did in fact have multiple home ballparks, there will be multiple rows in the table.

There are some demonstrations where we need data with some real heft—not so much that you can't run it on a single-node cluster, but enough that parallelizing the computation becomes important. In those cases, we'll go to the `games` table (100+ MB), which holds the final box score summary of every baseball game played, or to the full madness of the `events` table (1+ GB), which records every play for nearly every game back to the 1940s and before. These tables have nearly 100 columns each in their original form. Not to carry the joke quite so far, we've pared them back to only a few dozen columns each, with only a handful seeing actual use.

We denormalized the names of players, parks, and teams into some of the nonprime tables to make their records more recognizable. In many cases, you'll see us carry along the name of a player, ballpark, or team to make the final results more readable, even where they add extra heft to the job. We always try to show you sample code that represents the code we'd write professionally, and while we'd strip these fields from the script before it hit production, you're seeing just what we'd do in development. *Know your data.*

Acronyms and Terminology

We use the following acronyms (and, coincidentally, field names) in our baseball dataset:

G Games

PA Plate appearances (the number of completed chances to contribute offensively; for historical reasons, some stats use a restricted subset of plate appearances called AB, which stands for *at bats*, but should generally prefer PA to AB, and can pretend they represent the same concept)

H Hits—the value for this can be h1B (a single), h2B (a double), h3B (a triple), or HR (a home run)

BB Walks (pitcher presented too many unsuitable pitches)

HBP Hit by pitch (like a walk but more painful)

OBP On-base percentage (indicates effectiveness at becoming a potential run)

SLG   Slugging percentage (indicates effectiveness at converting potential runs into runs)

OPS   On-base-plus-slugging (a reasonable estimate of overall offensive contribution)

For those uninterested in baseball or who consider sporting events to be the dull province of jocks: when we say that the "on-base percentage" is a simple matter of finding (H + BB + HBP) / AB, just trust us that (a) it's a useful statistic; (b) that's how you find its value; and then (c) pretend it's the kind of numbers-in-a-table example abstracted from the real world that many books use.

The Rules and Goals

Major League Baseball teams play a game nearly every single day from the start of April to the end of September (currently, 162 per season). The team on offense sends its players to bat in order, with the goal of having its players reach base and advance the full way around the diamond. Each time a player makes it all the way to home, his team scores a run, and at the end of the game, the team with the most runs wins. We count these events as games (G), plate appearances on offense (PA), and runs (R).

The best way to reach base is by hitting the ball back to the fielders and reaching base safely before they can retrieve the ball and chase you down—this is called a hit (H). You can also reach base on a walk (BB) if the pitcher presents too many unsuitable pitches, or from a hit by pitch (HBP), which is like a walk but more painful. You advance on the basepaths when your teammates hit the ball or reach base; the reason a hit is valuable is that you can advance as many bases as you can run in time. Most hits are singles (h1B)— batter safely reaches first base. Even better is for the batter to get a double (h2B); a triple (h3B), which is rare and requires very fast running; or a home run (HR), usually by clobbering the ball out of the park.

Your goal as a batter is twofold: you want to become a potential run and you want to help convert players on base into runs. If the batter does not reach base, it counts as an out, and after three outs, all the players on base lose their chance to score and the other team comes to bat. (This threshold dynamic is what makes a baseball game exciting: the outcome of a single pitch could swing the score by several points and continue the offensive campaign, or it could squander the scoring potential of a brilliant offensive position.)

Performance Metrics

These baseball statistics are all "counting stats," and generally, the more games, the more hits and runs and so forth. For estimating performance and comparing players, it's better to use "rate stats" normalized against plate appearances.

On-base percentage (OBP) indicates how well the player meets offensive goal #1: get on base, thus becoming a potential run and *not* consuming a precious out. It is given as the fraction of plate appearances that are successful: ((H + BB + HBP) / PA).[1] An OBP over 0.400 is very good (better than 95% of significant seasons).

Slugging percentage (SLG) indicates how well the player meets offensive goal #2: advance the runners on base, thus converting potential runs into points toward victory. It is given by the total bases gained in hitting (one for a single, two for a double, etc.) divided by the number of at bats: ((H + h2B + 2*h3B + 3*HR) / AB). An SLG over 0.500 is very good.

On-base-plus-slugging (OPS) combines on-base and slugging percentages to give a simple and useful estimate of overall offensive contribution. It's found by simply adding the figures: (OBP + SLG). Anything above 0.900 is very good.

Just as a professional mechanic has an assortment of specialized and powerful tools, modern baseball analysis uses statistics significantly more nuanced than these. But when it comes time to hang a picture, they use the same hammer as the rest of us. You might think that using the OBP, SLG, and OPS figures to estimate overall performance is a simplification we made for you. In fact, these are quite actionable metrics that analysts will reach for when they want to hang a sketch that anyone can interpret.

Wrapping Up

In this chapter, we have introduced our dataset so that you can understand our examples without prior knowledge of baseball. You now have enough information about baseball and its metrics to work through the examples in this book. Whether you're a baseball fan or not, this dataset should work well for teaching analytic patterns. If you are a baseball fan, feel free to filter the examples to tell stories about your favorite team.

In Part II, we'll use baseball examples to teach analytic patterns—those operations that enable most kinds of analysis. First, though, we're going to learn about Apache Pig, which will dramatically streamline our use of MapReduce.

---

1 Although known as percentages, OBP and SLG are always given as fractions to three decimal places. For OBP, we're also using a slightly modified formula to reduce the number of stats to learn. It gives nearly identical results, but you will notice small discrepancies with official figures.

## CHAPTER 4

Introduction to Pig

In this chapter, we introduce the tools to teach analytic patterns in the chapters that comprise Part II of the book. To start, we'll set you up with chains of MapReduce jobs in the form of Pig scripts, and then we'll explain Pig's data model and tour the different datatypes. We'll also cover basic operations like LOAD and STORE. Next, we'll learn about UFOs and when people most often report them, and we'll dive into Wikipedia usage data and compare different projects. We'll also briefly introduce the different kind of analytic operations in Pig that we'll be covering in the rest of the book. Finally, we'll introduce you to two libraries of *user-defined functions* (UDFs): the Apache DataFu project and the Piggybank.

By the end of this chapter, you will be able to perform basic data processing on Hadoop using Pig.

Pig Helps Hadoop Work with Tables, Not Records

Apache Pig is an open source, high-level language that enables you to create efficient MapReduce jobs using clear, maintainable scripts. Its interface is similar to SQL, which makes it a great choice for folks with significant experience there. It's not identical, though, and things that are efficient in SQL may not be so in Pig (we will try to highlight those traps).

We use Pig, instead of Hive (another popular Hadoop tool), because it takes a procedural approach to data pipelines. A procedural approach lends itself to the implementation of complex data pipelines as clearly as possible, whereas nested SQL can get confusing, fast. A procedural approach also gives you the opportunity to optimize your data processing as you go, without relying on a *magic* query analyzer. When used in conjunction with Python, Pig forms the backbone of your data processing, while Python handles more complex operations.

You can run Pig in local mode with the following command:

```
pig -l /tmp -x local
```

Let's dive in with an example using the UFO dataset to estimate whether aliens tend to visit in some months over others:

```
sightings = LOAD '/data/gold/geo/ufo_sightings/ufo_sightings.tsv.bz2'  AS (
    sighted_at: chararray,    reported_at: chararray,    location_str: chararray,
    shape: chararray,         duration_str: chararray,   description: chararray,
    lng: float,               lat: float,                city: chararray,
    county: chararray,        state: chararray,          country: chararray );

-- Take the 6th and 7th character from the original string,
-- as in '2010-06-25T05:00:00Z', take '06'
month_count = FOREACH sightings GENERATE SUBSTRING(sighted_at, 5, 7) AS month;

-- Group by year_month,
-- and then count the size of the 'bag' this creates to get a total
ufos_by_month    = FOREACH (GROUP month_count BY month) GENERATE
  group AS month, COUNT_STAR(month_count) AS total;

STORE ufos_by_month INTO './ufos_by_month.out';
```

In a Python streaming or traditional Hadoop job, the focus is on the record, and you're best off thinking in terms of message passing or grouping. In Pig, the focus is much more on the structure, and you should think in terms of relational and set operations. In the preceding example, each line described an operation on the full dataset; we declared what change to make and Pig, as you'll see, executes those changes by dynamically assembling and running a set of MapReduce jobs.

To run the Pig job, go into the example code repository and run:

```
pig examples/ch_04/ufos_by_month.pig
```

If you consult the Job Browser, you should see a single MapReduce job; the dataflow Pig instructed Hadoop to run is essentially similar to the Python script you ran. What Pig ran was, in all respects, a Hadoop job. It calls on some of Hadoop's advanced features to help it operate, but nothing you could not access through the standard Java API.

To see the result of the Pig script, run the following:

```
cat ./ufos_by_month.out/*
```

You'll see the following results (also shown in Figure 4-1):

```
01   4263
02   3644
03   4170
04   4120
05   4220
06   6745
```

```
07   7361
08   6641
09   5665
10   5421
11   4954
12   3933
     256
```

Note that 256 records had no such value—data will often surprise you. You might filter these empty values, or look closer at the raw data to see what's going on. Also, did
you notice the output was sorted? That is no coincidence; as you saw in Chapter 2,
Hadoop sorted the results in order to group them. Sorting in this case is free! We'll
learn how to explicitly sort data in Pig in a future chapter.

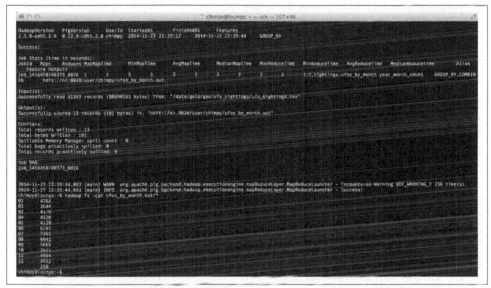

Figure 4-1. Running Pig on our Docker VM

Wikipedia Visitor Counts

Let's put Pig to a sterner test. Here's the same script from before, modified to run on
the much-larger Wikipedia dataset, and this time to assemble counts by hour:

```
/* Wikipedia pagecounts data described at https://dumps.wikimedia.org/other/
pagecounts-raw/ The first column is the project name. The second column is
the title of the page retrieved, the third column is the number of requests,
and the fourth column is the size of the content returned. */

-- LOAD the data, which is space-delimited
pageviews = LOAD '/data/rawd/wikipedia/page_counts/pagecounts-20141126-230000.gz'
    USING PigStorage(' ') AS (
        project_name:chararray,
        page_title:chararray,
```

```
        requests:long,
        bytes:long
);

-- Group the data by project name, then count
-- total pageviews & bytes sent per project
per_project_counts = FOREACH (GROUP pageviews BY project_name) GENERATE
    group AS project_name,
    SUM(pageviews.requests) AS total_pageviews,
    SUM(pageviews.bytes) AS total_bytes;

-- Order the output by the total pageviews, in descending order
sorted_per_project_counts = ORDER per_project_counts BY total_pageviews DESC;

-- Store the data in our home directory
STORE sorted_per_project_counts INTO 'sorted_per_project_counts.out';

/*
LOAD SOURCE FILE
GROUP BY PROJECT NAME
SUM THE PAGE VIEWS AND BYTES FOR EACH PROJECT
ORDER THE RESULTS BY PAGE VIEWS, HIGHEST VALUE FIRST
STORE INTO FILE
*/
```

Run the script just as you did in the previous section:

```
hadoop fs -cat sorted_per_project_counts.out/* | head -10
```

which should result in a top 10 list of Wikipedia projects by page views:

```
meta.m  14163318    42739631770
en  8464555 271270368044
meta.mw 8070652 10197686607
en.mw   4793661 113071171104
es  2105765 48775855730
ru  1198414 38771387406
es.mw   967440  16660332837
de  967435  20956877209
fr  870142  22441868998
pt  633136  16647117186
```

Until now, we have described Pig as authoring the same MapReduce job you would. In fact, Pig has automatically introduced the same optimizations an advanced practitioner have introduced, but with no effort on your part. Pig instructed Hadoop to use a combiner. In the naive Python job, every mapper output record was sent across the network to the reducer; in Hadoop, the mapper output files have already been partitioned and sorted. Hadoop offers you the opportunity to do preaggregation on those groups. Rather than send every record for, say, September 26, 2014, 8 p.m., the combiner outputs the hour and sum of visits emitted by the mapper.

The second script instructed Pig to explicitly sort the output by total page views or requests, an additional operation. We did not do that in the first example to limit it to a single job. As you will recall from Chapter 3, Hadoop uses a sort to prepare the reducer groups, so its output was naturally ordered. If there are multiple reducers, however, that would not be enough to give you a result file you can treat as ordered. By default, Hadoop assigns partitions to reducers using the RandomPartitioner, which is designed to give each reducer a uniform chance of claiming any given partition. This defends against the problem of one reducer becoming overwhelmed with an unfair share of records, but means the keys are distributed willy-nilly across machines. Although each reducer's output is sorted, you will see early records at the top of each result file and later records at the bottom of each result file.

What we want instead is a total sort—the earliest records in the first numbered file in order, the following records in the next file in order, and so on until the last numbered file. Pig's ORDER operator does just that. In fact, it does better than that. If you look at the JobTracker console, you will see Pig actually ran three MapReduce jobs. As you would expect, the first job is the one that did the grouping and summing, and the last job is the one that sorted the output records. In the last job, all the earliest records were sent to reducer 0, the middle range of records were sent to reducer 1, and the latest records were sent to reducer 2.

Hadoop, however, has no intrinsic way to make that mapping happen. Even if it figured out, say, that the earliest buckets were sooner and the latest buckets were later, if we fed it a dataset with skyrocketing traffic in 2014, we would end up sending an overwhelming portion of results to that reducer. In the second job, Pig sampled the set of output keys, brought them to the same reducer, and figured out the set of partition breakpoints to distribute records fairly.

In general, Pig offers many more optimizations beyond these. In our experience, as long as you're willing to give Pig a bit of coaching, the only times it will author a dataflow that is significantly less performant are when Pig is *overly* aggressive about introducing an optimization. And in those cases, the impact is more like a bunch of silly piglets making things take 50% longer than they should, rather than a stampede of boars blowing up your cluster. The ORDER BY example is a case in point: for small- to medium-sized tables, the intermediate sampling stage to calculate partitions can have a larger time cost than the penalty for partitioning badly would carry. Sometimes you're stuck paying an extra 20 seconds on top of each 1-minute job so that Pig and Hadoop can save you an order of magnitude off your 10-minute-and-up jobs.

Fundamental Data Operations

Pig's operators (and fundamental Hadoop processing patterns) can be grouped into several families: control operations, pipelinable operations, and structural operations.

A control operation either influences or describes the dataflow itself. A pipelinable operation is one that does not require a reduce step of its own: the records can each be handled in isolation, and so they do not have to be expensively assembled into context. All structural operations must put records into context: placing all records for a given key into common context; sorting each record into context with the record that precedes it and the record that follows it; eliminating duplicates by putting all potential duplicates into common context; and so forth.

Control Operations

The following control operations are essential to defining dataflows, or chains of data processing:

- Serialization operations (LOAD, STORE) load and store data into filesystems or datastores.
- Pig-specific directives (DESCRIBE, ILLUSTRATE, REGISTER, etc.) to Pig itself do not modify the data; rather, they modify Pig's execution (outputting debug information, registering external UDFs, etc.).

Pipelinable Operations

With no structural operations, these operations create a mapper-only job with the composed pipeline. When they come before or after a structural operation, they are composed into the mapper or reducer:

- Transformation operations (FOREACH, FOREACH..FLATTEN(*tuple*)) modify the contents of records individually. The count of output records is exactly the same as the count of input records, but the contents and schema of the records can change arbitrarily.
- Filtering operations (FILTER, SAMPLE, LIMIT, ASSERT) accept or reject each record individually. These can yield the same or a fewer number of records, but each record has the same contents and schema as its input.
- Repartitioning operations (SPLIT, UNION) don't change records; they just distribute them into new tables or dataflows. UNION outputs exactly as many records as the sum of its inputs. Because SPLIT is effectively several FILTERs run simultaneously, its total output record count is the sum of what each of its filters would produce.
- Ungrouping operations (FOREACH..FLATTEN(*bag*)) turn records that have bags of tuples into records with each such tuple from the bags in combination. It is most commonly seen after a grouping operation (and thus occurs within the reduce phase) but can be used on its own (in which case, like the other pipelinable oper-

ations, it produces a mapper-only job). FLATTEN itself leaves the bag contents unaltered and substitutes the bag field's schema with the schema of its contents. When you are flattening on a single field, the count of output records is exactly the count of elements in all bags (records with empty bags will disappear in the output). Multiple FLATTEN clauses yield a record for each possible combination of elements, which can be explosively higher than the input count.

Structural Operations

The following jobs require a map and reduce phase:

- Grouping operations (GROUP, COGROUP, CUBE, ROLLUP) place records into context with each other. They make no modifications to the input records' contents, but do rearrange their schema. You will often find them followed by a FOREACH that is able to take advantage of the group context. GROUP and COGROUP yield one output record per distinct GROUP value.

- Joining operations (JOIN, CROSS) match records between tables. JOIN is simply an optimized COGROUP/FLATTEN/FOREACH sequence, but it is important enough and different in use that we'll cover it separately. (The same is true about CROSS, except for the "important" part: we'll have very little to say about it and discourage its use).

- Sorting operations (ORDER BY, RANK) perform a total sort on their input; every record in file 00000 is in sorted order and comes before all records in 00001 and so forth for the number of output files. These require two jobs: first, a light mapper-only pass to understand the distribution of sort keys, and next a MapReduce job to perform the sort.

- Uniquing and (DISTINCT, specific COGROUP forms) select/reject/collapse duplicates, or find records associated with unique or duplicated records. These are typically accomplished with specific combinations of the above, but can involve more than one MapReduce job. We'll talk more about these later in Chapter 9.

That's everything you can do with Pig—and everything you need to do with data. Each of those operations leads to a predictable set of map and reduce steps, so it's very straightforward to reason about your job's performance. Pig is very clever about chaining and optimizing these steps.

Pig is an extremely sparse language. By having very few operators and a very uniform syntax,[1] the language makes it easy for the robots to optimize the dataflow and for humans to predict and reason about its performance.

We will not explore every nook and cranny of its syntax, only illustrate its patterns of use. The online Pig manual (*http://pig.apache.org/*) is quite good, and for a deeper exploration, consult *Programming Pig* by Alan Gates. If the need for a construction never arose naturally in a pattern demonstration or exploration,[2] we omitted it, along with options or alternative forms of construction that are either dangerous or rarely used.[3]

In the remainder of this chapter, we'll illustrate the mechanics of using Pig and the essentials of its control flow operations by demonstrating them in actual use. In Part II, we'll cover patterns of both pipelinable and structural operations. In each case, the goal is to understand not only its use, but also how to implement the corresponding patterns in a plain MapReduce approach—and therefore how to reason about their performance.

LOAD Locates and Describes Your Data

In order to analyze data, we need data to analyze. In this case, we'll start by looking at a record of the outcome of baseball games using the LOAD statement in Pig. Pig scripts need data to process, and so your Pig scripts will begin with a LOAD statement and have one or many STORE statements throughout. Here's a script to find all Wikipedia articles that contain the word *Hadoop*:

```
games = LOAD '/data/gold/sports/baseball/games_lite.tsv' AS (
  game_id:chararray,      year_id:int,
  away_team_id:chararray, home_team_id:chararray,
  away_runs_ct:int,       home_runs_ct:int
);

home_wins = FILTER games BY home_runs_ct > away_runs_ct;

STORE home_wins INTO './home_wins.tsv';
```

Note the output shows us how many records were read and written. This happens to tell us there are 206,015 games total, of which 111,890 (or 54.3%) were won by the home team. We have quantified the home field advantage!

```
Input(s):
Successfully read 206015 records (6213566 bytes) from:
```

---

1 Something SQL users but nonenthusiasts like your authors appreciate.

2 An example of the first is UNION ONSCHEMA—useful but not used.

3 It's legal in Pig to load data without a schema (but you shouldn't, so we're not going to tell you how).

```
"/data/gold/sports/baseball/games_lite.tsv"
```

```
Output(s):
Successfully stored 111890 records (3374003 bytes) in:
  "hdfs://nn:8020/user/chimpy/home_wins.tsv"
```

Simple Types

As you can see, in addition to telling Pig where to find the data, the LOAD statement also describes the table's schema. Pig understands 10 kinds of simple type, 6 of which are numbers: signed machine integers, as int (32 bit) or long (64-bit); signed floating-point numbers, as float (32-bit) or double (64-bit); arbitrary-length integers, as biginteger; and arbitrary-precision real numbers, as bigdecimal. If you're supplying a literal value for a long, you should append a capital L to the quantity: 12345L; if you're supplying a literal float, use an f: 123.45f.

The chararray type loads text as UTF-8 encoded strings (the only kind of string you should ever traffic in). String literals are contained in single quotes: 'hello, world'. Regular expressions are supplied as string literals, as in the previous example: '.*[Hh]adoop.*'. The bytearray type does no interpretation of its contents whatsoever, but be careful— the most common interchange formats (tsv, xml, and json) cannot faithfully round-trip data that is truly freeform.

Lastly, there are two special-purpose simple types. Time values are described with datetime, and should be serialized in the ISO-8601 format: 1970-01-01T00:00:00.000+00:00

Boolean values are described with boolean, and should bear the values true or false.

boolean, datetime, and the biginteger/bigdecimal types are recent additions to Pig, and you will notice rough edges around their use.

Complex Type 1, Tuples: Fixed-Length Sequence of Typed Fields

Pig also has three complex types, representing collections of fields. A tuple is a fixed-length sequence of fields, each of which has its own schema. They're ubiquitous in the results of the various structural operations you're about to learn. Here's how you'd load a listing of Major League ballpark locations (we usually don't serialize tuples, but so far LOAD is the only operation we've taught you):

```
-- The address and geocoordinates are stored as tuples. Don't do that, though.
ballpark_locations = LOAD 'ballpark_locations' AS (
    park_id:chararray, park_name:chararray,
    address:tuple(
      full_street:chararray, city:chararray, state:chararray, zip:chararray),
    geocoordinates:tuple(lng:float, lat:float)
);
```

```
ballparks_in_texas = FILTER ballpark_locations BY (address.state == 'TX');
STORE ballparks_in_texas INTO '/tmp/ballparks_in_texas.tsv'
```

Pig displays tuples using parentheses. It would dump a line from the input file as:

```
BOS07,Fenway Park,(4 Yawkey Way,Boston,MA,02215),(-71.097378,42.3465909)
```

As shown here, you address single values within a tuple using `tuple_name.sub` `field_name`—for example, `address.state` will have the schema `state:chararray`. You can also create a new tuple that projects or rearranges fields from a tuple by writing `tuple_name.(subfield_a, subfield_b, ...)`; for example, `address.(zip, city, state)` will have schema `address_zip_city_state:tuple(zip:chararray, city:chararray, state:chararray)` (Pig helpfully generated a readable name for the tuple).

Tuples can contain values of any type, even bags and other tuples, but that's nothing to be proud of. We follow almost every structural operation with a `FOREACH` to simplify its schema as soon as possible, and so should you—it doesn't cost anything and it makes your code readable.

Complex Type 2, Bags: Unbounded Collection of Tuples

A bag is an arbitrary-length collection of tuples, all of which are expected to have the same schema. Just like with tuples, they're ubiquitous yet rarely serialized. In the following code example, we demonstrate the creation and storing of bags, as well as how to load them again. Here we prepare, store, and load a dataset for each team listing the year and park ID of the ballparks it played in:

```
park_team_years = LOAD '/data/gold/sports/baseball/park_team_years.tsv'
    USING PigStorage('\t') AS (
        park_id:chararray, team_id:chararray, year:long,
        beg_date:chararray, end_date:chararray, n_games:long
);
team_park_seasons = FOREACH (GROUP park_team_years BY team_id) GENERATE
    group AS team_id,
    park_team_years.(year, park_id) AS park_years;

DESCRIBE team_park_seasons

STORE team_park_seasons INTO './bag_of_park_years.txt';

team_park_seasons = LOAD './bag_of_park_years.txt' AS (
    team_id:chararray,
    park_years: bag{tuple(year:int, park_id:chararray)}
    );

DESCRIBE team_park_seasons
```

A `DESCRIBE` of the data looks like this:

```
team_park_seasons: {
    team_id: chararray,park_years: {
        (year: long,park_id: chararray)}}
```

Let's look at a few lines of the relation team_park_seasons:

```
a = limit team_park_seasons 5;
dump a
```

They look like this:

```
(BFN,{(1884,BUF02),(1882,BUF01),(1883,BUF01),(1879,BUF01),(1885,MILA?),...])
(BFP,{(1890,BUF03)})
(BL1,{(1872,RAL02),(1873,BAL02),(1874,BAL02)})
(BL2,{(1887,BAL03),(1883,BAL03),(1889,BAL06),(1885,BAL03),(1888,BAL03),...})
(BL3,{(1891,BAL06),(1891,BAL07),(1890,BAL06)})
```

Defining the Schema of a Transformed Record

You can also address values within a bag using bag_name.(subfield_a, sub field_b), but this time the result is a bag with the given projected tuples. You'll see examples of this shortly when we discuss FLATTEN and the various group operations. Note that the *only* type a bag holds is tuple, even if there's only one field—a bag of just park IDs would have schema bag{tuple(park_id:chararray)}.

It is worth noting the way schema are constructed in the preceding example: using a FOREACH. The FOREACH in the snippet emits two fields of the elements of the bag park_team_years, and supplies a schema for each new field with the AS <schema> clauses.

STORE Writes Data to Disk

The STORE operation writes your data to the destination you specify (typically and by default, the HDFS). The current working directory and your home directory on HDFS is referenced by ./:

```
STORE my_records INTO './bag_of_park_years.txt';
```

As with any Hadoop job, Pig creates a *directory* (not a file) at the path you specify; each task generates a file named with its task ID into that directory. In a slight difference from vanilla Hadoop, if the last stage is a reduce, the files are named like *part-r-00000* (r for reduce, followed by the task ID); if a map, they are named like *part-m-00000*.

Try removing the STORE line from the preceding script, and run it again. You'll see nothing happen! Pig is declarative: your statements inform Pig how it could produce certain tables, rather than command Pig to produce those tables in order.

Note that we can view the files created by STORE using ls:

```
ls ./bag_of_park_years.txt
```

which gives us:

```
part-r-00000 _SUCCESS
```

The behavior of only evaluating on demand is an incredibly useful feature for development work. One of the best pieces of advice we can give you is to checkpoint all the time. Smart data scientists iteratively develop the first few transformations of a project, then save that result to disk; working with that saved checkpoint, they develop the next few transformations, then save it to disk; and so forth. Here's a demonstration:

```
great_start = LOAD '...' AS (...);
-- ...
-- lots of stuff happens, leading up to
-- ...
important_milestone = JOIN [...];

-- reached an important milestone, so checkpoint to disk.
STORE important_milestone INTO './important_milestone.tsv';
    important_milestone = LOAD './important_milestone.tsv' AS (...schema...);
```

In development, once you've run the job past the STORE important_milestone line, you can comment it out to make Pig skip all the preceding steps. Because there's nothing tying the graph to an output operation, nothing will be computed on behalf of important_milestone, and so execution will start with the following LOAD. The gratuitous save and load does impose a minor cost, so in production, comment out both the STORE and its following LOAD to eliminate the checkpoint step.

These checkpoints bring another benefit: an inspectable copy of your data at that checkpoint. Many newcomers to big data processing resist the idea of checkpointing often. It takes a while to accept that a terabyte of data on disk is cheap—but the cluster time to generate that data is far less cheap, and *the programmer time to create the job to create the data is most expensive of all*. We won't include the checkpoint steps in the printed code snippets of the book, but we've left them in the example code.

Development Aid Commands

Pig comes with several *helper* commands that assist you in writing Pig scripts, which we will now introduce: DESCRIBE, ASSERT, EXPLAIN, LIMIT..DUMP, and ILLUSTRATE.

DESCRIBE

DESCRIBE shows the schema of a table. You've already seen the DESCRIBE directive, which writes a description of a table's schema to the console. It's invaluable, and even as your project goes to production you shouldn't be afraid to leave these statements in where reasonable.

DUMP

DUMP shows data on the console, with great peril. The DUMP directive is actually equivalent to STORE, but (gulp) writes its output to your console. That's very handy when you're messing with data at your console, but a trainwreck when you unwittingly feed it a gigabyte of data. So you should never use a DUMP statement except as in the following stanza:

```
dumpable = LIMIT table_to_dump 10;
DUMP dumpable;
```

SAMPLE

SAMPLE pulls a certain ratio of data from a relation. The SAMPLE command does what it sounds like: given a relation and a ratio, it randomly samples the proportion of the ratio from the relation. SAMPLE is useful because it gives you a random sample of your data—as opposed to LIMIT/DUMP, which tends to give you a small, very *local* sorted piece of the data. You can combine SAMPLE, LIMIT, and DUMP:

```
-- Sample 5% of our data, then view 10 records from the sample
sampled = SAMPLE large_relation 0.05
limited = LIMIT sampled 10;
DUMP limited
```

ILLUSTRATE

ILLUSTRATE magically simulates your script's actions, except when it fails to work. The ILLUSTRATE directive is one of our best-loved, and most-hated, Pig operations. When it works, it is amazing. Unfortunately, it is often unreliable.

Even if you only want to see an example line or two of your output, using a DUMP or a STORE requires passing the full dataset through the processing pipeline. You might think, "OK, so just choose a few rows at random and run on that, but if your job has steps that try to match two datasets using a JOIN, it's exceptionally unlikely that any matches will survive the limiting. (For example, the players in the first few rows of the baseball players table belonged to teams that are not in the first few rows from the baseball teams table.) ILLUSTRATE previews your execution graph to intelligently mock up records at each processing stage. If the sample rows would fail to join, Pig uses them to generate fake records that will find matches. It solves the problem of running on ad hoc subsets, and that's why we love it.

However, not all parts of Pig's functionality work with ILLUSTRATE, meaning that it often fails to run. When is the ILLUSTRATE command most valuable? When applied to less widely used operations and complex sequences of statements, of course. What parts of Pig are most likely to lack ILLUSTRATE support or trip it up? Well, less widely used operations and complex sequences of statements, of course. And when it fails, it does so with perversely opaque error messages, leaving you to wonder if there's a problem in your script or if ILLUSTRATE has left you short. If you, eager reader, are looking for a good place to return some open source karma, consider making ILLUS TRATE into the tool it could be. Until somebody does, you should checkpoint often (as described in "STORE Writes Data to Disk" on page 49).

EXPLAIN

EXPLAIN shows Pig's execution graph. This command writes the "execution graph" of your job to the console. It's extremely verbose, showing *everything* Pig will do to your data, down to the typecasting it applies to inputs as they are read. We mostly find it useful when trying to understand whether Pig has applied some of the optimizations you'll learn about later.

Pig Functions

Pig functions act on fields. Pig wouldn't be complete without a way to *act* on the various fields. It offers a sparse but essential set of built-in functions as well as a rich collection of user-defined functions (UDFs) in the Piggybank (*http://bit.ly/ pig_piggybank*) and the Apache DataFu project (*http://datafu.incubator.apache.org/*). Part II is devoted to examples of Pig and MapReduce programs in practice, so we'll just list the highlights here:

- **Math functions** for all the things you'd expect to see on a good calculator: LOG/ LOG10/EXP, RANDOM, ROUND/ROUND_TO/FLOOR/CEIL, ABS, trigonometric functions, and so forth.
- **String comparison**:
  - matches tests a value against a regular expression.
  - Compare strings directly using ==. EqualsIgnoreCase does a case-insensitive match, while STARTSWITH/ENDSWITH test whether one string is a prefix or suffix of the other, respectively.
  - SIZE returns the number of characters in a chararray, and the number of bytes in a bytearray. Remember that characters often occupy more than one byte: the string *Motörhead* has 9 characters, but because of its umlauted ö, the string occupies 10 bytes. You can use SIZE on other types, too; but to find the number of elements in a bag, use COUNT_STAR and not SIZE.
  - INDEXOF finds the character position of a substring within a chararray.

- **Transform strings**:
  - CONCAT concatenates all its inputs into a new string; SPRINTF uses a supplied template to format its inputs into a new string; BagToString joins the contents of a bag into a single string, separated by a supplied delimiter.
  - LOWER converts a string to lowercase characters; UPPER to all uppercase.
  - TRIM strips leading and trailing whitespace.
  - REPLACE(string, 'regexp', 'replacement') substitutes the replacement string wherever the given regular expression matches, as implemented by java.string.replaceAll. If there are no matches, the input string is passed through unchanged.
  - REGEX_EXTRACT(string, regexp, index) applies the given regular expression and returns the contents of the indicated matched group. If the regular expression does not match, it returns NULL. The REGEX_EXTRACT_ALL function is similar, but returns a tuple of the matched groups.
  - STRSPLIT splits a string at each match of the given regular expression.
  - SUBSTRING selects a portion of a string based on position.
- **Datetime functions**, such as CurrentTime, ToUnixTime, SecondsBetween (duration between two given datetimes)
- **Aggregate functions** that act on bags:
  - AVG, MAX, MIN, SUM
  - COUNT_STAR reports the number of elements in a bag, including nulls; COUNT reports the number of non-null elements. IsEmpty tests that a bag has elements. Don't use the quite-similar-sounding SIZE function on bags: it's much less efficient.
- **Bag functions**:
  - Extremal
  - FirstTupleInBag
  - BagConcat
  - Stitch/Over
  - SUBTRACT(bag_a, bag_b) returns a new bag having all the tuples that are in the first but not in the second, and DIFF(bag_a, bag_b) returns a new bag having all tuples that are in either but not in both. These are rarely used, as the bags must be of modest size—in general, use an inner JOIN, as described in Chapter 7.

— TOP(num, column_index, bag) selects the top num of elements from each tuple in the given bag, as ordered by column_index. This uses a clever algorithm that doesn't require an expensive total sort of the data.

- **Conversion functions** to perform higher-level type casting: TOTUPLE, TOBAG, TOMAP

Pig has two libraries that add lots of features: Piggybank and Apache DataFu.

Piggybank

Piggybank comes with Pig—all you have to do to access it is REGISTER /usr/lib/pig/piggybank.jar;. To learn more about Pig, check the Piggybank documentation (*http://bit.ly/piggybank-lib*). At the time of writing, the Piggybank has the following Pig UDFs:

ABS	ASIN	ACOS
AllLoader	ATAN	ATAN2
AvroSchema2Pig	AvroSchemaManager	AvroStorage
AvroStorageInputStream	AvroStorageLog	AvroStorageUtils
Base	Bin	BinCond
CBRT	CEIL	CombinedLogLoader
CommonLogLoader	copySign	COR
COS	COSH	COV
CustomFormatToISO	CSVExcelStorage	CSVLoader
DateExtractor	DBStorage	Decode
DiffDate	DoubleAbs	DoubleBase
DoubleCopySign	DoubleDoubleBase	DoubleGetExponent
DoubleMax	DoubleMin	DoubleNextAfter
DoubleNextup	DoubleRound	DoubleSignum
DoubleUlp	EXP	EXPM1

ExtremalTupleByNthField	FixedWidthLoader	FixedWidthStorer
FloatAbs	FloatCopySign	FloatGetExponent
FloatMax	FloatMin	FloatNextAfter
FloatNextup	FloatRound	FloatSignum
FloatUlp	FLOOR	getExponent
HadoopJobHistoryLoader	HashFNV	HashFNV1
HashFNV2	HiveColumnarLoader	HiveColumnarStorage
HiveRCInputFormat	HiveRCOutputFormat	HiveRCRecordReader
HiveRCSchemaUtil	HostExtractor	HYPOT
IEEEremainder	IndexedStorage	INDEXOF
IntAbs	IntMax	IntMin
IsDouble	IsFloat	IsInt
IsLong	IsNumeric	ISODaysBetween
ISOHelper	ISOHoursBetween	ISOMinutesBetween
ISOMonthsBetween	ISOSecondsBetween	ISOToDay
ISOToHour	ISOToMinute	ISOToMonth
ISOToSecond	ISOToUnix	ISOToWeek
ISOToYear	ISOYearsBetween	JsonMetadata
LASTINDEXOF	LcFirst	LENGTH
LoadFuncHelper	LOG	LOG10
LOG1P	LongAbs	LongMax
LongMin	LookupInFiles	LOWER
MAX	MaxTupleBy1stField	MIN

MultiStorage	MyRegExLoader	nextAfter
NEXTUP	Over	PathPartitioner
PathPartitionHelper	PigAvroDatumReader	PigAvroDatumWriter
PigAvroInputFormat	PigAvroOutputFormat	PigAvroRecordReader
PigAvroRecordWriter	PigSchema2Avro	PigStorageSchema
POW	RANDOM	RegexExtract
RegexExtractAll	RegExLoader	RegexMatch
REPLACE	Reverse	RINT
ROUND	SCALB	SearchEngineExtractor
SearchTermExtractor	SearchQuery	SequenceFileLoader
SIGNUM	SIN	SINH
Split	SQRT	Stitch
Stuff	SUBSTRING	TAN
TANH	TestAllLoader	TestAvroStorage
TestAvroStorageUtils	TestCombinedLogLoader	TestCommonLogLoader
TestConvertDateTime	TestCSVExcelStorage	TestCSVStorage
TestDateExtractor	TestDBStorage	TestDecode
TestDiffDate	TestDiffDateTime	TestEvalString
TestExtremalTupleByNthField	TestFixedWidthLoader	TestFixedWidthStorer
TestHadoopJobHistoryLoader	TestHashFNV	TestHelper
TestHiveColumnarLoader	TestHiveColumnarStorage	TestHostExtractor
TestIndexedStorage	TestIsDouble	TestIsFloat
TestIsInt	TestIsLong	TestIsNumeric

TestLength	TestLoadFuncHelper	TestLookupInFiles
TestMathUDF	TestMultiStorage	TestMultiStorageCompression
TestMyRegExLoader	TestOver	TestPathPartitioner
TestPathPartitionHelper	TestRegex	TestRegExLoader
TestReverse	TestSearchEngineExtractor	TestSearchQuery
TestSearchTermExtractor	TestSequenceFileLoader	TestSplit
TestStat	TestStitch	TestStuff
TestToBagToTuple	TestTop	TestTruncateDateTime
TestUcFirst	TestXMLLoader	ToBag
toDegrees	Top	toRadians
ToTuple	Trim	UcFirst
ULP	UPPER	Util
UnixToISO	XMLLoader	XPath

To use a UDF, you must call on its full classpath. The DEFINE command can help you make a shortcut to the UDF. DEFINE can also add any initialization parameters the UDF requires:

```
REGISTER /usr/lib/pig/piggybank.jar

DEFINE Reverse org.apache.pig.piggybank.evaluation.string.Reverse();

b = FOREACH a GENERATE Reverse(char_field) AS reversed_char_field;
```

Apache DataFu

Apache DataFu is a collection of libraries for Pig that includes statistical and utility functions. To learn more about DataFu, check out the website (*https://datafu.incuba tor.apache.org/*). At the time of writing, Apache DataFu has the following Pig UDFs:

AbstractStableDistributionFunction	AliasableEvalFunc
AppendToBag	Assert

AssertUDF	BagConcat
BagGroup	BagJoin
BagLeftOuterJoin	BagSplit
Base64Decode	Base64Encode
BoolToInt	CachedFile
ChaoShenEntropyEstimator	Coalesce
CondEntropy	ContextualEvalFunc
Cosine	CountEach
CosineDistanceHash	DataFuException
DataTypeUtil	DistinctBy
DoubleVAR	EmpiricalCountEntropy
EmpiricalEntropyEstimator	EmptyBagToNull
EmptyBagToNullFields	Entropy
EntropyEstimator	EntropyUtil
Enumerate	FieldNotFound
FirstTupleFromBag	FloatVAR
HaversineDistInMiles	HyperLogLogPlusPlus
HyperplaneLSH	In
IntToBool	IntVAR
InUDF	L1
L1LSH	L1PStableHash
L2	L2LSH
L2PStableHash	LongVAR

LSH	LSHCreator
LSHFamily	LSHFunc
MarkovPairs	MD5
Median	MetricUDF
NullToEmptyBag	package-info
PageRank	PageRankImpl
POSTag	PrependToBag
ProgressIndicator	Quantile
QuantileUtil	RandInt
RandomUUID	RepeatingLSH
Reservoir	ReservoirSample
ReverseEnumerate	SampleByKey
Sampler	ScoredTuple
SelectStringFieldByName	SentenceDetect
SessionCount	Sessionize
SetDifference	SetIntersect
SetOperationsBase	SetUnion
SHA	SimpleEvalFunc
SimpleRandomSample	SimpleRandomSampleWithReplacementElect
SimpleRandomSampleWithReplacementVote	StreamingMedian
StreamingQuantile	TokenizeME
TokenizeSimple	TokenizeWhitespace
TransposeTupleToBag	UnorderedPairs

URLInfo	UserAgentClassify
VAR	WeightedReservoirSample
WeightedSample	WilsonBinConf

As in Piggybank, you must register the DataFu JAR and then call on the full classpath of the UDF, or use DEFINE to make a shortcut:

```
REGISTER /usr/lib/pig/datafu.jar

DEFINE COALESCE datafu.pig.util.Coalesce();

b = FOREACH a GENERATE COALESCE(field1, field2) AS coalesced;
```

Wrapping Up

This chapter was a gentle introduction to Pig and its basic operations. We introduced Pig's basic syntax: LOAD, STORE, SAMPLE, DUMP, ILLUSTRATE, and EXPLAIN. We listed Pig's basic operations. We introduced the Apache DataFu and Piggybank libraries of Pig UDFs. Using this knowledge, you can now write and run basic Pig scripts.

We used this new ability to dive in and perform some basic queries: we determined in which months people report the most UFOs, as well as which projects are most popular on Wikipedia. We've been able to do a lot already with very basic knowledge!

In the next two chapters, we'll build on what we've learned and see Pig in action, doing more with the tool as we learn analytics patterns.

## PART II

Tactics: Analytic Patterns

Now that you've met the fundamental analytic machinery (in both its MapReduce and table-operation form), it's time to put it to work.

This part of the book will equip you to think tactically (i.e., in terms of the changes you would like to make to the data). Each chapter introduces a repeatedly useful data transformation pattern, demonstrated in Pig (and, where we'd like to reinforce the record-by-record action, in Python as well).

One of this book's principles is to center demonstrations on an interesting and realistic problem from some domain. And whenever possible, we endeavor to indicate how the approach would extend to other domains, especially ones with an obvious business focus. The tactical patterns, however, are exactly those tools that crop up in nearly every domain: think of them as the screwdriver, torque wrench, lathe, and so forth of your toolkit. Now, if this book were called *Big Mechanics for Chimps*, we might introduce those tools by repairing and rebuilding a Volkswagen Beetle engine, or by building another lathe from scratch. Those lessons would carry over to anywhere machine tools apply: air conditioner repair, fixing your kid's bike, or building a rocketship to Mars.

So we will focus this part of the book on the dataset we just introduced, what Nate Silver calls "the perfect dataset": the sea of numbers surrounding the sport of baseball. The members of the Retrosheet and Baseball Databank projects have provided an extraordinary resource: comprehensive statistics from the birth of the game in the late 1800s until the present day, freely available and redistributable. Chapter 3 provides an overview of the stats we'll use. Even if you're not a baseball fan, we've minimized the number of concepts you'll need to learn.

In particular, we will be hopping in and out of two main storylines as each pattern is introduced. One is a graphical biography of each player and team—the data tables for a website that can display timelines, maps, and charts of the major events and people in the history of a team or player. This is explanatory analytics, where the goal is to summarize the answers to well-determined questions for presentation. We will demonstrate finding the geographical coordinates for each stadium or assembling the events in a player's career in a way that you can apply any time you want to show things on a map or display a timeline. When we demonstrate the self-join by listing each player's teammates, we're showing you how to list all other products purchased in the same shopping cart as a product, or all pages covisited by a user during a website session, and any other occasion where you want to extend a relationship by one degree.

The other storyline is to find indicators of exceptional performance, supplying a quantitative basis for the age-old question "Who are the greatest players in the game?" This is exploratory analytics, where the work is as much to determine the questions as to assemble the answers, quantifying "How many great seasons did this player have?" or "How many great players did this team have in which era?" As we pursue this exploration, you should recognize not just a way for fantasy baseball players to get an edge, but also strategies for quantifying the behavior of any sort of outlier. Here, it's baseball players, but similar questions will apply for examining agents posing security threats, load factor on public transit routes, factors causing manufacturing defects, cell strains with a significantly positive response, and many other topics of importance.

In many cases, though, a pattern has no natural demonstration in service of those primary stories, and so we'll find questions that could support an investigation of their own: "How can we track changes in each team's roster over time?" and "Is the stereotypical picture of the big brawny home-run hitter true?" For these, we will usually just show the setup and stop at the trailhead. But when the data comes forth with a story so compelling it demands investigation ("Does God really hate Cleveland?" and "Why are baseball players more likely to die in January and be born in August?"), we will take a brief side trip to follow the tale.

This means, however, that you may find yourself looking at a pattern and saying, "Geez, I don't see how this would apply to my work in quantitative finance/manufacturing/basket weaving/etc." It might be the case that it doesn't apply; a practicing air conditioner repairperson generally doesn't have much use for a lathe. In many other cases, it does apply, but you won't see how until some late night when your back's against the wall and you remember that one section that covered "Splitting a Table into Uniform Chunks" and an hour later you tweet "No doubt about it, I sure am glad I purchased *Big Data for Chimps*." Our belief and our goal is that it's most commonly the second scenario.

Each pattern is followed by a "pattern in use" synopsis that suggests alternative business contexts for this pattern, lists important caveats and associated patterns, and explains how to reason about its performance. These will become most useful once you've read the book a first time and (we hope) begin using it as your go-to reference. If you find the level of detail here to be a bit intense, skim past them on the first reading.

What's most important is that you learn the mechanics of each pattern, ignoring the story if you must. The best thing you can do is to grab a dataset of your own (e.g., from your work or research) and translate the patterns to that domain. Don't worry about finding an overarching theme like our performance-outliers storyline—just get a feel for the craft of using Hadoop at scale.

## CHAPTER 5

Map-Only Operations

This chapter begins the *Analytic Patterns* section of the book. In this chapter (and those beyond), we will walk you through a series of analytic patterns, an example of each, and a summary of information about when and where you might use them. As we go, you will learn and accumulate new abilities in your analytic toolkit.

This chapter focuses exclusively on what we'll call *map-only operations*. A map-only operation is one that can handle each record in isolation, like the translator chimps from Chimpanzee and Elephant Inc's first job. That property makes those operations trivially parallelizable: they require no reduce phase of their own.

Technically, these operations can be run in the map or reduce phase of MapReduce. When a script exclusively uses map-only operations, they give rise to one mapper-only job, which executes the composed pipeline stages.

All of these are listed first and together for two reasons. One, they are largely fundamental; it's hard to get much done without FILTER or FOREACH. Two, the way you reason about the performance impact of these operations is largely the same. Because these operations are trivially parallelizable, they scale efficiently and the computation cost rarely impedes throughput. And when pipelined, their performance cost can be summarized as "kids eat free with purchase of an adult meal." For datasets of any material size, it's very rare that the cost of preliminary or follow-on processing rivals the cost of the reduce phase. Finally, because these operations handle records in isolation, their memory impact is modest. So learn to think of these together.

Pattern in Use

Blocks like the following will show up after each of the patterns or groups of patterns we cover (not every field will be present every time, as there's not always anything interesting to say):

Where You'll Use It (The business or programming context.)

Everywhere. Like the f-stop on your camera, composing a photo begins and ends with throttling its illumination.

Standard Snippet (Just enough of the code to remind you how it's spelled.)

```
some_records = FILTER myrecords BY (criteria AND criteria ...);
```

Hello, SQL Users (A sketch of the corresponding SQL command, and important caveats for people coming from a SQL background.)

```
SELECT bat_season.* FROM bat_season WHERE year_id >= 1900;
```

Important to Know (Caveats about its use. Things that you likely won't understand or buy into the first time through the book, but will probably like to know later.)

- Filter early, filter often. The best thing you can do with a large dataset is make it smaller.

- SQL users take note: ==, != (not = or anything else)

- Programmers take note: AND, OR (not &&, ||)

Output Count (How many records in the output: fewer, same, more, explosively more?)

Zero to 100% of the input record count. Data size will decrease accordingly.

Records (A sketch of what the records coming out of this operation look like.)

Identical to input.

Dataflow (The Hadoop jobs this operation gives rise to. In this chapter, all the lines will look like this one; in the next chapters, that will change.)

Map-only: it's composed onto the end of the preceding map or reduce, and if it stands alone becomes a map-only job.

Exercises for You (A mission to carry forward, if you choose. Don't go looking for an answer section—we haven't done any of them. In many cases, you'll be the first to find the answer.)

Play around with nulls and the conditional operators until you have a good sense of its quirks.

See Also (Besides the patterns in its section of the book, what other topics might apply if you're considering this one? Sometimes this is another section in the book, sometimes it's a pointer elsewhere.)

The distinct operations, some set operations, and some joins are also used to eliminate records according to some criteria. See especially the sections on selecting or rejecting matches against a large list of keys ("Selecting Only Records That Lack a Match in Another Table (Anti-Join)" on page 164 and "Selecting Only Records That Possess a Match in Another Table (Semi-Join)" on page 164).

Eliminating Data

The first round of patterns will focus on methods to shrink your dataset. This may sound counterintuitive to the novice ear: isn't the whole point of big data that we get to work with the entire dataset at once? We ultimately develop models based on the entire population, not a sample thereof, so why should we scale down our data?

The primary reason is to focus on a subset of records: only website requests with an external referrer, only security events with high threat levels, only accounts of more than $1 million. And even when you work with every *record* in a dataset, you may be interested in a subset of *fields* relevant to your research. For reasons of memory and computational efficiency, and also your sanity, you'd do yourself a favor to immediately trim a working dataset down to just those records and fields relevant to the task at hand. Last, but not least, you may want to draw a random sample just to spot-check a dataset when it's too computationally expensive to inspect every element.

Working with a subset of data will simplify debugging. It also plays to our favorite refrain of *know your data*. If you're working on a dataset and there are additional fields or records you don't plan to use, can you be certain they won't somehow creep into your model? The worst-case scenario here is what's called a feature leak, wherein your target variable winds up in your training data. In essence: imagine saying you can predict today's high temperature, so long as you are first provided today's high temperature. A feature leak can lead to painful surprises when you deploy this model to the real world.

Furthermore, you may wish to test some code on a small sample before unleashing it on a long-running job. This is generally a good habit to develop, especially if you're one to kick off jobs before leaving the office, going to bed, or boarding a long-haul flight.

The goal of course isn't to *eliminate* data—rather, it's to be *selective* about your data. In the sections that follow, we'll introduce you to a variety of techniques for doing so.

Selecting Records That Satisfy a Condition: FILTER and Friends

The first step to eliminating (or being selective about) data is to reject records that don't match certain criteria. Pig's `FILTER` statement does this for you. It doesn't remove the data (all data in Hadoop and thus Pig is immutable); rather, like all Pig operations, it creates a new table that omits certain records from the input.

The baseball stats go back to 1871 (!), but it took a few decades for the game to reach its modern form. Let's say we're only interested in seasons since 1900. In Pig, we apply the FILTER operation:[1]

```
modern_bats = FILTER bats BY (year_id >= 1900);
```

The range of conditional expressions you'd expect are present: == (double-equals) to express an equality condition; != for not-equals; >, >=, <, and <= for inequalities; IN for presence in a list; and MATCHES for string pattern matching.

Selecting Records That Satisfy Multiple Conditions

In a data exploration, it's often important to exclude subjects with sparse data, either to eliminate small-sample-size artifacts, or because they are not in the focus of interest. In our case, we will often want to restrict analysis to regular players (i.e., those who have seen significant playing time in a season, while allowing for injury or situational replacement). Major League players come to bat a bit over 4 times per game on average in a season of 154 to 162 games (it increased in 1960), so we can take 450 plate appearances (roughly 2/3 of the maximum) as our threshold.[2]

In Pig, you can also combine conditional statements with AND, OR, and NOT. The following selects what we'll call "qualified modern seasons"—regular players, competing in the modern era, in either of the two modern leagues:

```
modsig_stats = FILTER bats BY
  (PA >= 450) AND (year_id >= 1900) AND ((lg_id == 'AL') OR (lg_id == 'NL'));
```

Selecting or Rejecting Records with a null Value

Another table we'll be working with is the people table. It describes players' vital statistics (their names, where and when they were born and died, when their career started and ended, their height and weight, etc.). The data is quite comprehensive, but in some cases, the fields have null values. nulls are used in practice for many things:

Missing/unknown value
   This is the case for a fraction of early players' birthplaces or birth dates.

No value applies
   Players who are still alive have null in the fields for date and location of death.

---

1 In this and in subsequent scripts, we're going to omit the LOAD, STORE, and other boilerplate except to prove a point. See the example code (*https://github.com/bd4c/big_data_for_chimps-code*) for fully working snippets.

2 Not coincidentally, that figure of 450 PA is close to the "qualified" season threshold of 3.1 plate appearances per team game that are required for seasonal performance awards.

Ill-formed value

If a corrupt line creates an unparseable cell (e.g., a value of `'Bob'` for an `int`), Pig will write a warning to the log but otherwise load it without complaint as `null`.

Illegal value

Division by zero and similar misbehavior results in a `null` value (and not an error, warning, or log statement).

"Other"

People will use a `null` value in general to represent "it's complicated, but maybe some other field has details."

We can exclude players whose birth year or birth place is unknown with a `FILTER` statement:

```
borned = FILTER people BY (birth_year IS NOT NULL) AND (birth_place IS NOT NULL);
```

For those coming from a SQL background, Pig's handling of `null` values will be fairly familiar. For the rest of us, good luck. `null` values generally disappear without notice from operations, and generally compare as `null` (which signifies neither `false` nor `true`). And so `null` is not less than 5.0, it is not greater than 5.0, and it is not equal to 5.0. A `null` value is not equal to `null`, and is not *unequal* to `null`. You can see why for programmers it can be hard to track all this. All the fiddly collection of rules is well detailed in the Pig manual, so we won't go deep into that here—we've found the best way to learn what you need is to just see lots of examples, which we endeavor to supply in abundance.

Selecting Records That Match a Regular Expression (MATCHES)

A `MATCHES` expression employs regular expression pattern matching against string values. Regular expressions are given as plain `chararray` strings; there's no special syntax, as Python/Ruby/Perl/etc. enthusiasts might have hoped. See "Important Notes About String Matching" on page 70 for important details and references that will help you master this important tool.

This operation uses a regular expression to select players with names similar to either of your authors' names:

```
-- Name is `Russ`, or `Russell`;
-- is `Flip` or anything in the Philip/Phillip/... family.
-- (?i) means be case-insensitive:
namesakes = FILTER people
        BY (name_first MATCHES '(?i).*(russ|russell|flip|phil+ip).*');
```

It's easy to forget that people's names can contain spaces, dots, dashes, apostrophes; start with lowercase letters or apostrophes; and have accented or other non-Latin characters.[3] So as a less silly demonstration of MATCHES, this snippet extracts all names that do not start with a capital letter or that contain a nonword, nonspace character:

```
funnychars = FILTER people BY (name_first MATCHES '^([^A-Z]|.*[^\\w\\s]).*');
```

There are many players with nonword, nonspace characters, but none whose names are represented as starting with a lowercase character. However, in early drafts of the book, this query caught a record with the value name_first—the header rows from a source datafile had contaminated the table. Sanity checks like these are a good idea always, even more so in big data. When you have billions of records, a one-in-a-million exception will appear thousands of times.

Important Notes About String Matching

Regular expressions are incredibly powerful, and we urge all readers to acquire basic familiarity with them. There is no better path to mastery than the Regular-Expressions.info website (*http://regexp.info*). Here are some essential clarifications about Pig in particular:

- Regular expressions in Pig are supplied to the MATCHES operator as plain strings. A single backslash serves the purposes of the string literal and does not appear in the string sent to the regexp engine. To pass along the shorthand [^\\w\\s] (nonword, nonspace characters), we have to use two backslashes.

  Yes, that means matching a literal backslash in the target string is done with four backslashes: \\\\

- Options for matching are supplied within the string. For example, (?i) matches without regard to case (as shown in the preceding example), (?m) is used to do multiline matches, and so forth (see the documentation).

- Pig regular expressions are implicitly anchored at the beginning and end of the string, the equivalent of adding ^ at the start and $ at the end (this mirrors Java but is unlike most other languages). Use .* at both ends, as we did before, to regain the conventional "greedy" behavior. Supplying explicit ^ or $ when intended is a good habit for readability.

- MATCHES is an expression, like AND or == (e.g., you write str MATCHES regexp). The other regular expression mechanisms you'll meet are functions—you write REGEX_EXTRACT(str, regexp, 1). You will forget we told you so the moment you finish this book.

- Appearing in the crop of results: Peek-A-Boo Veach, Quincy Trouppe, and Flip Lafferty.

---

[3] A demonstration of the general principle that if you believe an analysis involving people will be simple, you're probably wrong.

- You're allowed to have the regular expression be a value from the record, though Pig is able to precompile a constant (literal) regexp string for a nice speedup.

- Pig doesn't offer an exact equivalent to the SQL `%` expression for simple string matching. The rough equivalents are dot-star (`.*`) for the SQL `%` (zero or more arbitrary characters), dot (`.`) for the SQL `_` (a single character), and square brackets (e.g., `[a-z]`) for a character range, similar to SQL.

- The string equality expression is case sensitive: `'Peek-A-Boo'` does not equal `'peek-a-boo'`. For case-insensitive string matching, use the `EqualsIgnoreCase` function: `EqualsIgnoreCase('Peek-A-Boo', 'peek-a-boo')` is true. This simply invokes Java's `String.equalsIgnoreCase()` method and does not support regular expressions.

 Sadly, the Nobel Prize–winning physicists Gerard 't Hooft, Louis-Victor Pierre Raymond de Broglie, and Tomonaga Shin'ichirō never made the Major Leagues (or tried out, as far as we know). But their names are great counterexamples to keep in mind when dealing with names. Prof. de Broglie's full name is 38 characters long, has a last name that starts with a lowercase letter, and is nontrivial to segment. "Tomonaga" is a family name, though it comes first. You'll see Prof. Tomonaga's name given variously as "Tomonaga Shin'ichirō," "Sin-Itiro Tomonaga," or "朝永 振一郎," each one of them correct, and the others not, depending on context. Prof 't Hooft's last name starts with an apostrophe and a lowercase letter, and contains a space. You're well advised to start a little curio shelf in your workshop for counterexample collections such as these, and we'll share some of ours throughout the book.

Pattern in use

Where You'll Use It

Wherever you need to select records by a string field, for selecting against small lists, for finding ill-formed records, and for matching against a subsection of a composite key. Can you figure out what `game_id MATCHES '...(19|20).*'` in the games table does?

Standard Snippet

`FILTER recs BY (str MATCHES '.*pattern.*')`, sure, but also `FOREACH recs GENERATE (str MATCHES '.*(kitty|cat|meow).*' ? 'cat' : 'notcat') AS catness`.

Hello, SQL Users

Similar to but more powerful than the `LIKE` operator. See "Important Notes About String Matching" on page 70 for a conversion guide.

Important to Know

- These are incredibly powerful, and even if they seem arcane now they're much easier to learn than it first seems.

- You're far better off learning one extra thing to do with a regular expression than most of the other string conditional functions Pig offers.

- …There are enough other "Importants to Know" that we made a sidebar of them ("Important Notes About String Matching" on page 70).

Records

You can use this in a filter clause but also anywhere else an expression is permitted, like the preceding snippet.

Dataflow

Map-only: it's composed onto the end of the preceding map or reduce, and if it stands alone becomes a map-only job.

Exercises for You

Follow the Regular-Expressions.info tutorial (*http://regexp.info/tutorial.html*), but *only up to the part on Grouping & Capturing*. The rest you are far better off picking up once you find you need it.

See Also

The Pig `REGEX_EXTRACT` and `REPLACE` (*http://bit.ly/pig_replace*) functions, and Java's Regular Expression documentation (*http://bit.ly/regex_docs*) for details on its peccadilloes (but not for an education about regular expressions).

Matching Records Against a Fixed List of Lookup Values

If you plan to filter by matching against a small static list of values, Pig offers the handy `IN` expression: true if the value is equal (case-sensitive) to any of the listed values. This selects the stadiums used each year by the current teams in baseball's AL-east division:

```
al_east_parks = FILTER park_team_years BY
    team_id IN ('BAL', 'BOS', 'CLE', 'DET', 'ML4', 'NYA', 'TBA', 'TOR', 'WS2');
```

Sometimes a regular expression alternative can be the right choice instead. For example, this:

```
bubba MATCHES 'shrimp (kabobs|creole|gumbo|soup|stew|salad|and potatoes|burger
                      |sandwich)'
OR bubba MATCHES '(pineapple|lemon|coconut|pepper|pan.fried|deep.fried
                  |stir.fried) shrimp'
```

is more readable than:

```
`bubba IN ('shrimp kabobs', 'shrimp creole', 'shrimp gumbo', ...)`.
```

When the list grows somewhat larger, an alternative is to read it into a set-membership data structure,[4] but ultimately large datasets belong in datafiles.

The general case is handled by using a join, as described in "Selecting Only Records That Lack a Match in Another Table (Anti-Join)" on page 164. See in particular the specialized merge join and HashMap (replicated) join, which can offer a great speedup if you meet their qualifications. Finally, you may find yourself with an extremely large table but with few elements expected to match. In that case, a Bloom filter may be appropriate.

Pattern in use

Where You'll Use It
> File types or IP addresses to select/reject from web logs; keys for exemplar records you're tracking through a dataflow; or stock symbols you're researching. Together with "Summarizing Multiple Subsets of a Group Simultaneously" on page 139, enumerate members of a cohort ((state IN ('CA', 'WA', 'OR') ? 1 : 0) AS is_western, ...).

Standard Snippet
> foo IN ('this', 'that', 'the_other'), or any of the other variants given above.

Hello, SQL Users
> This isn't anywhere near as powerful as SQL's IN expression. Most importantly, you can't supply another table as the list.

Important to Know
> A regular expression alternation is often the right choice instead.

Output Count
> As many records as the cardinality of its key (i.e., the number of distinct values). Data size should decrease greatly.

Dataflow
> Map-only: it's composed onto the end of the preceding map or reduce, and if it stands alone becomes a map-only job.

---

4 For a dynamic language such as Ruby, it can often be both faster and cleaner to reformat the table into the language itself than to parse a datafile. Loading the table is now a one-liner (require "lookup_table"), and there's nothing the Ruby interpreter does faster than interpret Ruby.

Project Only Chosen Columns by Name

While a FILTER selects *rows* based on an expression, Pig's FOREACH selects specific *fields* chosen by name. The fancy word for this simple action is "projection." We'll try to be precise in using *project* for choosing columns, *select* for choosing rows by any means, and *filter* where we specifically mean selecting rows that satisfy a conditional expression.

The tables we're using come with an overwhelming wealth of stats, but we only need a few of them to do fairly sophisticated explorations. The gamelogs table has more than 90 columns; to extract just the teams and the final score, use a FOREACH:

```
game_scores = FOREACH games GENERATE
  away_team_id, home_team_id, home_runs_ct, away_runs_ct;
```

Using a FOREACH to Select, Rename, and Reorder fields

You're not limited to simply restricting the number of columns; you can also rename and reorder them in a projection. Each record in the game_scores relation has *two* game outcomes, one for the home team and one for the away team. We can represent the same data in a table listing outcomes purely from each team's perspective:

```
games_a = FOREACH games GENERATE
  year_id, home_team_id AS team,
  home_runs_ct AS runs_for, away_runs_ct AS runs_against, 1 AS is_home:int;

games_b = FOREACH games GENERATE
  away_team_id AS team,     year_id,
  away_runs_ct AS runs_for, home_runs_ct AS runs_against, 0 AS is_home:int;

team_scores = UNION games_a, games_b;

DESCRIBE team_scores;
--   team_scores:
                {
  team: chararray,year_id: int,runs_for: int,runs_against: int,is_home: int}
```

The first projection puts the home_team_id into the team slot, renaming it team; leaves the year_id field unchanged; and files the home and away scores under runs_for and runs_against. Lastly, we slot in an indicator field for home games, supplying both the name and type as a matter of form. Next, we generate the corresponding table for away games, then stack them together with the UNION operation (to which you'll be properly introduced in a few pages). All the tables have the identical schema shown, even though their values come from different columns in the original tables.

Pattern in use

Where You'll Use It
> Nearly everywhere. If `FILTER` is the f-stop of our camera, this is the zoom lens.

Standard Snippet
```
FOREACH recs GENERATE only, some, columns;
```

Important to Know
> As you can see, we take a lot of care visually aligning subexpressions within the code snippets. That's not because we've tidied up the house for students coming over; this is what the code we write and the code our teammates expect us to write looks like.

Output Count
> Exactly the same as the input.

Records
> However you define them to be.

Dataflow
> Map-only: it's composed onto the end of the preceding map or reduce, and if it stands alone becomes a map-only job.

See Also
> "Assembling Literals with Complex Types" on page 84

Extracting a Random Sample of Records

Another common operation is to extract a *uniform* sample—one where every record has an equivalent chance of being selected. For example, you could use this to test new code before running it against the entire dataset (and possibly having a long-running job fail due to a large number of mishandled records). By calling the `SAMPLE` operator, you ask Pig to pluck out some records at random

The following Pig code will return a randomly selected 10% (that is, 1/10 = 0.10) of the records from our baseball dataset:

```
some_seasons_samp = SAMPLE bat_seasons 0.10;
```

The `SAMPLE` operation does so by generating a random number to select records, which means each run of a script that uses `SAMPLE` will yield a different set of records. Sometimes this is what you want, or at the very least, you don't mind. In other cases, you may want to draw a uniform sample once, then repeatedly work through those *same* records. (Consider our example of spot-checking new code against a dataset:

you'd need to run your code against the same sample in order to confirm your changes work as expected.)

Experienced software developers will reach for a "seeding" function—such as R's `set.seed()` or Python's `random.seed()`—to make the randomness a little less so. At the moment, Pig does not have an equivalent function. Even worse, it is not consistent *within the task*—if a map task fails on one machine, the retry attempt will generate different data sent to different reducers. This rarely causes problems, but for anyone looking to contribute back to the Pig project, this is a straighforward high-value issue to tackle.

Pattern in use

Where You'll Use It
> At the start of the exploration, to cut down on data size, and in many machine learning algorithms. Don't use it for simulations—you need to be taking aggressive charge of the sampling algorithm.

Important to Know
> - A consistent sample is a much better practice, though we admit that can be more of a hassle. But records that dance around mean you can't *know thy data* as you should.
>
> - The DataFu package has UDFs for sampling with replacement and other advanced features.

Output Count
> Determined by the sampling fraction. As a rule of thumb, variances of things are square-root-ish; expect the size of a 10% sample to be in the 7%–13% range.

Records
> Identical to the input.

Dataflow
> Map-only: it's composed onto the end of the preceding map or reduce, and if it stands alone becomes a map-only job.

Exercises for You
> Modify Pig's `SAMPLE` function to accept a seed parameter, and submit that patch back to the open source project. This is a bit harder to do than it seems: sampling is key to efficient sorting and so the code to sample data is intertwingled with a lot of core functionality.

Extracting a Consistent Sample of Records by Key

A good way to stabilize the sample from run to run is to use a *consistent hash digest*. A hash digest function creates a fixed-length fingerprint of a string whose output is otherwise unpredictable from the input and uniformly distributed—that is, you can't tell which string the function will produce except by computing the digest, and every string is equally likely. For example, the hash function might give the hexadecimal-string digest 3ce3e909 for *Chimpanzee* but 07a05f9c for *Chimp*. Because all hexadecimal strings have effectively equal likelihood, one-sixteenth of them will start with a zero, and so this filter would reject Chimpanzee but select Chimp.

Unfortunately, Pig doesn't have a good built-in hash digest function! Do we have to give up all hope? You'll find the answer later in "Calling a User-Defined Function from an External Package" on page 91,[5] but for now instead of using a good built-in hash digest function, let's use a terrible hash digest function. A bit under 10% of player_ids start with the letter *s*, and any coupling between a player's name and performance would be far more subtle than we need to worry about. So the following simple snippet gives a 10% sample of batting seasons whose behavior should reasonably match that of the whole:

```
some_seasons = FILTER bat_seasons BY (SUBSTRING(player_id, 0, 1) == 's');
```

We called this a terrible hash function, but it does fit the bill. When applied to an arbitrary serial identifier it's not terrible at all—the Twitter firehose provides a 1% service tier that returns only tweets from users whose numeric ID ends in 00, and a 10% tier with user IDs ending in 0. We'll return to the subject with a proper hash digest function later on in the chapter, once you're brimming with even more smartitude than you are right now.

Pattern in use

Where You'll Use It
  At the start of the exploration

Important to Know
  • If you'll be spending a bunch of time with a dataset, using any kind of random sample to prepare your development sample might be a stupid idea. You'll notice that Red Sox players show up frequently in our examples—that's because our development samples are "seasons by Red Sox players" and "seasons from 2000 to 2010," which lets us make good friends with the data.

---

5 Spoiler alert: no, you don't have to give up all hope when Pig lacks a built-in function you require.

Output Count
> Determined by the sampling fraction. As a rule of thumb, variances of things are square-root-ish; expect the size of a 10% sample to be in the 7%–13% range.

Records
> Identical to the input.

Dataflow
> Map-only: it's composed onto the end of the preceding map or reduce, and if it stands alone becomes a map-only job.

Sampling Carelessly by Only Loading Some part- Files

Sometimes you just want to knock down the data size while developing your script, and don't much care about the exact population. If you find a prior stage has left you with 20 files, `part-r-00000` through `part-r-00019`, specifying `part-r-0000[01]` (the first 2 out of 20 files) as the input to the next stage is a hamfisted but effective way to get a 10% sample. You can cheat even harder by adjusting the parallelism of the preceding stage to get you the file granularity you need. As long as you're mindful that some operations leave the reducer with a biased selection of records, toggling back and forth between, say, `my_data/part-r-0000[01]` (two files) and `my_data/` (all files in that directory) can really speed up development.

Selecting a Fixed Number of Records with LIMIT

A much blunter way to create a smaller dataset is to take some fixed number K of records. Pig offers the `LIMIT` operator for this purpose. To select 25 records from our `bat_seasons` data, you would run:

```
some_players = LIMIT bat_seasons 25;
```

This is somewhat similar to running the `head` command in Unix-like operating systems, or using the `LIMIT` clause in a SQL `SELECT` statement. However, unless you have explicitly imparted some order to the table (probably by sorting it with `ORDER`, which we'll cover in Chapter 8), Pig gives you *no guarantee over which records it selects*. In the big data regime, where your data is striped across many machines, there's no intrinsic notion of a record order. Changes in the number of mappers or reducers in the data or in the cluster may change which records are selected. In practice, you'll find that it takes the first K records of the first-listed file (and so, as opposed to `SAMPLE`, generally gives the same outcome run-to-run), but it's irresponsible to rely on that.

When you have a very large dataset, as long as you really just need any small piece of it, you can apply the previous trick as well and just specify a single input file. Invoking LIMIT on one file will prevent a lot of trivial map tasks from running.

Other Data Elimination Patterns

There are two tools we'll introduce in the next chapter that can be viewed as data elimination patterns as well. The DISTINCT and related operations are used to identify duplicated or unique records. Doing so requires putting each record in context with its possible duplicates—meaning they are not pure pipeline operations like the others here. Earlier, we gave you a few special cases of selecting records against a list of values. We'll see the general case—selecting records having or lacking a match in another table (also known as semi-join and anti-join)—when we meet all the flavors of the JOIN operation in Chapter 7.

Transforming Records

Besides getting rid of old records, the second-most exciting thing to do with a big dataset is to rip through it manufacturing new records.[6] We've been quietly sneaking FOREACH into snippets, but it's time to make its proper acquaintance.

Transforming Records Individually Using FOREACH

The FOREACH lets you develop simple transformations based on each record. It's the most versatile Pig operation and the one you'll spend the most time using.

To start with a basic example, this FOREACH statement combines the fields giving the city, state, and country of birth for each player into the familiar comma-space separated combined form (Austin, TX, USA):[7]

```
birthplaces = FOREACH people GENERATE
    player_id,
    StringConcat(birth_city, ', ', birth_state, ', ', birth_country) AS birth_loc
    ;
```

The syntax should be largely self-explanatory: this runs through the people table, and outputs a table with two columns: the player ID and our synthesized string. In the output, you'll see that when StringConcat encounters records with null values, it returned null as well without an error.

---

6 Although you might rerank things when we show you how to misuse Hadoop to stress-test a web server with millions of concurrent requests per minute.

7 The country field uses some ad-hoc mixture of full name and arbitrary abbreviations. In practice, we would have converted the country fields to use ISO two-letter abbreviations.

For the benefit of SQL aficionados, here's an equivalent SQL query:

```
SELECT
    player_id,
    CONCAT(birth_city, ', ', birth_state, ', ', birth_country) AS birth_loc
  FROM people;
```

You'll recall we took some care when loading the data to describe the table's schema, and Pig makes it easy to ensure that the data continues to be typed. Run DESCRIBE birthplaces; to return the schema:

```
birthplaces: {player_id: chararray,birth_loc: chararray}
```

Because player_id carries through unchanged, its name and type convey to the new schema. Pig figures out that the result of CONCAT is a chararray, but it's up to us to award it with a new name (birth_loc).

A FOREACH won't cause a new Hadoop job stage: it's chained onto the end of the preceding operation (and when it's on its own, like this one, there's just a single mapper-only job). It always produces exactly the same count of output records as input records, although as you've seen it can change the number of columns.

A Nested FOREACH Allows Intermediate Expressions

Earlier, we promised you a storyline in the form of an extended exploration of player performance. We've now gathered enough tactical prowess to set out.[8]

The stats in the bat_seasons table are all "counting stats" (total numbers of hits, of games, etc.), and certainly from the team's perspective, the more hits the better. But for comparing players, the counting stats don't distinguish between the player who eared 70 hits in a mere 200 trips to the plate before a season-ending injury, and the player who squandered 400 of his team's plate appearances getting to a similar total.[9] We should also form "rate stats," normalizing those figures against plate appearances. The following simple metrics do quite a reasonable job of characterizing players' performance:

- On-base percentage (OBP) indicates how well the player meets offensive goal #1: get on base, thus becoming a potential run and *not* consuming a precious out. It is given as the fraction of plate appearances that are successful: ((H + BB +

---

8 We also warned you we'd wander away from it frequently—the bulk of it sits in the next chapter.

9 Here's to you, Rod Carew (1970) and Mario Mendoza (1979).

HBP) / PA).[10] An OBP over 0.400 is very good (better than 95% of significant seasons).

- Slugging percentage (SLG) indicates how well the player meets offensive goal #2: advance the runners on base, thus converting potential runs into points toward victory. It is given by the total bases gained in hitting (one for a single, two for a double, etc.) divided by the number of at bats: (TB / AB, where TB := (H + h2B + 2*h3B + 3*HR)). An SLG over 0.500 is very good.

- On-base-plus-slugging (OPS) combines on-base and slugging percentages to give a simple and useful estimate of overall offensive contribution. We find it by simply adding the figures: (OBP + SLG). Anything above 0.900 is very good.

Doing this with the simple form of FOREACH we've been using would be annoying and hard to read: for one thing, the expressions for OBP and SLG would have to be repeated in the expression for OPS, because the full statement is evaluated together. Pig provides a fancier form of FOREACH (a *nested* FOREACH) that allows intermediate expressions:

```
bat_seasons = FILTER bat_seasons BY PA > 0 AND AB > 0;
core_stats  = FOREACH bat_seasons {
   TB   = h1B + 2*h2B + 3*h3B + 4*HR;
   OBP  = 1.0f*(H + BB + HBP) / PA;
   SLG  = 1.0f*TB / AB;
   OPS  = SLG + OBP;
   GENERATE
     player_id, name_first, name_last,    -- $0-$2
     year_id,   team_id,    lg_id,        -- $3-$5
     age, G,    PA, AB,    HBP, SH,  BB,  -- $6-$12
     H,    h1B, h2B, h3B,  HR,  R,   RBI, -- $13-$19
     SLG, OBP, OPS;                       -- $20-$22
};
```

This alternative { (curly braces) form of FOREACH lets you describe its transformations in smaller pieces, rather than smushing everything into the single GENERATE clause. New identifiers within the curly braces (such as player) only have meaning within those braces, but they do inform the schema.

You'll notice that we multiplied by 1.0 while calculating OBP and SLG. If all the operands were integers, Pig would use integer arithmetic; instead of fractions between 0 and 1, the result would always be integer 0. Multiplying by the floating-point value 1.0 forces Pig to use floating-point math, preserving the fraction. Using a

---

10 Although known as percentages, OBP and SLG are always given as fractions to three decimal places. For OBP, we're also using a slightly modified formula to reduce the number of stats to learn. It gives nearly identical results, but you will notice small discrepancies with official figures.

typecast (i.e., SLG = (float)TB / AB), as described next, is arguably more efficient but inarguably uglier. The preceding code is what we'd write in practice.

By the way, the filter used here is sneakily doing two things. It obviously eliminates records where PA is equal to zero, but it also eliminates records where PA is null. (See "Selecting or Rejecting Records with a null Value" on page 68 for details.)

In addition to applying arithmetic expressions and functions, you can apply a set of *operations* (ORDER, DISTINCT, FOREACH, FILTER, LIMIT) to bags within a nested FORE ACH. We'll wait until Chapter 6 to introduce their nested FOREACH ("inner bag") forms.

Formatting a String According to a Template

The SPRINTF function is a great tool for assembling a string for humans to look at. It uses the printf-style templating convention common to C and many other languages to assemble strings with consistent padding and spacing. You'll learn it best by seeing it in action:

```
formatted = FOREACH bat_seasons GENERATE
  SPRINTF('%4d\t%-9s %-20s\tOBP %5.3f / %-3s %-3s\t%4$012.3e',
    year_id, player_id,
    CONCAT(name_first, ' ', name_last),
    1.0f*(H + BB + HBP) / PA,
    (year_id >= 1900 ? '.'   : 'pre'),
    (PA >= 450       ? 'sig' : '.')
  ) AS OBP_summary:chararray;
```

So you can follow along, here are some scattered lines from the results:

```
1954    aaronha01 Hank Aaron        OBP 0.318 / .   sig    0003.183e-01
1897    ansonca01 Cap Anson         OBP 0.372 / pre sig    0003.722e-01
1970    carewro01 Rod Carew         OBP 0.407 / .   .      0004.069e-01
1987    gwynnto01 Tony Gwynn        OBP 0.446 / .   sig    0004.456e-01
2007    pedrodu01 Dustin Pedroia    OBP 0.377 / .   sig    0003.769e-01
1995    vanlawi01 William Van Land...OBP 0.149 / .  .      0001.489e-01
1941    willite01 Ted Williams      OBP 0.553 / .   sig    0005.528e-01
```

The parts of the template are as follows:

%4d

Render an integer, right aligned, in a four-character slot. All the year_id values have exactly four characters, but if Pliny the Elder's rookie season from 43 AD showed up in our dataset, it would be padded with two spaces: 43. Writing %04d (i.e., with a zero after the percent) causes zero-padding: 0043.

\t *(backslash-t)*

Renders a literal tab character. This is done by Pig, not in the SPRINTF function.

`%-9s`

A nine-character string. Because it has a minus sign, it is left aligned.

`%-20s`

Like `%-9s`, this has a minus sign, so it is left aligned. You usually want this for strings. Some additional notes:

- We prepared the name with a separate `CONCAT` statement and gave it a single string slot in the template, rather than using, say, `%-8s %-11s`. In our formulation, the first and last name are separated by only one space and share the same 20-character slot. Try modifying the script to see what happens with the alternative.

- Any value shorter than its slot width is padded to fit, either with spaces (as seen here) or with zeros (as seen in the last field). A value longer than the slot width is not truncated—it is printed at full length, shifting everything after it on the line out of place. When we chose the 19-character width, we didn't count on William Van Landingham's corpulent cognomen contravening character caps, correspondingly corrupting columnar comparisons. Still, that only messes up Mr. Van Landingham's line—subsequent lines are unaffected.

`OBP`

Any literal text you care to enter just carries through. In case you're wondering, you can render a literal percent sign by writing `%%`.

`%5.3f`

For floating-point numbers, you supply two widths. The first is the width of the full slot, including the sign, the integer part, the decimal point, and the fractional part. The second number gives the width of the fractional part. A lot of scripts that use arithmetic to format a number to three decimal places (as in the prior section) should be using `SPRINTF` instead.

`%-3s %-3s`

Strings indicating whether the season is premodern (`\<\= 1900`) and whether it is significant (`>= 450 PA`). We could have used `true`/`false`, but doing it as we did here—one value tiny, the other with visual weight—makes it much easier to scan the data. By inserting the `/` delimiter and using different phrases for each indicator, we make it easy to `grep` for matching lines later (e.g., `grep -e '/.*sig'`) without picking up lines having `'sig'` in the player ID.

`%4$12.3e`

Two things to see here:

- Each of the preceding has pulled its value from the next argument in sequence. Here, the 4$ part of the specifier uses the value of the fourth non-template argument (the OBP) instead.

- The remaining 012.3e part of the specifier says to use scientific notation, with three decimal places and 12 total characters. Because the strings don't reach full width, their decimal parts are padded with zeros. When you're calculating the width of a scientific notation field, don't forget to include the *two* sign characters: one for the number and one for the exponent.

We won't go any further into the details, as the SPRINTF function (*http://bit.ly/ pig_sprintf*) is well documented, and examples of printf-style templating abound on the Web. But this is a useful and versatile tool, and if you're able to mimic the elements used here you understand its essentials.

Assembling Literals with Complex Types

Another reason you may need the nested form of FOREACH is to assemble a complex literal. If we wanted to draw key events in a player's history (e.g., birth, death, start and end of career) on a timeline, or wanted to place the location of his birth and death on a map, it would make sense to prepare generic baskets of events and location records. We will solve this problem in a few different ways to demonstrate assembling complex types from simple fields.

 In order to use the functions in Piggybank and DataFu, we have to REGISTER their JAR files so Pig knows about them. This is accomplished with the REGISTER command:

```
REGISTER /usr/lib/pig/datafu.jar
```

Parsing a date

Parsing dates in Pig is easy with the ToDate function and SPRINTF:

```
REGISTER /usr/lib/pig/datafu.jar
DEFINE Coalesce datafu.pig.util.Coalesce();
DEFINE SPRINTF datafu.pig.util.SPRINTF();

-- Assembling complex types (Only for Pig >= 0.14.0)
people = FILTER people BY (beg_date IS NOT NULL) AND
                         (end_date IS NOT NULL) AND
                         (birth_year IS NOT NULL) AND
                         (death_year IS NOT NULL);

date_converted = FOREACH people {
    beg_dt   = ToDate(CONCAT(beg_date, 'T00:00:00.000Z'));
    end_dt   = ToDate(end_date, 'yyyy-MM-dd', '+0000');
```

```
birth_dt = ToDate(
    SPRINTF(
    '%s-%s-%sT00:00:00Z',
    birth_year, Coalesce(birth_month,1), Coalesce(birth_day,1))
);
death_dt = ToDate(
    SPRINTF(
    '%s-%s-%sT00:00:00Z',
    death_year, Coalesce(death_month,1), Coalesce(death_day,1))
);

GENERATE player_id, birth_dt, death_dt, beg_dt, end_dt, name_first,
    name_last;
};
```

One oddity of the people table's structure as it arrived to us is that the birth/death dates are given with separate fields, while the beginning/end of career dates are given as ISO date strings. We left that alone because this kind of inconsistency is the reality of datasets in practice—in fact, this is about as mild a case as you'll find. So one thing we'll have to do is pick a uniform date representation and go forward with it.

You may have heard the saying "The two hardest things in computer science are cache coherency and naming things." Our nominations for the two most horrible things in computer science are time zones and character encoding.[11] Elsewhere, you'll hear "Our rule for time zones is *put it in UTC immediately and never speak of it again.*"[12] A final step in rendering data for an end-user interface may convert to local time, but *at no point in data analysis should you tolerate anything but UTC.* We're only working with dates right here, but we'll repeat that rule every chance we have in the book.

There are two and a half defensible ways to represent a date or time:

As an ISO 8601 date/time string in the UTC time zone
   It sounds scary when we say "ISO 8601" (*http://bit.ly/iso_8601*), but it's self-explanatory and you see it all over the place: '2007-08-09T10:11:12Z' is an example of a time, and '2007-08-09' is an example of a date. It's compact enough to not worry about, there's little chance of it arriving in that format by accident, everything everywhere can parse it, and you can do ad hoc manipulation of it using string functions (e.g., (int)SUBSTRING(end_date,0,4) to extract a year). Use this format only if you are representing instants that come after the 1700s, if you only need seconds-level precision, and where human readability is more important than compactness (which we encourage).

---

11 Many people add "…and off-by-one errors" to the hardest-things list. If we are allowed to reuse the same joke, the two most horrible things in computer science are 1) time zones, 2) character encoding, 2) Threads.ding.

12 You can guess our rule for character encoding: "put it in UTF-8 *immediately* and never speak of it again."

As an integer number of epoch milliseconds in the UTC time zone
>   This means the number of elapsed milliseconds since midnight January 1, 1970 UTC, (you may see this referred to as "UNIX time"). It allows you to easily calculate durations, and is nearly universal as well. Its value fits nicely in an unsigned 64-bit long. We believe using fractional epoch time (e.g., 1186654272892.657 to mean 657 microseconds into the given second) is carrying the joke too far. If you care about micro- or nanoseconds, then you need to care about floating-point error, and the leading part of the number consumes too much of your precision. Use this format only if you are representing instants that come after the start of the epoch, only need millisecond precision, and don't care about leap seconds.

Using a domain representation chosen judiciously by an expert
>   If neither of the previous representations will work for you, then sorry: you need to get serious. Astronomers and anyone else working at century scale will likely use some form of Julian Date (*http://bit.ly/julian_day*); those working at nanosecond scale should look at TAI (*http://bit.ly/int_atomic_time*); and there are dozens of others. You'll probably have to learn things about leap seconds or sidereal times or the fluid space–time discontinuum that is the map of time zones, and you will wish you didn't have to. We're not going to deal with this category as it's far, far beyond the scope of the book.

In general, we will leave times in their primitive datatype (long for epoch milliseconds, chararray for ISO strings) until we need them to be proper datetime data structures. The lines above show a couple of ways to create datetime values; here's the fuller catalog.

We can easily convert epoch milliseconds by calling ToDate(my_epoch_millis). For an ISO format string with date, time, and time zone, pass it as a single chararray string argument: ToDate(beg_date). If its lacks the time-of-day or time zone part, you must fill it out first: ToDate(CONCAT(beg_date, 'T00:00:00.000Z')). If the string has a nonstandard format, supply two additional arguments: a template according to Java's SimpleDateFormat (*http://bit.ly/simpledateformat*), and unless the input has a time zone, the UTC time zone string +0000.

For composite year-month-day-etc. fields, create an ISO-formatted string and pass it to ToDate. Here's the snippet we used, in slow motion this time:

```
ToDate(
  SPRINTF('%s-%s-%sT00:00:00Z',                        -- ISO format template
    birth_year,                                        -- if year is NULL, value also null
    (birth_month IS NULL ? 1 : birth_month),           -- but coerce null month/day to 1
    (birth_day IS NULL ? 1 : birth_day)
  ));
```

Apart from subtracting one epoch milliseconds from another to get a duration in milliseconds, you must *never do any date/time manipulation except through a best-in-class date library*. You can't calculate the difference of one year by adding one to the year field (which brought down Microsoft's cloud storage product (*http://bit.ly/ disruption_summary*) on the leap day of February 29, 2012), and you can't assume that the time difference from one minute to the next is 60 seconds (which brought down HBase servers worldwide (*http://bit.ly/leap_sec_troubles*) when the leap second of `2012-06-30T23:59:60Z`—note the `:60`—occurred). This is no joke: companies go out of business because of mistakes like these.

Assembling a bag

Sometimes it can be useful to create complex objects to be referenced and processed later. While we try to keep schemas as simple as possible, sometimes you want a bag.

We can take things further and assemble truly complex records of bags of tuples, and nested tuples:

```
graphable = FOREACH people {
    birth_month = Coalesce(birth_month, 1); birth_day = Coalesce(birth_day, 1);
    death_month = Coalesce(death_month, 1); death_day = Coalesce(death_day, 1);
    beg_dt   = ToDate(beg_date);
    end_dt   = ToDate('yyyy-MM-dd', end_date);
    birth_dt = ToDate(SPRINTF('%s-%s-%s', birth_year, birth_month, birth_day));
    death_dt = ToDate(SPRINTF('%s-%s-%s', death_year, death_month, death_day));
    --
    occasions = {
        ('birth', birth_year, birth_month, birth_day),
        ('death', death_year, death_month, death_day),
        ('debut',
            (int)SUBSTRING(beg_date,0,4),
            (int)SUBSTRING(beg_date,5,7),
            (int)SUBSTRING(beg_date,8,10)
        ),
        ('lastg',
            (int)SUBSTRING(end_date,0,4),
            (int)SUBSTRING(end_date,5,7),
            (int)SUBSTRING(end_date,8,10)
        )
    };
    --
    places = (
        (birth_dt, birth_city, birth_state, birth_country),
        (death_dt, death_city, death_state, death_country)
    );

    GENERATE
    player_id,
    occasions AS occasions:bag{occasion:(name:chararray, year:int, month:int,
```

```
                                    day:int)},
    places        AS places:tuple( birth:tuple(date, city, state, country),
                                   death:tuple(date, city, state, country) )
       ;
   };
```

The occasions intermediate alias is a bag of event tuples holding a chararray and three ints. Bags are disordered (unless you have transiently applied an explicit sort), and so we've prefixed each event with a slug naming the occasion.

You can do this inline (non-nested FOREACH) but we wouldn't, as it is not readable.

Manipulating the Type of a Field

We used StringConcat to combine players' city, state, and country of birth into a combined field without drama. But if we tried to do the same for their date of birth by writing StringConcat(birth_year, '-', birth_month, '-', birth_day), Pig would throw an error:

```
Could not infer the matching function for org.apache.pig.builtin.StringConcat...
```

You see, StringConcat understandably wants to consume and deliver strings, and so isn't in the business of guessing at and fixing up types. What we need to do is coerce the int values (e.g., 1961, a 32-bit integer) into chararray values (e.g., '1961', a string of four characters). You do so using C-style typecast expression: (charar ray)birth_year. Here it is in action:

```
birthplaces = FOREACH people GENERATE
    player_id,
    StringConcat(
        (chararray)birth_year, '-',
        (chararray)birth_month, '-',
        (chararray)birth_day
    ) AS birth_date
  ;
```

In other cases, you don't need to manipulate the type going into a function—you need to manipulate the type going out of your FOREACH.

Here are several takes on a FOREACH statement to find the slugging average:

```
obp_1 = FOREACH bat_seasons {
  OBP = 1.0f * (H + BB + HBP) / PA; -- constant is a float
  GENERATE OBP;                     -- making OBP a float
};
-- obp_1: {OBP: float}
```

The first stanza matches what was used earlier. We wrote the literal value as 1.0f (which signifies the float value 1.0), thus giving OBP the implicit type float as well:

```
obp_2 = FOREACH bat_seasons {
  OBP = 1.0 * (H + BB + HBP) / PA;  -- constant is a double
  GENERATE OBP;                     -- making OBP a double
};
-- obp_2: {OBP: double}
```

In the second stanza, we instead wrote the literal value as 1.0 (type double), giving OBP the implicit type double as well:

```
obp_3 = FOREACH bat_seasons {
  OBP = (float)(H + BB + HBP) / PA; -- typecast forces floating-point arithmetic
  GENERATE OBP AS OBP;              -- making OBP a float
};
-- obp_3: {OBP: float}
```

The third stanza takes a different tack: it forces floating-point math by typecasting the result as a float, thus also implying type float for the generated value:[13]

```
obp_4 = FOREACH bat_seasons {
  OBP = 1.0 * (H + BB + HBP) / PA;  -- constant is a double
  GENERATE OBP AS OBP:float;        -- but OBP is explicitly a float
};
-- obp_4: {OBP: float}
```

In the fourth stanza, the constant was given as a double. However, this time, the AS clause specifies not just a name but an explicit type, and that takes precedence:[14]

```
broken = FOREACH bat_seasons {
  OBP = (H + BB + HBP) / PA;        -- all int operands means integer math
                                    -- and zero as result
  GENERATE OBP AS OBP:float;        -- even though OBP is explicitly a float
};
-- broken: {OBP: float}
```

The fifth and final stanza exists just to reprove the point that if you care about the types Pig will use, say something. Although the output type is a float, the intermediate expression is calculated with integer math and so all the answers are zero. Even if that worked, you'd be a chump to rely on it: use any of the preceding four stanzas instead.

---

13 As you can see, for most of the stanzas Pig picked up the name of the intermediate expression (OBP) as the name of that field in the schema. Weirdly, the typecast in the third stanza makes the current version of Pig lose track of the name, so we chose to provide it explicitly.

14 Is the intermediate result calculated using double-precision math because it starts with a double and then converts to float? Or is it calculated with single-precision math because the result is a float? We don't know, and even if we did we wouldn't tell you. Don't resolve language edge cases by consulting the manual; resolve them by using lots of parentheses and typecasts and explicitness. If you learn fiddly rules like that (operator precedence is another case in point), there's a danger you might actually rely on them. Remember, you write code for humans to read and only incidentally for robots to run.

Ints and Floats and Rounding, Oh My!

Another occasion for type conversion comes when you are trying to round or truncate a fractional number.

The first four fields of the following statement turn the full-precision result of calculating OBP (0.31827113) into a result with three fractional digits (0.318), as OBP is usually represented:

```
rounded = FOREACH bat_seasons GENERATE
  (ROUND(1000.0f*(H + BB + HBP) / PA)) / 1000.0f AS round_and_typecast,
  ((int)(1000.0f*(H + BB + HBP) / PA)) / 1000.0f AS typecast_only,
  (FLOOR(1000.0f*(H + BB + HBP) / PA)) / 1000    AS floor_and_typecast,
  ROUND_TO( 1.0f*(H + BB + HBP) / PA, 3)         AS what_we_would_use,
  SPRINTF('%5.3f', 1.0f*(H + BB + HBP) / PA)     AS if_u_want_a_string_say_so,
  1.0f*(H + BB + HBP) / PA                        AS full_value
  ;
```

The round_and_typecast field shows a fairly common (and mildly flawed) method for chunking or partially rounding values: scale-truncate-rescale. Multiplying 0.31827113 by 1000.0f gives a float result 318.27113; rounding it gets an integer value 318; rescaling by 1000.0f gives a final result of 0.318f, a float. The second version works mostly the same way, but has no redeeming merits. Use a typecast expression when you want to typecast, not for its side effects. This muddy formulation leads off with a story about casting things to type int, but only a careful ticking off of parentheses shows that we swoop in at the end and implicitly cast to float. If you want to truncate the fractional part, say so by using the function for truncating the fractional part, as the third formulation does. The FLOOR method uses machine numeric functions to generate the value. This is likely more efficient, and it is certainly more correct.

Floating-point arithmetic, like Unicode normalization and anything cryptography, has far more complexity than anyone who wants to get things done can grasp. At some point, take time to become aware of the built-in math functions (*http://bit.ly/method_summary*) that are available.[15] You don't have to learn them; just stick the fact of their existence in the back of your head. If the folks at the IEEE have decided every computer on the planet should set aside silicon for a function to find the log of 1 plus *x* (log1p), or a function to find the remainder when dividing two numbers (IEEEremainder), you can bet there's a really good reason why your stupid way of doing it is some mixture of incorrect, inaccurate, or fragile.

That is why the formulation we would actually use to find a rounded number is the fourth one. It says what we mean ("round this number to three decimal places") and it

---

15 Either as Pig built-ins, or through the Piggybank UDF library.

draws on Java library functions built for just this purpose. The error between the ROUND formulation and the ROUND_TO formulation is almost certainly miniscule. But multiply "miniscule" by a billion records and you won't like what comes out.

Calling a User-Defined Function from an External Package

You can extend Pig's functionality with user-defined functions (UDFs) written in Java, Python, Ruby, JavaScript, and others. These have first-class functionality—almost all of Pig's native functions are actually Java UDFs that just happen to live in a built-in namespace.

The DataFu package is a collection of Pig extensions open-sourced by LinkedIn, and in our opinion everyone who uses Pig should install it. It provides the most important flavors of hash digest and checksum you need in practice, and explains how to choose the right one. For consistent hashing purposes, the right choice is the "Mumur 3" function,[16] and because we don't need many bytes, we'll use the 32-bit flavor.

You must do two things to enable use of a UDF. First, so that Pig can load the UDF's code, call the REGISTER command with the path to the UDF's JAR file. You only need to REGISTER a JAR once, even if you'll use more than one of its UDFs.

Second, use the DEFINE command to construct it. DEFINE takes two arguments, separated by spaces: the short name you will use to invoke the command, and the fully qualified package name of its class (e.g., datafu.pig.hash.Hasher). Some UDFs, including the one we're using, accept or require constructor arguments (always strings). These are passed function-call style, in the following code (there's nothing wrong with DEFINE-ing a UDF multiple times with different constructor arguments; for example, adding a line DEFINE DigestMD5 datafu.pig.hash.Hasher('md5'); would create a hash function that used the MD5 algorithm):

```
-- Register the jar containing the UDFs
REGISTER /usr/lib/pig/datafu.jar
-- Murmur3, 32 bit version: a fast statistically smooth hash digest function
DEFINE Digest datafu.pig.hash.Hasher('murmur3-32');

bat_seasons = LOAD '/data/gold/sports/baseball/bat_seasons.tsv'
  USING PigStorage('\t') AS (
    player_id:chararray, name_first:chararray, name_last:chararray,
    year_id:int,        team_id:chararray,     lg_id:chararray,
    age:int,  G:int,     PA:int,   AB:int,  HBP:int,  SH:int,   BB:int,
    H:int,    h1B:int,  h2B:int,  h3B:int, HR:int,   R:int,    RBI:int
```

---

16 Those familiar with the MD5 or SHA hashes might have expected we'd use one of them. Those would work as well, but Murmur3 is faster and has superior statistical properties; for more, see the DataFu documentation (*http://bit.ly/datafu_1_1_0*). Oh, and if you're not familiar with any of the stuff we just said: don't worry about it, just know that 'murmur3-32' is what you should type in.

```
);
bat_seasons = FILTER bat_seasons BY PA > 0 AND AB > 0;

-- Prepend a hash of the player_id
keyed_seasons = FOREACH bat_seasons GENERATE Digest(player_id) AS keep_hash, *;

-- Prepare a reproducible sample of bat seasons
some_seasons  = FOREACH (
    FILTER keyed_seasons BY (SUBSTRING(keep_hash, 0, 1) == '0')
  ) GENERATE $0..;
```

Operations That Break One Table into Many

Pig Latin is a language defined by the manipulation of dataflows. In Pig, we often load an entire dataset at once and manipulate it in a stream. Streams needn't remain singular—they can split and merge like real rivers, flowing through different filters and operations before rejoining further on. It can help in writing Pig scripts to visualize your data as a dataflow. Now let's learn about SPLIT and UNION.

Directing Data Conditionally into Multiple Dataflows (SPLIT)

The careers table gives the number of times each player was elected to the All-Star Game (indicating extraordinary performance during a season) and whether he was elected to the Hall of Fame (indicating a truly exceptional career).

Demonstration in Pig

Separating those records into different dataflows isn't straightforward in MapReduce, but it's very natural using Pig's SPLIT operation:

```
SPLIT bat_seasons
  INTO young   IF age <= 30,
       middle  IF (age >= 30) AND (age < 40),
       old OTHERWISE
  ;
STORE young  INTO 'young_players';
STORE middle INTO 'middle_age_players';
STORE old    INTO 'old_players';
```

The SPLIT operator does not short-circuit: every record is tested against every condition, so a player who is 30 will be written to both young_players and mid dle_age_players.

The most natural use of the SPLIT operator is when you really do require divergent processing flows. In the next chapter, you'll use a JOIN LEFT OUTER to geolocate (derive longitude and latitude from place name) records. That method is susceptible to missing matches, and so in practice a next step might be to apply a fancier but more costly geolocation tool. This is a strategy that arises often in advanced machine learning applications: run a first pass with a cheap algorithm that can estimate its error rate, isolate the low-confidence results for harder processing, and then reunite the whole dataset.

The syntax of the SPLIT command does not have an equals sign to the left of it; the new table aliases are created in its body.

Operations That Treat the Union of Several Tables as One

The counterpart to splitting a table into pieces is to treat many pieces as a single table. This really only makes sense when all those pieces have the same schema, so that's the only case we'll handle here.

Treating Several Pig Relation Tables as a Single Table (Stacking Rowsets)

In Pig, you can rejoin several pipelines using the UNION operation. The tables we've been using so far cover only batting stats; there is another set of tables covering stats for pitchers, and in rare cases a player may only appear in one or the other. To find the name and ID of all players that appear in either table, we can project the fields we want (earning a uniform schema) and then unify the two streams:

```
-- Unions can bring relations with the same schema together
young_player_seasons = LOAD 'young_player_seasons' USING PigStorage('\t') AS (
    player_id:chararray, name_first:chararray, name_last:chararray,
    year_id:int,         team_id:chararray,    lg_id:chararray,
    age:int,  G:int,     PA:int,   AB:int,  HBP:int,  SH:int,   BB:int,
    H:int,    h1B:int,   h2B:int,  h3B:int, HR:int,   R:int,    RBI:int
);
middle_age_player_seasons = LOAD 'middle_age_player_seasons'
USING PigStorage('\t') AS (
    player_id:chararray, name_first:chararray, name_last:chararray,
    year_id:int,         team_id:chararray,    lg_id:chararray,
    age:int,  G:int,     PA:int,   AB:int,  HBP:int,  SH:int,   BB:int,
    H:int,    h1B:int,   h2B:int,  h3B:int, HR:int,   R:int,    RBI:int
);
old_player_seasons = LOAD 'old_player_seasons'
USING PigStorage('\t') AS (
    player_id:chararray, name_first:chararray, name_last:chararray,
    year_id:int,         team_id:chararray,    lg_id:chararray,
    age:int,  G:int,     PA:int,   AB:int,  HBP:int,  SH:int,   BB:int,
    H:int,    h1B:int,   h2B:int,  h3B:int, HR:int,   R:int,    RBI:int
);

young_names = FOREACH young_player_seasons GENERATE
player_id, name_first, name_last;
middle_age_names = FOREACH middle_age_player_seasons GENERATE
player_id, name_first, name_last;
old_names = FOREACH old_player_seasons GENERATE
```

```
player_id, name_first, name_last;

all_players = UNION young_names, middle_age_names, old_names;
all_unique_players = DISTINCT all_players;
```

Note that this is not a join (which requires a reduce, and changes the schema of the records); it's more like stacking one table atop another, making no changes to the records (schema or otherwise), and does not require a reduce.

A common use of the UNION statement comes in *symmetrizing* a relationship. For example, each line in the games table describes in a sense two game outcomes: one for the home team and one for the away team. We might reasonably want to prepare another table that listed game *outcomes*: game_id, team, opponent, team's home/away position, team's score, opponent's score. The game between BAL playing at BOS on XXX (final score BOS Y, BAL Z) would get two lines—GAMEIDXXX BOS BAL 1 Y Z and GAMEID BAL BOS 0 Z Y:

```
games = LOAD '/data/gold/sports/baseball/games_lite.tsv' AS (
  game_id:chararray,       year_id:int,
  away_team_id:chararray,  home_team_id:chararray,
  away_runs_ct:int,        home_runs_ct:int
);

games_a = FOREACH games GENERATE
  year_id, home_team_id AS team,
  home_runs_ct AS runs_for, away_runs_ct AS runs_against, 1 AS is_home:int;

games_b = FOREACH games GENERATE
  away_team_id AS team,    year_id,
  away_runs_ct AS runs_for, home_runs_ct AS runs_against, 0 AS is_home:int;

team_scores = UNION games_a, games_b;

STORE team_scores INTO 'team_scores';

DESCRIBE team_scores;
-- team_scores: {
-- team: chararray,year_id: int,runs_for: int,runs_against: int,is_home: int}
```

The UNION operation does not remove duplicate rows as a set-wise union would. It simply tacks one table onto the end of the other, and so the last line eliminates those duplicates (more on DISTINCT in Chapter 6). The UNION operation also does not provide any guarantees on ordering of rows. Some SQL users may fall into the trap of doing a UNION-then-GROUP to combine multiple tables. This is terrible in several ways, and you should instead use the COGROUP operation.

The UNION operator is easy to overuse. For one example, in the next chapter we'll extend the first part of this code to prepare win-loss statistics by team. A plausible first guess would be to follow the UNION statement with a GROUP statement, but a much better approach would use a COGROUP instead (both operators are explained in the next chapter). The UNION statement is mostly harmless but fairly rare in use; give it a second look any time you find yourself writing it into a script.

Wrapping Up

The operations in this chapter do not require a reduce on their own, which makes them very efficient. These operations can be chained one after the other without causing a reduce to occur. Although we call them *map-only* operations, they can be executed during either the map or at the tail of the reduce phase. The ability to chain map-only operations really helps MapReduce scale during complex operations. Arbitrarily long combinations of map-only operations can be chained one after the other and accomplished in a single phase of a Hadoop MapReduce job.

You can now LOAD, STORE, FILTER, UNION, SPLIT, LIMIT, and FOREACH/GENERATE. You can accomplish quite a bit with these operations alone. For instance, you could open an Apache web server logfile, search for a particular IP address, and print only those records. Or you could load stock ticker data, and home in on just one or two stocks.

This chapter gives you a powerful toolkit with which to modify individual records in isolation. The really interesting applications, however, come when we put data into context by grouping similar records in the reduce phase of MapReduce. This is the subject of the next chapter: grouping data.

## CHAPTER 6

Grouping Operations

Some content contributed by Q. Ethan McCallum (@qethanm)

In this chapter, we will introduce grouping operations in Pig and MapReduce. We'll teach you the schemas behind grouped data, how to inspect and sample grouped data relations, how to count records in groups, and how to use aggregate functions to calculate arbitrary statistics about groups. We'll teach you to describe and summarize individual records, fields, or entire data tables. In so doing, we'll explore questions such as, "Does God hate Cleveland?" and "Who are the best players for each phase of their career?"

The GROUP BY operation is fundamental to data processing, both in MapReduce and in the world of SQL. In this chapter, we will cover grouping operations in Pig, which are *one-liners*, or one line of Pig code to perform. This is part of Pig's power. We'll learn how grouping operations relate to the reduce phase of MapReduce and how to combine map-only operations with GROUP BY operations to perform arbitrary operations on data relations.

Grouping operations are at the heart of MapReduce—they make use of and define the *reduce* operation of MapReduce, in which records with the same reduce key are grouped on a single reducer in sorted order. Thus it is possible to define a single MapReduce job that performs any number of map-only operations, followed by a grouping operation, followed by more map-only operations after the reduce. This simple pattern enables MapReduce to perform a wide array of operations, implementing a wide array of algorithms.

Grouping Records into a Bag by Key

The `GROUP BY` operation is at the heart of every structural operation. `GROUP BY` is responsible for collecting records for other operations to occur on them as they are grouped together.

Let's dive right in. Grouping data in Pig is easy: it's a one-liner in Pig to collect all the stadiums a team has called home in its history:

```
park_teams_g = GROUP park_team_years BY team_id;
```

The result of a `GROUP BY` operation is always a field called *group*, followed by one field per grouped table, each named for the table it came from. The shape of the `group` field depends on whether you specified one or many group keys. If you specified a single key, the new `group` field is a scalar with the same schema. If you specified multiple keys, the new `group` field is a tuple whose schema corresponds to those keys. In this example, we grouped on the `team_id` chararray, and so the `group` field is a scalar `chararray` as well. In a moment, we'll group on `year_id` and `team_id`, and so the `group` field would have schema `group:tuple(year_id:int, team_id:charar ray)`.

Each of the following fields is a bag, holding tuples whose schema matches the corresponding table. Notice that the name we used to refer to the *table* is now also the name for a *field*. This will confuse you at first, but soon become natural, especially if you use `DESCRIBE` liberally:

```
DESCRIBE park_teams_g;

/*

park_teams_g: {
    group: chararray,
    park_team_years: {
        (
            park_id: chararray,
            team_id: chararray,
            year_id: long,
            beg_date: chararray,
            end_date: chararray,
            n_games: long
        )
    }
}

*/

A = LIMIT park_teams_g 2;
dump A
```

Notice that the *full record* is kept, even including the keys:

```
(ALT,{(ALT01,ALT,1884,1884-04-30,1884-05-31,18)})
(ANA,{(ANA01,ANA,2001,2001-04-10,2001-10-07,81),
       (ANA01,ANA,2010,2010-04-05,2010-09-29,81),...})
```

To eliminate the redundant data, you'll almost always immediately project using a FOREACH. This lets you trim the fields in the group to those you are interested in. Pig allows you to put the GROUP statement inline within a FOREACH:

```
team_pkyr_pairs = FOREACH (GROUP park_team_years BY team_id) GENERATE
    group AS team_id,
    park_team_years.(park_id, year_id) AS park_team_years;
-- (ALT,{(ALT01,1884)})
-- (ANA,{(ANA01,2001),(ANA01,2010),(ANA01,2002),...})
```

Note that we used an AS clause within our FOREACH/GENERATE call, to give an explicit name, park_team_years, to park_team_years.(park_id, year_id). It is easier to give explicit names as a part of managing our schemas, so that a field can be explicitly referred to later on.

Also notice the park_team_years.(park_id, year_id) form, which gives us a bag of (park_id, year_id) pairs. Using park_teams.park_id, park_teams.year_id instead gives two bags, one with park_id tuples and one with year_id tuples:

```
team_pkyr_bags = FOREACH (GROUP park_team_years BY team_id) GENERATE
    group AS team_id,
    park_team_years.park_id AS park_ids,
    park_team_years.year_id AS park_years;

-- (ALT, {(ALT01)}, {(1884)})
-- (ANA, {(ANA01),(ANA01),(ANA01),...}, {(2001),(2010),(2002),...})

DESCRIBE team_pkyr_pairs;

/*
team_pkyr_pairs: {
    team_id: chararray,
    park_team_years: {
        (park_id: chararray,year_id: long)
    }
}
*/

DESCRIBE team_pkyr_bags;

/*
team_pkyr_bags: {
    team_id: chararray,
    park_ids: {
        (park_id: chararray)
    },
```

```
        park_years: {
            (year_id: long)
        }
    }
*/
```

You can group on multiple fields. For each team and year, we can find the park(s) that team called home:

```
team_yr_parks_g = GROUP park_team_years BY (year_id, team_id);
```

The first field is still called *group*, but it's now a tuple:

```
DESCRIBE team_yr_parks_g;

/*
team_yr_parks_g: {
    group:
        (
            year_id: long,
            team_id: chararray
        ),
    park_team_years: {
        (
            park_id: chararray,
            team_id: chararray,
            year_id: long,
            beg_date: chararray,
            end_date: chararray,
            n_games: long
        )
    }
}
*/
```

Our FOREACH statement now looks a bit different:

```
team_yr_parks = FOREACH(GROUP park_team_years BY (year_id, team_id)) GENERATE
    group.team_id, park_team_years.park_id AS park_ids;

just_4 = LIMIT team_yr_parks 4; DUMP @;

--    (BS1,{(BOS01),(NYC01)})
--    (CH1,{(NYC01),(CHI01)})
--    (CL1,{(CIN01),(CLE01)})
--    (FW1,{(FOR01)})
```

If you have multiple group keys, and want all of the group keys back, you can flatten the group tuple and cast it, as in:

```
year_team = FOREACH (GROUP park_team_years BY (year_id, team_id)) GENERATE
    FLATTEN(group) AS (year_id, team_id);

DESCRIBE year_team;
```

```
year_team: {
    year_id: long,
    team_id: chararray
}
```

Pattern in Use

Where You'll Use It
> Rarely on its own, but otherwise everywhere.

Standard Snippet
```
FOREACH (GROUP recs BY (key1, key2)) GENERATE group.key1,
group.key2, recs AS bag_of_recs_records;.
```

Hello, SQL Users
> Similar to the windowed functionality supplied by high-end SQL databases (MySQL, PostgreSQL, etc., don't have similar functionality).

Output Count
> As many records as the cardinality of its key (i.e., the number of distinct values).

Records
> Output is group, bag of records, with record contents within the bag unchanged.

Dataflow
> Map and reduce.

Counting Occurrences of a Key

The typical reason to group records is to operate on the bag of values the group forms, and that's how we'll spend much of this chapter—the data bag is a very powerful concept. Let's take a quickie tour of what we can do to a group; afterward, we'll see the internals of how a group works before moving on to its broader applications.

You'll notice from the result of the last query that sometimes a team has more than one "home" stadium in a season. That's a bit unexpected, but consider that teams occasionally face stadium repairs or late-season makeups for canceled games. Nonetheless, cases where there were even three home parks should be quite rare. Let's confirm our feel for the data using COUNT_STAR, which counts all elements of a bag:

```
team_n_parks = FOREACH (GROUP park_team_years BY (team_id,year_id)) GENERATE
    group.team_id,
    COUNT_STAR(park_team_years) AS n_parks;

DESCRIBE team_n_parks;
```

```
/*
team_n_parks: {
    team_id: chararray,
    n_parks: long
}
*/

vagabonds = FILTER team_n_parks BY n_parks >= 3;

DUMP vagabonds;
(CL4,7)
(CLE,5)
(WS3,4)
(CLE,3)
(DET,3)
...
```

Always, always look through the data and seek *second stories*.

Our script is reporting that CL4 (the Cleveland Spiders) called seven (!) different stadiums home during a season. Is this some weirdness in the data? Could we possibly have messed up this three-line script? Or is it really the case that some teams have had four, five, even seven home stadiums? This demands a closer look.

Pattern in use

Where You'll Use It
   Anywhere you're summarizing counts.

Standard Snippet
   FOREACH   (GROUP   recs   BY   mykey)   GENERATE   group   AS   mykey, COUNT_STAR(recs) AS ct;.

Hello, SQL Users
   SELECT key, COUNT(*) as CT from recs GROUP BY key;. Remember: COUNT_STAR(recs), not COUNT(*).

Important to Know
   See "Pattern in use" on page 111.

Output Count
   As many records as the cardinality of its key (i.e., the number of distinct values).

Records
   Output is mykey, ct:long.

Dataflow
   Map, combiner, and reduce; combiners are very effective unless cardinality is extremely high.

Representing a Collection of Values with a Delimited String

Let's keep the count of parks, but also list the parks themselves for inspection. We could keep dumping the values in Pig's oddball output format, but this is a good opportunity to introduce a very useful pattern: denormalizing a collection of values into a single delimited field.

The format Pig uses to dump bags and tuples to disk wastes characters and is not safe to use in general: any string containing a comma or bracket will cause its record to be misinterpreted. For simple data structures such as a list, we are better off concatenating the values together using a delimiter: a character with no other meaning that does not appear in any of the values. This preserves the rows-and-columns representation of the table that Pig handles best. It also lets us keep using the oh-so-simple TSV format for interchange with Excel, cut and other command-line tools, and later runs of Pig itself. Storing data this way means we do have to pack and unpack the value ourselves, which is an added burden when we need access to the array members. But if accessing the list contents is less frequent, this can act as a positive feature: we can move the field around as a simple string and only pay the cost of constructing the full data structure when necessary.

The BagToString function will serialize a bag of values into a single delimited field as follows:

```
team_year_w_parks = FOREACH (GROUP park_teams BY (team_id, year_id)) GENERATE
  group.team_id,
  COUNT_STAR(park_teams) AS n_parks,
  BagToString(park_teams.park_id, '^') AS park_ids;

DESCRIBE team_year_w_parks;

/*
team_year_w_parks: {
    team_id: chararray,
    n_parks: long,
    park_ids: chararray
}
/*

top_team_year_w_parks = ORDER team_year_w_parks BY n_parks DESC;
top_20 = LIMIT top_team_year_w_parks 20; DUMP @;

/*
(CL4,7,CHI08^CLL01^CLE05^PHI09^ROC03^STL05^ROC02)
(CLE,5,CLE05^DAY01^FOR03^CAN01^COL03)
(WS3,4,BAL01^WAS01^NYC01^CIN01)
(CL3,3,GEA01^NEW03^CLE03)
(CL4,3,IND06^CLE03^DET01)
(BFN,3,ELM01^MIL02^BUF02)
```

```
(WS6,3,BAL02^WAS01^RIC01)
*/
```

This script ouputs four fields: park ID, year, count of stadiums, and the names of the stadiums used separated by a caret (^) delimiter. Like colon (:), comma (,), and slash (/), it doesn't need to be escaped at the command line; like those and semicolon (;), pipe (|), and bang (!), it is visually lightweight and can be avoided within a value. Don't use the wrong delimiter for addresses ("Fargo, ND"), dates ("2014-08-08T12:34:56+00:00"), paths (/tmp/foo), or unsanitized free text (It's a girl! ^_^ \m/ |:-)). If you are considering the use of quoting or escaping to make your strings delimiter safe, you're getting carried away. Stop, step away from the delimiter, and see "Representing a Complex Data Structure with a JSON-Encoded String" on page 106.

Because the park IDs are formed from the first characters of the city name, we can recognize that the Spiders' home fields include two stadiums in Cleveland plus "home" stadiums in Philadelphia, Rochester, St. Louis, and Chicago. These aren't close enough to be alternatives in case of repairs, and baseball did not call for publicity tours in 1898. Were they rotating among these fields, or just spending a day or so at each? Let's see how many games were played at each stadium.

Pattern in use

Where You'll Use It
> Creating a URL for a batch request; hiding a list you don't always want to deserialize; writing a table in a format that will work everywhere.

Standard Snippet
> ```
> FOREACH (GROUP recs BY key) GENERATE group AS mykey, BagToString(recs, '|') AS recs_list;.
> ```

Hello, SQL Users
> Similar to GROUP_CONCAT, but you prepare the input bag first; no fiddly inline DISTINCT calls.

Important to Know
> Be careful with your choice of delimiter. Keep it simple. Don't stringify huge groups.

Output Count
> As many records as the cardinality of its key (i.e., the number of distinct values).

Records
> Output is mykey, recs_list:chararray.

Map and reduce; no real data reduction or explosion, as assumedly you're turning all the data into strings.

Representing a Complex Data Structure with a Delimited String

Instead of serializing the simple list of park IDs we had before, we'd now like to prepare and serialize the collection of park ID/number of games pairs. We can handle this by using two delimiters—one for separating list elements and one for delimiting its contents (this is also how you would handle an object with simple attribute-value pairs such as a hash map):

```
team_year_w_pkgms = FOREACH (GROUP park_team_years BY (team_id, year_id)) {
    /* Create 'park ID'/'game count' field */
    pty_ordered     = ORDER park_team_years BY n_games DESC;
    pk_ng_pairs     = FOREACH pty_ordered GENERATE
        CONCAT(park_id, ':', (chararray)n_games) AS pk_ng_pair;

    /* Generate team/year, number of parks and list of parks/games played */
    GENERATE group.team_id, group.year_id,
        COUNT_STAR(park_team_years) AS n_parks,
        BagToString(pk_ng_pairs,'|') AS pk_ngs;
    };

top_team_parks = ORDER team_year_w_pkgms BY n_parks DESC;
top_20 = LIMIT top_team_parks 20;
-- DUMP @;
STORE top_20 INTO 'park_teams_report';
```

which results in:

```
(CL4,1898,7,CLE05:40|PHI09:9|STL05:2|CLL01:2|ROC02:2|CHTAR:1|ROC03:1)
(CLE,1902,5,CLE05:60|FOR03:2|COL03:1|CAN01:1|DAY01:1)
(WS3,1871,4,WAS01:11|BAL01:1|NYC01:1|CIN01:1)
(CL3,1888,3,CLE03:56|GEA01:3|NEW03:1)
(CL4,1890,3,CLE03:63|IND06:6|DET01:1)
(BFN,1885,3,BUF02:50|ELM01:2|MIL02:1)
(WS6,1875,3,WAS01:8|RIC01:2|BAL02:2)
(BS1,1875,3,BOS01:35|SPR01:1|PRO01:1)
(MID,1872,3,MID01:7|HRT02:3|SPR01:1)
(CHU,1884,3,CHI05:35|PIT03:5|BAL04:1)
...
```

There are a few new things going on here. We've snuck the ORDER BY statement into a few previous examples even though it won't be covered until Chapter 8, but always as a full-table operator. Here we're using it within the body of a FOREACH to sort each bag locally, rather than as a total sort of the whole table. One nice thing about this ORDER BY: it's essentially free, as Pig just instructs Hadoop to do a secondary sort on the data as it lands on the reducer. So there's no reason not to make the data easier to read.

After the ORDER BY statement, we use a *nested* FOREACH to staple each park onto the number of games at that park, delimited with a colon. (Along the way you'll see we also typecast the n_games value, as the CONCAT method expects a chararray.) The final GENERATE line creates records naming the team, the count of parks, and the list of park-usages pairs:

```
hadoop fs -cat park_teams_report/*

CL4  1898    7    CLE05:40|PHI09:9|STL05:2|CLL01:2|ROC02:2|CHI08:1|ROC03:1
CLE  1902    5    CLE05:60|FOR03:2|COL03:1|CAN01:1|DAY01:1
WS3  1871    4    WAS01:11|BAL01:1|NYC01:1|CIN01:1
CL3  1888    3    CLE03:56|GEA01:3|NEW03:1
CL4  1890    3    CLE03:63|IND06:6|DET01:1
BFN  1885    3    BUF02:50|ELM01:2|MIL02:1
WS6  1875    3    WAS01:8|RIC01:2|BAL02:2
BS1  1875    3    BOS01:35|SPR01:1|PRO01:1
MID  1872    3    MID01:7|HRT02:3|SPR01:1
CHU  1884    3    CHI05:35|PIT03:5|BAL04:1
...
```

Out of 156 games (*http://bit.ly/1898_spiders*) that season, the Spiders played only 42 in Cleveland. Between the 15 "home" games in other cities, and their *99* away games, they spent nearly three-quarters of their season on the road.

The Baseball Library Chronology (*http://bit.ly/baseball_1898*) sheds some light. It turns out that labor problems prevented play at their home or any other stadium in Cleveland for a stretch of time, and so they relocated to Philadelphia while that went on. What's more, on June 19th, police *arrested the entire team* during a home game[1] for violating the Sunday "blue laws."[2] Little wonder the Spiders decided to take their talents away from Cleveland! The following year they played 50 straight on the road, won fewer than 13% of their games overall (20–134, the worst single-season record ever), and immediately disbanded at season's end.

Pattern in use

Refer to "Pattern in use" on page 104.

Representing a Complex Data Structure with a JSON-Encoded String

So the result for the Spiders isn't a mistake. Is the team a sole anomalous outlier, or are there other cases, less extreme but similar? The Spiders' season stands out for at

---

1 The Baseball Library Chronology does note that "not so coincidentally, the Spiders had just scored to go ahead 4–3, so the arrests assured Cleveland of a victory." Sounds like the officers, not devoid of hometown pride, might have enjoyed a few innings of the game first.

2 As late as 1967, selling cookery on Sunday in Ohio was still enough to get you convicted. (*http://bit.ly/state_v_heaton*)

least these three reasons: an unusual number of alternative parks, "home" games played in other cities, and a premodern (1898) setting. So let's include a field for the city (we'll take the first three characters of the park ID to represent the city name) and not throw away the field for year:

```
-- Prepare the city field
pktm_city = FOREACH park_team_years GENERATE
    team_id,
    year_id,
    park_id,
    n_games,
    SUBSTRING(park_id, 0,3) AS city;

-- First grouping: stats about each city of residence
pktm_stats = FOREACH (GROUP pktm_city BY (team_id, year_id, city)) {
    pty_ordered   = ORDER   pktm_city BY n_games DESC;
    pk_ct_pairs   = FOREACH pty_ordered GENERATE
                StringConcat(park_id, ':', (chararray)n_games);
    GENERATE
        group.team_id,
        group.year_id,
        group.city                 AS city,
        COUNT_STAR(pktm_city)      AS n_parks,
        SUM(pktm_city.n_games)     AS n_city_games,
        MAX(pktm_city.n_games)     AS max_in_city,
        BagToString(pk_ct_pairs,'|') AS parks
        ;
};
top_parks = ORDER pktm_stats BY n_parks DESC; DUMP @;
```

DUMP shows us:

```
(BR3,1889,NYC,3,71,49,NYC08:49|NYC18:14|NYC05:8)
(BSN,1894,BOS,3,63,32,BOS05:32|BOS04:27|BOS03:4)
(PHI,1894,PHI,3,71,43,PHI06:43|PHI14:22|PHI08:6)
(NY1,1911,NYC,3,75,45,NYC14:45|NYC13:28|NYC10:2)
(PHI,1927,PHI,2,78,66,PHI09:66|PHI11:12)
(LS3,1893,LOU,2,53,52,LOU03:52|LOU02:1)
(NY4,1884,NYC,2,55,33,NYC06:33|NYC03:22)
(CLE,1946,CLE,2,77,41,CLE07:41|CLE06:36)
(CLE,1945,CLE,2,77,46,CLE07:46|CLE06:31)
...
```

The records we're forming are significantly more complex this time. With fields of numbers or constrained categorical values, stapling together delimited values is a fine approach. But when fields become this complex, or when there's any danger of stray delimiters sneaking into the record, if you're going to stick with TSV, you are better off using JSON encoding to serialize the field. It's a bit more heavyweight but nearly as portable, and it happily bundles complex structures and special characters to hide within TSV files:[3]

```
-- Next, assemble full picture:
farhome_gms = FOREACH (GROUP pktm_stats BY (team_id, year_id)) {
    pty_ordered   = ORDER    pktm_stats BY n_city_games DESC;
    city_pairs    = FOREACH pty_ordered GENERATE
        CONCAT(city, ':', (chararray)n_city_games);
    n_home_gms    = SUM(pktm_stats.n_city_games);
    n_main_city   = MAX(pktm_stats.n_city_games);
    n_main_park   = MAX(pktm_stats.max_in_city);
    -- a string versus a blank makes it easy to scan the data for patterns:
    is_modern     = (group.year_id >= 1905 ? 'mod' : NULL);
    --
    GENERATE group.team_id, group.year_id,
        is_modern                          AS is_modern,
        n_home_gms                         AS n_home_gms,
        n_home_gms - n_main_city           AS n_farhome_gms,
        n_home_gms - n_main_park           AS n_althome_games,
        COUNT_STAR(pktm_stats)             AS n_cities,
        BagToString(city_pairs,'|')        AS cities,
        BagToString(pktm_stats.parks,'|')    AS parks
        ;
};

farhome_gms = ORDER farhome_gms BY n_cities DESC, n_farhome_gms DESC;

STORE farhome_gms INTO 'json_test' USING JsonStorage();
```

Here's a sample of the output:

```
{
    "team_id":"BSN",
    "year_id":1894,
    "city":"BOS",
    "n_parks":3,
    "n_city_games":63,
    "max_in_city":32,
    "parks":"BOS05:32|BOS04:27|BOS03:4"
}
{"team_id":"PHI","year_id":1894,"city":"PHI","n_parks":3,"n_city_games":71,
    "max_in_city...
{"team_id":"NY1","year_id":1911,"city":"NYC","n_parks":3,"n_city_games":75,
    "max_in_city...
{"team_id":"PHI","year_id":1927,"city":"PHI","n_parks":2,"n_city_games":78,
    "max_in_city...
{"team_id":"LS3","year_id":1893,"city":"LOU","n_parks":2,"n_city_games":53,
```

---

3 And if neither JSON nor simple-delimiter is appropriate, use Parquet or Trevni, big data–optimized formats that support complex data structures. Those are your three choices: TSV with delimited fields, TSV with JSON fields or JSON lines on their own, or Parquet/Trevni. We don't recommend anything else.

```
    "max_in_city...
{"team_id":"NY4","year_id":1884,"city":"NYC","n_parks":2,"n_city_games":55,
    "max_in_city...
{"team_id":"CLE","year_id":1946,"city":"CLE","n_parks":2,"n_city_games":77,
    "max_in_city...
{"team_id":"CLE","year_id":1945,"city":"CLE","n_parks":2,"n_city_games":77,
    "max_in_city...
    ...
```

Pattern in use

Where You'll Use It

Creating the POST body for a JSON batch request; hiding a complex value you don't always want to deserialize; writing a table in a format that will work everywhere; creating a string free of nonkeyboard characters.

Standard Snippet

```
STORE my_relation INTO 'my_relation' USING JsonStorage();.
```

Output Count

As many records as the relation contains.

Records

Output is one JSON object per line.

Dataflow

Map and reduce; mild data expansion as JSON repeats the subfield names on each row.

Does God hate Cleveland?

Probably. But are the Spiders a particularly anomalous exhibition? No. Considered against the teams of their era, they look much more normal. In the early days, baseball was still literally getting its act together and teams hopped around frequently. Since 1905, no team has seen home bases in three cities, and the three cases where a team spent any significant time in an alternative city each tell a notable story.

In 2003 and 2004, *les pauvres* Montreal Expos were sentenced to play 22 "home" games in San Juan (Puerto Rico) and only 59 back in Montreal. The rudderless franchise had been sold back to the league itself and was being shopped around in preparation for a move to Washington, DC. With no real stars, no hometown enthusiasm, and no future in Montreal, MLB took the opportunity to build its burgeoning fanbase in Latin America and so deployed the team to Puerto Rico part-time. The 1968–1969 Chicago White Sox (CHA) were similarly team building in Milwaukee; the owner of the 1956–1957 Brooklyn Dodgers slipped them away for a stint in New Jersey in order to pressure Brooklyn for a new stadium.

You won't always want to read a second story to the end as we have here, but it's important to at least identify unusual features of your dataset—they may turn out to explain more than you'd think.

 In traditional analysis with sampled data, edge cases undermine the data, presenting the spectre of a nonrepresentative sample or biased result. In big data analysis on comprehensive data, the edge cases *prove* the data. Here's what we mean. Since 1904, only a very few teams have multiple home stadiums, and no team has had more than two home stadiums in a season. Home-field advantage gives a significant edge: the home team plays the deciding half of the final inning, the roster is constructed to take advantage of the ballpark's layout, and players get to eat home-cooked meals, enjoy the cheers of encouraging fans, and spend a stretch of time in one location. The Spiders and les Expos and a few others enjoyed only part of those advantages.

With a dataset this small, there's no good way to control for these unusual circumstances, and so they represent outliers that taint our results. With a large and comprehensive dataset, those small fractions would represent analyzable populations of their own. With millions of seasons, we could conceivably baseline the jet-powered, computer-optimized schedules of the present against the night-train *wanderjahr* of the Cleveland Spiders and other early teams.

Group and Aggregate

Some of the happiest moments you can have analyzing a massive dataset come when you are able to make it a slightly less massive dataset. Aggregate functions (i.e., ones that turn the whole of a group into a scalar value) are the best path to this joy.

Aggregating Statistics of a Group

In Chapter 5, we used each player's seasonal counting stats (hits, home runs, etc.) to estimate seasonal rate stats—that is, how well they get on base (OPS), how well they clear the bases (SLG), and an overall estimate of offensive performance (OBP). But because we were focused on pipeline operations, we only did so on a season-by-season basis. The group-and-aggregate pattern lets us combine those seasonal stats in order to characterize each player's career:

```
bat_careers = FOREACH (GROUP bat_seasons BY player_id) {
    totG   = SUM(bat_seasons.G);
    totPA  = SUM(bat_seasons.PA);  totAB  = SUM(bat_seasons.AB);
    totHBP = SUM(bat_seasons.HBP); totSH  = SUM(bat_seasons.SH);
    totBB  = SUM(bat_seasons.BB);  totH   = SUM(bat_seasons.H);
    toth1B = SUM(bat_seasons.h1B); toth2B = SUM(bat_seasons.h2B);
```

```
        toth3B  = SUM(bat_seasons.h3B); totHR  = SUM(bat_seasons.HR);
        totR    = SUM(bat_seasons.R);   totRBI = SUM(bat_seasons.RBI);
        OBP     = 1.0*(totH + totBB + totHBP) / totPA;
        SLG     = 1.0*(toth1B + 2*toth2B + 3*toth3B + 4*totHR) / totAB;
        team_ids = DISTINCT bat_seasons.team_id;
        GENERATE
            group                       AS player_id,
            COUNT_STAR(bat_seasons)     AS n_seasons,
            COUNT_STAR(team_ids)        AS card_teams,
            MIN(bat_seasons.year_id)    AS beg_year,
            MAX(bat_seasons.year_id)    AS end_year,
            totG    AS G,
            totPA AS PA,   totAB  AS AB,  totHBP AS HBP,   -- $6 -  $8
            totSH AS SH,   totBB  AS BB,  totH   AS H,     -- $9 - $11
            toth1B AS h1B, toth2B AS h2B, toth3B AS h3B,   -- $12 - $14
            totHR AS HR,   totR   AS R,   totRBI AS RBI,   -- $15 - $17
            OBP AS OBP, SLG AS SLG, (OBP + SLG) AS OPS     -- $18 - $20
        ;
    };

    STORE bat_careers INTO 'bat_careers';
```

We first gather together all seasons by a player by grouping on player_id, then throw a barrage of SUM, COUNT_STAR, MIN, and MAX functions at the accumulated fields to find the career totals. Using the nested FOREACH form means we can use intermediate values such as totPA in both the calculation of OBP and as a field in the new table directly.

The nested FOREACH also lets us apply the DISTINCT bag operation, creating a new bag holding only the distinct team_id values across all seasons. That statement has, in principle, two steps: projection of a bag-with-just-team_id followed by DISTINCT to eliminate duplicates. But behind the scenes, Pig uses a special kind of bag (Distinct DataBag) that in all respects meets the data bag interface, but that uses an efficient internal data structure to eliminate duplicates as they're added. So rather than (list of seasons) → (list of team IDs) → (list of distinct team IDs), you only have to pay for (list of seasons) → (list of distinct team IDs).

We will use the bat_careers table in several later demonstrations, so keep its output file around.

Pattern in use

Where You'll Use It

Everywhere: turning manufactured items into statistics about batches; summarizing a cohort; rolling up census block statistics to state-level statistics; and so on.

```
FOREACH (GROUP recs BY key) GENERATE group AS mykey, AggregateFunc
tion(recs), AggregateFunction(recs), ...;.
```

Hello, SQL Users

Directly comparable for the most part.

Output Count

As many records as the cardinality of its key (i.e., the number of distinct values); big decrease in output size from turning bags into scalars.

Records

Something like `mykey, aggregated_value, aggregated_value, ...`.

Dataflow

Map, combiner, and reduce; combiners are quite effective unless cardinality is very high.

In addition, see "Pattern in use" on page 114.

Completely Summarizing a Field

In the preceding case, the aggregate functions were used to create an output table with similar structure to the input table, but at a coarser-grained relational level: career rather than season. The result was a new table to analyze, not a conceptual report. Statistical aggregations also let you summarize groups and tables with well-understood descriptive statistics. By sketching their essential characteristics at dramatically smaller size, we make the data easier to work with but more importantly, we make it possible to comprehend.

The following functions are built into Pig:

- Count of all values: `COUNT_STAR(bag)`
- Count of non-null values: `COUNT(bag)`
- Minimum/maximum non-null value: `MIN(bag)` / `MAX(bag)`
- Sum of non-null values: `SUM(bag)`
- Average of non-null values: `AVG(bag)`

There are a few additional summary functions that aren't native features of Pig, but are offered by LinkedIn's might-as-well-be-native DataFu package.[4] This is important material, though. Every painter of landscapes must know how to convey the essence of a happy little tree (*http://bit.ly/happy_little_clouds*) using a few deft strokes and not the prickly minutiae of its 500 branches; these functions are your brushes:[5]

- Cardinality (i.e., the count of distinct values): combine the DISTINCT operation and the COUNT_STAR function as demonstrated below, or use the DataFu HyperLo gLogPlusPlus UDF
- Variance of non-null values: VAR(bag), using the datafu.pig.stats.VAR UDF
- Standard deviation of non-null values: SQRT(VAR(bag))
- Quantiles: Quantile(bag) or StreamingQuantile(bag)
- Median (50th percentile value) of a bag: Median(bag) or StreamingMedian(bag)

Chapter 5 has details on how to use UDFs, and so we're going to leave the details of that to the sample code. You'll also notice we list two functions for quantile and for median. Finding the exact median or other quantiles (as the Median/Quantile UDFs do) is costly at large scale, and so a good approximate algorithm (StreamingMedian/ StreamingQuantile) is well appreciated. Because the point of this stanza is to characterize the values for our own sense making, the approximate algorithms are appropriate:

```
weight_yr_stats = FOREACH (GROUP bat_seasons BY year_id) {
    dist         = DISTINCT bat_seasons.weight;
    sorted_a     = FILTER   bat_seasons.weight BY weight IS NOT NULL;
    sorted       = ORDER    sorted_a BY weight;
    some         = LIMIT    dist.weight 5;
    n_recs       = COUNT_STAR(bat_seasons);
    n_notnulls   = COUNT(bat_seasons.weight);
    GENERATE
      group,
      AVG(bat_seasons.weight)          AS avg_val,
      SQRT(VAR(bat_seasons.weight))    AS stddev_val,
      MIN(bat_seasons.weight)          AS min_val,
      FLATTEN(ApproxEdgeile(sorted))   AS (p01, p05, p50, p95, p99),
      MAX(bat_seasons.weight)          AS max_val,
      --
```

---

4 If you've forgotten/never quite learned what those functions mean, hang on for just a bit and we'll demonstrate them in context. If that still doesn't do it, set a copy of *Naked Statistics* (*http://bit.ly/naked_stats*) or *Head First Statistics* next to this book. Both do a good job of efficiently imparting what these functions mean and how to use them without assuming prior expertise or interest in mathematics.

5 Artist/educator Bob Ross: "Anyone can paint; all you need is a dream in your heart and a little bit of practice"—hopefully you're feeling the same way about big data analysis.

```
        n_recs                       AS n_recs,
        n_recs - n_notnulls          AS n_nulls,
        COUNT_STAR(dist)             AS cardinality,
        SUM(bat_seasons.weight)      AS sum_val,
        BagToString(some, '^')       AS some_vals
        ;
    };
```

Pattern in use

Where You'll Use It

> Everywhere: quality statistics on manufacturing batches; response times of web server requests; A/B testing in ecommerce; and so on.

Standard Snippet

> `FOREACH (GROUP recs BY key) { ... ; GENERATE ...; };`.

Hello, SQL Users

> Directly comparable for the most part.

Important to Know

> - Say `COUNT_STAR(recs)`, not `COUNT_STAR(recs.myfield)`. The latter creates a new bag and interferes with combiner'ing.
>
> - Use `COUNT_STAR` and never `SIZE` on a bag.
>
> - Say `SUM(recs.myfield)`, not `SUM(myfield)` (which isn't in scope).
>
> - Get in the habit of writing `COUNT_STAR` and never `COUNT`, unless you explicitly mean to only count non-nulls.

Output Count

> As many records as the cardinality of its key (i.e., the number of distinct values); big decrease in output size from turning bags into scalars.

Records

> Something like `mykey, aggregated_value, aggregated_value, ...`.

Dataflow

> Map, combiner, and reduce; combiners are quite effective unless cardinality is very high.

Summarizing Aggregate Statistics of a Full Table

To summarize the statistics of a full table, we use a `GROUP ALL` statement. That is, instead of GROUP *table* BY *key*, write GROUP *table* ALL. Everything else is as usual:

```
REGISTER /usr/lib/pig/datafu.jar

DEFINE VAR datafu.pig.stats.VAR();
DEFINE ApproxEdgeile datafu.pig.stats.StreamingQuantile(
  '0.01','0.05', '0.50', '0.95', '0.99');


...

weight_summary = FOREACH (GROUP people ALL) {
    dist        = DISTINCT people.weight_lb;
    sorted_a    = FILTER   people.weight_lb BY weight_lb IS NOT NULL;
    sorted      = ORDER    sorted_a BY weight_lb;
    some        = LIMIT    dist.weight_lb 5;
    n_recs      = COUNT_STAR(people);
    n_notnulls  = COUNT(people.weight_lb);
    GENERATE
        group,
        AVG(people.weight_lb)            AS avg_val,
        SQRT(VAR(people.weight_lb))      AS stddev_val,
        MIN(people.weight_lb)            AS min_val,
        FLATTEN(ApproxEdgeile(sorted))   AS (p01, p05, p50, p95, p99),
        MAX(people.weight_lb)            AS max_val,
        n_recs                           AS n_recs,
        n_recs - n_notnulls              AS n_nulls,
        COUNT_STAR(dist)                 AS cardinality,
        SUM(people.weight_lb)            AS sum_val,
        BagToString(some, '^')           AS some_vals
    ;
};
```

As we hope you readily recognize, using the GROUP ALL operation can be dangerous, as it requires bringing all the data onto a single reducer.

We're safe here, even on larger datasets, because all but one of the functions we supplied are efficiently *algebraic*: they can be significantly performed in the map phase and combiner'ed. This eliminates most of the data before the reducer. The cardinality calculation, done here with a nested DISTINCT operation, is the only real contributor to reducer-side data size. For this dataset, its size is manageable, and if it weren't, there is a good approximate cardinality function. You'll get a good feel for what is and isn't efficient through the examples in this chapter.

Pattern in use

Where You'll Use It
  Getting to know your data: computing relative statistics or normalizing values; topline totals and summaries; and so on.

Hello, SQL Users
  Aggregate functions *without* a GROUP BY.

Important to Know

- You're sending all the data to one reducer, so make sure the aggregate functions are highly reductive.

- Note the syntax of the full-table GROUP statement—there's no I in TEAM, and no BY in GROUP ALL.

Output Count

Single row.

Dataflow

Map, combiner, and *single* reducer.

In addition, see "Pattern in use" on page 114.

Summarizing a String Field

In Example 6-1 we'll analyze the distribution of the lengths of a string field.

Example 6-1. Summary of a string field (ch_06/bat_seasons.pig)

```
name_first_summary_0 = FOREACH (GROUP bat_seasons ALL) {
    dist       = DISTINCT bat_seasons.name_first;
    lens       = FOREACH  bat_seasons GENERATE SIZE(name_first) AS len;
    --
    n_recs     = COUNT_STAR(bat_seasons);
    n_notnulls = COUNT(bat_seasons.name_first);
    --
    examples   = LIMIT    dist.name_first 5;
    snippets   = FOREACH  examples GENERATE
        (SIZE(name_first) > 15 ? CONCAT(SUBSTRING(name_first, 0, 15),'…') :
            name_first) AS val;
    GENERATE
        group,
        'name_first'               AS var:chararray,
        MIN(lens.len)              AS minlen,
        MAX(lens.len)              AS maxlen,
        --
        AVG(lens.len)              AS avglen,
        SQRT(VAR(lens.len))        AS stdvlen,
        SUM(lens.len)              AS sumlen,
        --
        n_recs                     AS n_recs,
        n_recs - n_notnulls        AS n_nulls,
        COUNT_STAR(dist)           AS cardinality,
        MIN(bat_seasons.name_first) AS minval,
        MAX(bat_seasons.name_first) AS maxval,
        BagToString(snippets, '^') AS examples,
        lens  AS lens
    ;
```

```
};

name_first_summary = FOREACH name_first_summary_0 {
    sortlens    = ORDER lens BY len;
    pctiles     = ApproxEdgeile(sortlens);
    GENERATE
        var,
        minlen, FLATTEN(pctiles) AS (p01, p05, p10, p50, p90, p95, p99), maxlen,
        avglen, stdvlen, sumlen,
        n_recs, n_nulls, cardinality,
        minval, maxval, examples
    ;
};
```

Pattern in use

Where You'll Use It

Getting to know your data: sizing string lengths for creating a database schema; making sure there's nothing ill-formed or outrageously huge; making sure all values for a categorical field or string key are correct; and so on.

Hello, SQL Users

Corresponding functions *without* a GROUP BY.

Important to Know

- You're sending all the data to one reducer, so make sure the aggregate functions are highly reductive.

- Note the syntax of the full-table GROUP statement—there's no I in TEAM, and no BY in GROUP ALL.

Output Count

Single row.

Dataflow

Map, combiner, and single reducer.

In addition, see "Pattern in use" on page 114.

Calculating the Distribution of Numeric Values with a Histogram

One of the most common uses of a group-and-aggregate is to create a histogram showing how often each value (or range of values) of a field occurs. This calculates the distribution of seasons played (i.e., it counts the number of players whose career lasted only a single season, who played for two seasons, etc.):

```
vals = FOREACH bat_careers GENERATE n_seasons AS bin;
seasons_hist = FOREACH (GROUP vals BY bin) GENERATE
    group AS bin, COUNT_STAR(vals) AS ct;

DUMP vals;

/*
(1,4781)
(2,2461)
(3,1583)
(4,1162)
...
(23,13)
(24,5)
(25,3)
(26,1)
(27,1)
*/
```

Referring back to the `bat_seasons` relation, we can compute a histogram with example data:

```
vals = FOREACH (GROUP bat_seasons BY (player_id, name_first, name_last)) GENERATE
    COUNT_STAR(bat_seasons) AS bin, flatten(group);
seasons_hist = FOREACH (GROUP vals BY bin) {
    some_vals = LIMIT vals 3;
    GENERATE group AS bin, COUNT_STAR(vals) AS ct, BagToString(some_vals, '|');
};

DUMP seasons_hist

/*
(1,4781,1|zay01|William|Zay|1|zoccope01|Pete|Zoccolillo|1|zimmero01|Roy|...)
(2,2461,2|moranbi01|Bill|Moran|2|moranal01|Al|Moran|2|stewasc01|Scott|...)
(3,1583,3|wilshwh01|Whitey|Wilshere|3|drisktr01|Travis|Driskill|3|dellwh01|...)
(4,1162,4|mahonji01|Jim|Mahoney|4|deanwa01|Wayland|Dean|4|ceccaar01|Art|...)
*/
```

So the pattern here is to:

- Project only the values
- Group by the values
- Produce the group as key and the count as value

Pattern in Use

Where You'll Use It

Anywhere you need a more detailed sketch of your data than average/standard deviation or simple quantiles can provide.

```
vals = FOREACH recs GENERATE myfield AS bin; hist = FOREACH (GROUP
vals BY bin) GENERATE group AS bin, COUNT_STAR(vals) AS ct;.
```

Output Count

As many records as the cardinality of its key (i.e., the number of distinct values).

Records

Output is bin, ct:long; you've turned records-with-values into values-with-counts.

Dataflow

Map, combiner, and reduce; combiners are very effective unless cardinality is extremely high.

Binning Data for a Histogram

Generating a histogram for games just as we did in the previous section produces mostly useless output. There's no material difference between a career of 2,000 games and one of 2,001 games, but each value receives its own count—making it hard to distinguish the density of 1-, 2-, and 3-count bins near 1,000 games from the 1-, 2-, and 3-count bins near 1,500 games:

```
-- Meaningless
G_vals = FOREACH bat_careers GENERATE G AS val;
G_hist = FOREACH (GROUP G_vals BY val) GENERATE
    group AS val,
    SUM(G_vals) AS ct;

DUMP G_hist;

/*
(1,658)
(2,946)
(3,1164)
...
(3298,3298)
(3308,3308)
(3562,3562)
*/
```

Instead, we will bin the data: divide by the bin size (50 in this case), and then multiply back by the bin size. The result of the division is an integer (because both the value and the bin size are of type int), and so the resulting value of bin is always an even multiple of the bin size. Values of 0, 12, and 49 all go to the 0 bin; 150 games goes to the 150 bin; and Pete Rose's total of 3,562 games played becomes the only occupant of bin 3550:

```
-- Binning makes it sensible
G_vals = FOREACH bat_careers GENERATE 50*FLOOR(G/50) AS val;
G_hist = FOREACH (GROUP G_vals BY val) GENERATE
    group AS val,
    COUNT_STAR(G_vals) AS ct;

DUMP G_hist;

/*
(0.0,6638)
(50.0,1916)
(100.0,1176)
...
(3250.0,1)
(3300.0,1)
(3550.0,1)
*/
```

Histogram of career games played

The histogram on the binned data is now quite clear, as shown in Figure 6-1.

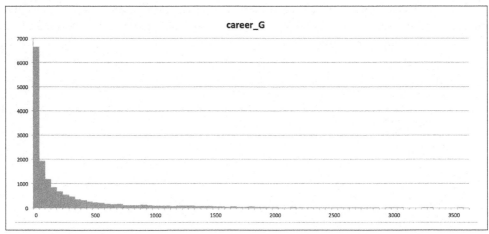

Figure 6-1. Career total games played

Choosing a Bin Size

How do you choose a bin size? Figures 6-2, 6-3, and 6-4 zoom in on the tail (2,000 or more games) to show bin sizes that are too large, too small, and just right.

Bin size too large

As shown in Figure 6-2, a bin size of 200 is too coarse, washing out legitimate gaps that tell a story.

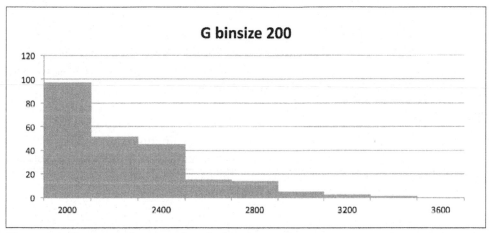

Figure 6-2. Career total games played—bin size too large

Bin size too small

The bin size of 2 is too fine—the counts are small, there are many trivial gaps, and there is a lot of nonmeaningful bin-to-bin variation (Figure 6-3).

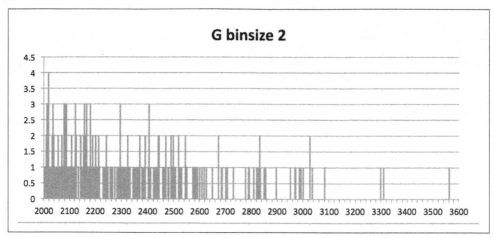

Figure 6-3. Career total games played—bin size too small

Bin size just right

The bin size we chose, 50 games, works well. It's a meaningful number (50 games represents about 1/3 of a season), it gives meaty counts per bin even when the population starts to become sparse, and yet it preserves the gaps that demonstrate the epic scope of Pete Rose and other outliers' careers. See Figure 6-4.

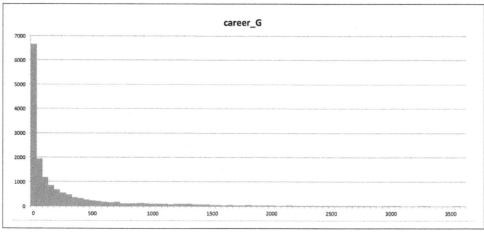

Figure 6-4. Career total games played—bin size just right

Bin sizing is where your skill as a storyteller comes through.

Interpreting Histograms and Quantiles

Different underlying mechanics will give different distributions.

Games played: linear

The histogram of career games shows that most players see only one game their whole career, and the counts drop off continuously at higher and higher career totals (Figure 6-5). You can't play 30 games unless you were good enough to make it into 29 games; you can't play 100 games unless you continued to be good, didn't get injured, didn't get old, didn't go to war between the 30th and 99th game, and so on.

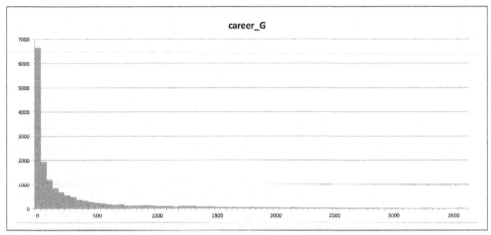

Figure 6-5. Career total games played—linear

Games played: log-log plot

Distributions, such as this one, that span many orders of magnitude in value and count, are easier to understand using a *log-log graph*. The "log" is short for "logarithm," in which successive values represent orders of magnitude difference. On a log log graph, then, the axes arrange the displayed values so that the same distance separates 1 from 10 as separates 10 from 100, and so on, for any *ratio* of values.

Though the career games data shows a very sharp dropoff, it is *not* a long-tail distribution, as you can see by comparing a power-law fit (which is always a straight line on a log-log graph) to the actual histogram. See Figure 6-6.

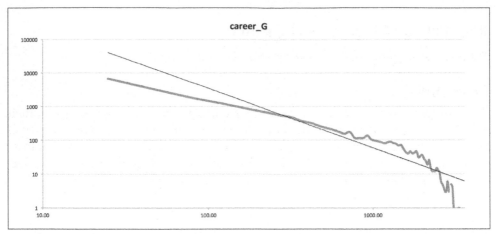

Figure 6-6. Career total games played—log-log

Binning Data into Exponentially Sized Buckets

In contrast, web page views are known to be one of many phenomena that obey the "long-tail" distribution, as we can see by generating a histogram of hourly pageview counts for each Wikipedia page (Figure 6-7).[6] Because the data is so sharply exponential, we are better off binning it *logarithmically*. To do so, we take the log of the value, chunk it (using the multiply-floor-undo method again), and then take the exponential to restore a representative value for the bin (you'll notice we avoid trouble taking the logarithm of zero by feeding it an insignificantly small number instead—this lets zero be included in the processing without materially altering the result):

```
pageviews = LOAD '/data/rawd/wikipedia/page_counts/pagecounts-20141126-230000.gz'
    USING PigStorage(' ') AS (
    project_name:chararray,
    page_title:chararray,
    requests:long,
    bytes:long
);

SET eps 0.001;

view_vals = FOREACH pageviews GENERATE
    (long)EXP( FLOOR(LOG((requests == 0 ? $eps : requests)) * 10)/10.0 ) AS bin;

hist_wp_view = FOREACH (GROUP view_vals BY bin) GENERATE
    group AS bin,
    COUNT_STAR(view_vals) AS ct;
```

---

6 For 11 p.m. UTC on November 26, 2014 (which is the date this section was written).

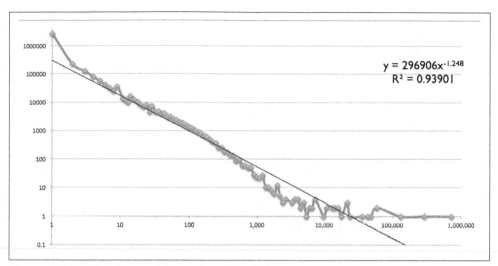

Figure 6-7. Wikipedia pageviews—logarithmic bins

The result indeed is a nice sharp line on the log-log plot, and the logarithmic bins did a nice job of accumulating robust counts while preserving detail. Logarithmic bins are generally a better choice any time you're using a logarithmic x-axis, because it means that the span of each bin is visually the same size, aiding interpretation.

As you can see, you don't have to only bin linearly. Apply any function that takes piecewise segments of the domain and maps them sequentially to the integers, then undo that function to map those integers back to a central value of each segment. The Wikipedia web server log data also includes the total *bytes* transferred per page; this data spans such a large range that we end up binning both logarithmically (to tame the upper range of values) and linearly (to tame the lower range of values)—see the sample code for details.

Pattern in use

Where You'll Use It

> Anywhere the values make sense exponentially (e.g., values make sense as 1, 100, 1000, ..., 10 million rather than 1 million, 2 million, ..., 10 million); anywhere you will use a logarithmic x-axis for displaying the bin values.

Important to Know

> The result is a representative value from the bin (e.g., `100`), and not the log of that value (e.g., `log(100)`); decide whether the representative should be a central value from the bin or the minimum value in the bin.

Standard Snippet

> (long)EXP(FLOOR(LOG((val == 0 ? $eps : val)) * bin_sf)/bin_sf) for scale factor `bin_sf`; instead of substituting `$eps` for zero, you might prefer to filter them out.

In addition, see "Pattern in Use" on page 118.

Creating Pig Macros for Common Stanzas

Rather than continuing to write the histogram recipe over and over, let's take a moment and generalize. Pig allows you to create macros that parameterize multiple statements:

```
DEFINE histogram(table, key) RETURNS dist {
    vals = FOREACH $table GENERATE $key;
    $dist = FOREACH (GROUP vals BY $key) GENERATE
        group AS val,
        COUNT_STAR(vals) AS ct;
};

DEFINE binned_histogram(table, key, binsize, maxval) RETURNS dist {
    -- A list of numbers from 0-9999
    numbers = LOAD '/data/gold/numbers10k.txt' AS (number:int);
    vals = FOREACH $table
        GENERATE (long)(FLOOR($key / $binsize) * $binsize) AS bin;
    all_bins = FOREACH numbers GENERATE (number * $binsize) AS bin;
    all_bins = FILTER  all_bins BY (bin <= $maxval);
    $dist = FOREACH (COGROUP vals BY bin, all_bins BY bin) GENERATE
        group AS bin,
        (COUNT_STAR(vals) == 0L ? 0L : COUNT_STAR(vals)) AS ct;
};
```

You'll notice we load a relation called `numbers`. This is a trick to fill in empty bins in the histogram with 0. If you can't follow this, don't worry—we'll cover COGROUP in Chapter 7.

Distribution of Games Played

Call the histogram macro on the batting career data as follows:

```
career_G_hist     = binned_histogram(bat_careers, 'G', 50, 3600);
career_G_hist_2   = binned_histogram(bat_careers, 'G', 2, 3600);
career_G_hist_200 = binned_histogram(bat_careers, 'G', 200, 3600);
```

And on the people data as follows:

```
height_hist  = binned_histogram(people, 'height_in', 40, 80);
weight_hist  = binned_histogram(people, 'weight_lb', 10, 300);

birthmo_hist = histogram(people, 'birth_month');
deathmo_hist = histogram(people, 'death_month');
```

Now that finding a histogram is effortless, let's examine more shapes of distributions.

Extreme Populations and Confounding Factors

To reach the major leagues, a player must possess multiple extreme attributes: ones that are easy to measure, like being tall or being born in a country where baseball is popular; and ones that are not, like field vision, clutch performance, the drive to put in outlandishly many hours practicing skills. Any time you are working with extremes as we are, you must be very careful to assume their characteristics resemble the overall population's. See Figures 6-8 and 6-9.

Here again are the graphs for players' height and weight, but now graphed against (in light blue) the distribution of height/weight for U.S. males aged 20–29.[7]

The overall-population distribution is shown with light blue bars, overlaid with a normal distribution curve for illustrative purposes. The population of baseball players deviates predictably from the overall population: it's an advantage to be taller. The distribution of player weights, meanwhile, is shifted somewhat but with a dramatically smaller spread.

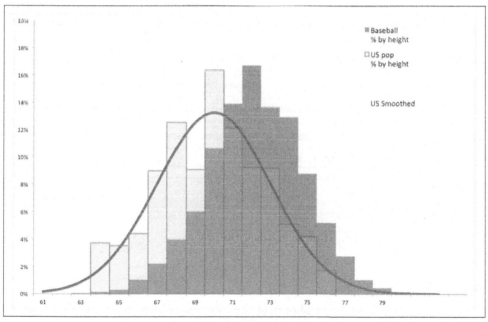

Figure 6-8. Baseball player heights vs. general population

---

7 U.S. Census Department, Statistical Abstract of the United States. Tables 206 and 209, Cumulative Percent Distribution of Population by (Weight/Height) and Sex, 2007–2008; uses data from the U.S. National Center for Health Statistics.

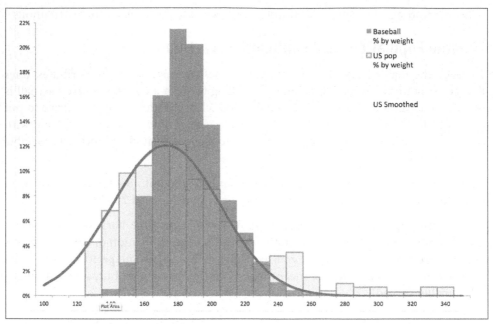

Figure 6-9. Baseball player weights vs. general population

Distribution of birth and death day of year

Surely at least baseball players are born and die like the rest of us, though?

With a little Pig action, we can generate some histograms to answer that question:

```
vitals = FOREACH people GENERATE
    height_in,
    10*CEIL(weight_lb/10.0) AS weight_lb,
    birth_month,
    death_month;

birth_month_hist = histogram(vitals, 'birth_month');
death_month_hist = histogram(vitals, 'death_month');
height_hist = histogram(vitals, 'height_in');
weight_hist = histogram(vitals, 'weight_lb');
```

Baseball player deaths

Figure 6-10 shows the relative seasonable distribution of death rates, with adjustment for the fact that there are fewer days in February than July and so forth. As before, the background U.S. rates are shown as darker outlined bars and the results from our dataset as solid blue bars.

We were surprised to see how seasonal the death rate is. We all probably have a feel there's more birthday party invitations in September than in March, but hopefully not so much for funerals. This pattern is quite consistent, and as you might guess, inverted in the Southern Hemisphere. Most surprisingly of all, it persists even in places with a mild climate (*http://j.mp/seasonal_deaths*). The most likely cause of fewer deaths in the summer is *not* fewer snow-covered driveways to shovel, but rather that people take vactions—lowering stress, improving mood, and synthesizing vitamin D. (And there's no clear signal of "hanging on for Christmas" in the data.)

The baseball distribution is lumpier, as you'd expect from its smaller sample size,[8] but matches the background distribution. Death treats baseball players, at least in this regard, as it does us all.

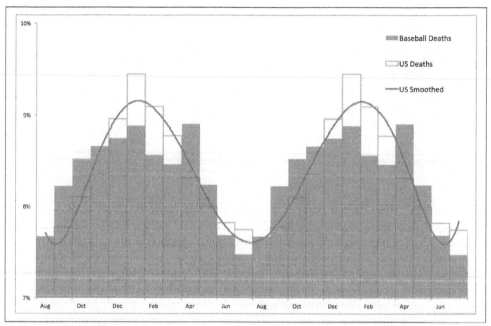

Figure 6-10. Month of death for baseball players vs. general population

Baseball player births

That is not true for the birth data! The format of Figure 6-11 is the same as Figure 6-10, and again we see a seasonal distribution—with a peak nine months after the cold winter temperatures induce people to stay home and find alternative recreations. But the baseball data does *not* match the background distribution at all. The sharp spike in August following the nadir in May and June appears nowhere in the background data, and its phase (where it crosses the centerline) is shifted later by

---

8 We don't think the April spike is anything significant ("Hanging on for one more Opening Day celebration?"); sometimes lumpy data is lumpy.

several months. In this dataset, a player born in August is about 25% more likely to make the Major Leagues than a player born in June; restricting it to players from the United States born after 1950 makes August babies *50%* more likely to earn a baseball card than June babies.

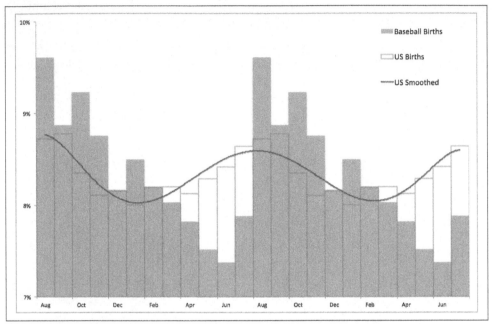

Figure 6-11. Baseball player births by month vs. general population

The reason is that since the 1940s, American youth leagues have used July 31st as an age cutoff. If Augusta were born on August 1st, then four calendar years and 364 days later, she would still technically be four years old. Julien, who showed up the day before her and thus has spent five years and no days orbiting the Sun, is permitted to join the league as a five-year-old. The Augustas may be initially disappointed, but when they do finally join the league as five-year-and-364-day-old kids, they have nearly an extra year of growth compared to the Juliens who sign up with them, which on the whole provides a huge advantage at young ages. This earns the Augustas extra attention from their coaches, extra validation of their skill, and extra investment of "I'm good at baseball!" in their identity.

Don't Trust Distributions at the Tails

A lot of big data analyses explore population extremes: manufacturing defects, security threats, disease carriers, peak performers. Elements arrive into these extremes exactly because multiple causative features drive them there (such as an advantageous height or birth month), and a host of other conflated features follow from those deviations (such as those stemming from the level of fitness athletes maintain).

So whenever you are examining populations of outliers, you cannot depend on their behavior resembling the universal population. Normal distributions may not remain normal and may not even retain a central tendency; independent features in the general population may become tightly coupled in the outlier group; and a host of other easy assumptions become invalid. Stay alert.

Calculating a Relative Distribution Histogram

The histograms we've calculated have results in terms of counts. The results do a better general job of enforcing comparisons if we express them as relative frequencies: as fractions of the total count. You know how to find the total:

```
HR_stats = FOREACH (GROUP bat_careers ALL)
    GENERATE COUNT_STAR(bat_careers) AS n_players;
```

The problem is that HR_stats is a single-row table, and so not something we can use directly in a FOREACH expression. Pig gives you a piece of syntactic sugar for this specific case of a one-row table:[9] project the value as *table.field.* as if it were an inner bag, but slap the field's type (in parentheses) in front of it like a typecast expression:

```
HR_stats = FOREACH (GROUP bat_careers ALL)
    GENERATE COUNT_STAR(bat_careers) AS ct;
HR_hist  = FOREACH (GROUP bat_careers BY HR) {
    ct = COUNT_STAR(bat_careers);
    GENERATE group as val,
        ct/( (double)HR_stats.ct ) AS freq,
        ct;
};
STORE HR_stats INTO 'HR_stats';
```

Typecasting the projected field as if you were simply converting the schema of a field from one scalar type to another acts as a promise to Pig that what looks like a column of possibly many values will turn out to have only one row. In return, Pig will understand that you want a sort of über-typecast of the projected column into what is effectively its literal value.

Pattern in use

Where You'll Use It
    Histograms on sampled populations; whenever you want frequencies rather than counts (i.e., proportions rather than absolute values).

---

9 Called *scalar projection* in Pig terminology.

Standard Snippet

> Same as for a histogram, but with `COUNT_STAR(vals)/((long)recs_info.ct)`
> `AS freq`.

In addition, see "Pattern in Use" on page 118 and "Reinjecting Global Values" on page 132.

Reinjecting Global Values

Sometimes things are more complicated, and what you'd like to do is perform light synthesis of the results of some initial Hadoop jobs, then bring them back into your script as if they were some sort of "global variable." But a Pig script just orchestrates the top-level motion of data: there are no good intrinsic ways to bring the result of a step into the declaration of following steps. You can use a backhoe to tear open the trunk of your car, but it's not really set up to push the trunk latch button. The proper recourse is to split the script into two parts, and run it within a workflow tool like Rake, Drake, or Oozie. The workflow layer can fish those values out of the HDFS and inject them as runtime parameters into the next stage of the script.

In the case of global counts, it would be much faster if we could sum the group counts to get the global totals; however, that would mean a job to get the counts, a job to get the totals, and a job to get the relative frequencies. Ugh.

If the global statistic is relatively static, there are occasions where we prefer to cheat. Write the portion of the script that finds the global count and stores it, then comment that part out and inject the values statically—the sample code shows you how to do it using the `cat` Grunt shell statement:

```
-- cheat mode:
-- HR_stats = FOREACH (GROUP bat_careers ALL)
     GENERATE COUNT_STAR(bat_careers) AS n_total;
-- STORE HR_stats INTO 'HR_stats';
SET HR_stats_n_total=`cat HR_stats`;

HR_hist  = FOREACH (GROUP bat_careers BY HR) {
    ct = COUNT_STAR(bat_careers);
    GENERATE
        HR as val,
        ct AS ct,
        ct/( (double)HR_stats_n_total) AS freq,
        ct;
};
```

As we said, this is a cheat-to-win scenario: using it to knock three minutes off an eight-minute job is canny when used to make better use of a human data scientist's time, foolish when applied as a production performance optimization.

Calculating a Histogram Within a Group

As long as the groups in question do not rival the available memory, we can easily count how often each value occurs within a group using the DataFu `CountEach` UDF (*http://bit.ly/bag_operations*):

```
sig_seasons = FILTER bat_seasons BY ((year_id >= 1900) AND
                                     (lg_id == 'NL' OR lg_id == 'AL') AND
                                     (PA >= 450));

REGISTER /usr/lib/pig/datafu.jar
DEFINE CountVals datafu.pig.bags.CountEach('flatten');

binned = FOREACH sig_seasons GENERATE
    ( 5 * ROUND(year_id/ 5.0f)) AS year_bin,
    (20 * ROUND(H       /20.0f)) AS H_bin;

hist_by_year_bags = FOREACH (GROUP binned BY year_bin) {
    H_hist_cts = CountVals(binned.H_bin);
    GENERATE
        group AS year_bin,
        H_hist_cts AS H_hist_cts;
};
```

We want to normalize this to be a relative-fraction histogram, so that we can make comparisons across eras even as the number of active players grows. Finding the total count to divide by is a straightforward COUNT_STAR on the group, but a peccadillo of Pig's syntax makes using it a bit frustrating (annoyingly, a nested FOREACH can only "see" values from the bag it's operating on, so there's no natural way to reference the calculated total from the FOREACH statement):

```
-- Won't work:
hist_by_year_bags = FOREACH (GROUP binned BY year_bin) {
    H_hist_cts = CountVals(binned.H_bin);
    tot        = 1.0f*COUNT_STAR(binned);
    H_hist_rel = FOREACH H_hist_cts GENERATE
        H_bin,
        (float)count/tot;
    GENERATE
        group AS year_bin,
        H_hist_cts AS H_hist_cts,
        tot AS tot;
};
```

The best current workaround is to generate the whole-group total in the form of a bag having just that one value. Then we use the CROSS operator to graft it onto each (bin,count) tuple, giving us a bag with (bin,count,total) tuples—yes, every tuple in the bag will have the same groupwide value. Finally, iterate across the tuples to find the relative frequency.

It's more verbose than we'd like, but the performance hit is limited to the CPU and garbage collection (GC) overhead of creating three bags ({(result,count)}, {(result,count,total)}, {(result,count,freq)}) in quick order:

```
hist_by_year_bags = FOREACH (GROUP binned BY year_bin) {
    H_hist_cts = CountVals(binned.H_bin);
    tot        = COUNT_STAR(binned);
    GENERATE
        group      AS year_bin,
        H_hist_cts AS H_hist,
        {(tot)}    AS info:bag{(tot:long)}; -- 1-tuple bag we can feed to CROSS
};

hist_by_year = FOREACH hist_by_year_bags {
    -- Combines H_hist bag {(100,93),(120,198)...} and dummy tot bag {(882.0)}
    -- to make new (bin,count,total) bag: {(100,93,882.0),(120,198,882.0)...}
    H_hist_with_tot = CROSS H_hist, info;
    -- Then turn the (bin,count,total) bag into the (bin,count,freq) bag we want
    H_hist_rel = FOREACH H_hist_with_tot GENERATE
        H_bin,
        count AS ct,
        count/((float)tot) AS freq;

    GENERATE
        year_bin,
        H_hist_rel;
};
```

Pattern in use

Where You'll Use It

Summarizing cohorts; comparatively plotting histograms as a small multiples plot or animation.

Standard Snippet

DEFINE CountVals datafu.pig.bags.CountEach('flatten'); FOREACH (GROUP recs BY bin) GENERATE group, CountVals(recs.bin); (must download and enable the DataFu package; see "Apache DataFu" on page 57).

Important to Know

This is done largely in-memory at the reducer, so watch your data sizes.

Output Count

As many records as the cardinality of its key (i.e., the number of distinct values).

Records

Output is group, bag of (count, bin) tuples; you've turned bags of records-with-values into bags of values-with-counts.

Dataflow

Map and reduce; `CountEach` is not an algebraic, but is an accumulator.

Dumping Readable Results

We are of course terribly anxious to find out the results, so much so that having to switch over to R to graph our totals is more delay than we can bear. It's also often nice to have production jobs dump a visual summary of the results that an operator can easily scan and sanity-check. And so let's apply the pattern discussed in "Formatting a String According to a Template" on page 82 to dump a readable summary of our results to the screen:

```
year_hists_H = FOREACH year_hists {
        -- put all bins in regular order
    H_hist_rel_o = ORDER H_hist_rel BY bin ASC;

        -- The PA threshold makes the lower bins ragged, exclude them
    H_hist_rel_x = FILTER H_hist_rel_o BY (bin >= 90);

        -- Format each bin/freq into a readable string
    H_hist_vis   = FOREACH H_hist_rel_x GENERATE
        SPRINTF('%1$3d: %3$4.0f', bin, ct, (double)ROUND(100*freq));

        -- Combine those strings into readable table
    GENERATE
        year_bin,
        BagToString(H_hist_vis, ' ');
};
```

In this snippet, we first put all bins in regular order and exclude the lower bins (the minimum-plate appearances threshold makes them ragged). Next, we transform each bin-count-frequency triple into a readable string using SPRINTF. Because we used positional specifiers (the 1$ part of %1$3d), it's easy to insert or remove fields in the display depending on what question you're asking. Here, we've omitted the count, as it wasn't helpful for the main question we have: "What are the long-term trends in offensive production?" Finally, we use BagToString to format the row. We first met that combination of formatting-elements-formatting-bag in "Representing a Complex Data Structure with a Delimited String" on page 105. (We hope you're starting to feel like Daniel-san in *Karate Kid* when all his work polishing cars comes together as deadly martial arts moves.) Here are the results:

```
1900    100:    21  125:    38  150:    27  175:    9  200:    2  225:    1
1905    100:    30  125:    37  150:    20  175:    4  200:    2
1910    100:    22  125:    40  150:    25  175:    9  200:    1  225:    1
1915    100:    25  125:    38  150:    20  175:    6  200:    1  225:    0
1920    100:    12  125:    26  150:    29  175:    21  200:    9  225:    1  250: 0
1925    100:    13  125:    29  150:    26  175:    19  200:    9  225:    2  250: 0
1930    100:    12  125:    30  150:    26  175:    20  200:    9  225:    1  250: 0
1935    100:    13  125:    29  150:    29  175:    19  200:    8  225:    1
```

Year	100:	125:	150:	175:	200:	225:	250:
1940	20	35	29	11	2		
1945	26	36	22	11	2	1	
1950	21	29	32	12	3		
1955	27	31	22	14	2		
1960	24	29	29	12	3	0	
1965	26	34	24	8	2	0	
1970	26	35	23	9	2	0	
1975	23	33	26	11	3	0	
1980	22	34	25	11	3	0	
1985	27	31	26	9	3	0	
1990	29	33	24	10	1		
1995	20	31	29	14	3	0	
2000	22	30	29	13	3	0	0
2005	19	32	28	15	3	0	
2010	22	36	26	11	2		

Year	0:	10:	20:	30:	40:	50:	60:	70:
1900	97	3						
1905	99	1						
1910	93	6	0					
1915	96	3	1					
1920	77	18	3	1	1	0		
1925	71	20	4	3	1	0	0	
1930	62	25	6	5	2	0		
1935	57	27	10	4	1	0		
1940	64	24	8	3	0			
1945	58	27	10	4	1	1		
1950	39	33	18	7	3			
1955	34	32	23	8	4	1		
1960	33	34	22	8	3	0	0	
1965	38	34	19	8	2	0		
1970	39	34	20	5	2			
1975	42	33	19	6	1	0		
1980	41	34	18	6	1			
1985	33	34	25	8	1			
1990	36	35	20	7	2	0		
1995	24	32	25	13	6	1	0	0
2000	19	35	26	14	5	1	0	0
2005	22	34	28	12	3	1		
2010	24	37	27	11	2	0		

We'll need to draw graphs to get any nuanced insight, but the long-term trends in production of hits and home runs is strong enough that this chart tells a clear story. Baseball has seen two offensive booms: one in the 1920–1939 period, and one in the 1990–2009 period. However, the first was an on-base boom, with a larger proportion of players crossing the 200-hit mark than ever have since. The recent one was decidedly a power-hitting boom. There is an increase in the fraction of players reaching high seasonal hit totals, but the table above shows how large the increase in the proportion of players hitting 30, 40, and 50 home runs per year is.

Pattern in use

Where You'll Use It

In production jobs, to give the operator a readable summary that the job not only ran to completion but gave meaningful results; in development, to *know thy data*.

Standard Snippet

A mashup of the format with a template, represent complex data structures, and group-and-aggregate patterns.

Important to Know

This is more valuable, and more frequently used by experts, than you might think (you'll see).

Records

Up to you: enough for your brain, not too much for your eyes.

Exercises for you

Create a macro to generate such a table (it should accept parameters for sprintf template, filter limits, and sort key).

The Summing Trick

There's a pattern-of-patterns we like to call the "summing trick", a frequently useful way to act on subsets of a group without having to perform multiple GROUP BY or FILTER operations. Call it to mind every time you find yourself thinking "gosh, this sure seems like a lot of reduce steps on the same key." Before we describe its generic nature, it will help to see an example.

Counting Conditional Subsets of a Group—The Summing Trick

Whenever you are exploring a dataset, you should determine figures of merit for each of the key statistics—easy-to-remember values that separate qualitatively distinct behaviors. You probably have a feel for the way that 30° C / 85° F reasonably separates a "warm" day from a "hot" one; and if I tell you that a sub-three-hour marathon time distinguishes "really impress your friends" from "really impress other runners," you are equipped to recognize how ludicrously fast a 2:15 (the pace of a world-class runner) marathon is.

For our purposes, we can adopt 180 hits (H), 30 home runs (HR), 100 runs batted in (RBI), a 0.400 on-base percentage (OBP), and a 0.500 slugging percentage (SLG) each as the dividing line between a good and a great performance.

One reasonable way to define a great career is to ask how many great seasons a player had. We can answer that by counting how often a player's season totals exceeded each figure of merit. The obvious tactic would seem to involve filtering and counting each bag of seasonal stats for a player's career; that is cumbersome to write, brings most of the data down to the reducer, and exerts GC pressure materializing multiple bags:

```
mod_seasons = FILTER bat_seasons BY (
    (year_id >= 1900) AND (lg_id == 'NL' OR lg_id == 'AL'));

standards = FOREACH mod_seasons {
    OBP     = 1.0*(H + BB + HBP) / PA;
    SLG     = 1.0*(h1B + 2*h2B + 3*h3B + 4*HR) / AB;

    GENERATE
        player_id,
        (H   >=    180 ? 1 : 0) AS hi_H,
        (HR  >=     30 ? 1 : 0) AS hi_HR,
        (RBI >=    100 ? 1 : 0) AS hi_RBI,
        (OBP >= 0.400 ? 1 : 0) AS hi_OBP,
        (SLG >= 0.500 ? 1 : 0) AS hi_SLG
    ;
};
```

Next, count the seasons that pass the threshold by summing the indicator value:

```
career_standards = FOREACH (GROUP standards BY player_id) GENERATE
    group AS player_id,
    COUNT_STAR(standards) AS n_seasons,
    SUM(standards.hi_H)    AS hi_H,
    SUM(standards.hi_HR)   AS hi_HR,
    SUM(standards.hi_RBI) AS hi_RBI,
    SUM(standards.hi_OBP) AS hi_OBP,
    SUM(standards.hi_SLG) AS hi_SLG
;
```

The summing trick involves projecting a new field whose value is based on whether it's in the desired set, forming the desired groups, and aggregating on those new fields. Irrelevant records are assigned a value that will be ignored by the aggregate function (typically zero or null), and so although we operate on the group as a whole, only the relevant records contribute.

In this case, instead of sending all the stats (hits, home runs, etc.) directly to the reducer to be bagged and filtered, we send a 1 for seasons above the threshold and 0 otherwise. After the group, we find the *count* of values meeting our condition by simply *summing* the values in the indicator field. This approach allows Pig to use combiners (and thus less data to the reducer), and more importantly, it doesn't cause a bag of values to be collected, only a running sum (and thus involves way less GC pressure).

Another example will help you see what we mean—next, we'll use one GROUP operation to summarize multiple subsets of a table at the same time.

First, though, a side note on these figures of merit. As it stands, this isn't a terribly sophisticated analysis: the numbers were chosen to be easy to remember, and not based on the data. A 0.400 OBP is a number you can hold in your hand and your head; you can go click around ESPN (*http://bit.ly/2015_mlb_obp*) and see that it selects about the top 10–15 players in most seasons; you can use paper and pencil to feed it to a run expectancy table and see what it says a 0.400-on-base hitter would produce. We've shown you how useful it is to identify exemplar records; learn to identify these touchstone values as well.

Summarizing Multiple Subsets of a Group Simultaneously

We can use the summing trick to apply even more sophisticated aggregations to conditional subsets. How did each player's career evolve? A brief brilliant flame? A rise to greatness? Sustained quality? Let's classify a player's seasons by whether he is young" (age 21 and below), "prime" (22–29 inclusive) or "older" (30 and older). We can then tell the story of his career by finding his OPS (our overall performance metric) both overall and for the subsets of seasons in each age range.[10]

The complication here over the previous exercise is that we are forming compound aggregates on the group. To apply the formula career SLG = (career TB) / (career AB), we need to separately determine the career values for TB and AB and then form the combined SLG statistic.

Project the numerator and denominator of each offensive stat into the field for that age bucket. Only one of the subset fields will be filled in; as an example, an age-25 season will have values for PA_all and PA_prime and zeros for PA_young and PA_older:

```
age_seasons = FOREACH mod_seasons {
    young = (age <= 21                ? true : false);
    prime = (age >= 22 AND age <= 29 ? true : false);
    older = (age >= 30               ? true : false);
    OB = H + BB + HBP;
    TB = h1B + 2*h2B + 3*h3B + 4*HR;
    GENERATE
        player_id, year_id,
        PA AS PA_all, AB AS AB_all, OB AS OB_all, TB AS TB_all,
        (young ? 1 : 0) AS is_young,
        (young ? PA : 0) AS PA_young, (young ? AB : 0) AS AB_young,
        (young ? OB : 0) AS OB_young, (young ? TB : 0) AS TB_young,
        (prime ? 1 : 0) AS is_prime,
        (prime ? PA : 0) AS PA_prime, (prime ? AB : 0) AS AB_prime,
        (prime ? OB : 0) AS OB_prime, (prime ? TB : 0) AS TB_prime,
        (older ? 1 : 0) AS is_older,
        (older ? PA : 0) AS PA_older, (older ? AB : 0) AS AB_older,
        (older ? OB : 0) AS OB_older, (older ? TB : 0) AS TB_older
```

---

10 These breakpoints are based on where FanGraphs research (*http://bit.ly/star_hitters_age*) showed a performance drop-off by 10% from peak.

```
    ;
};
```

After the group, we can sum across all the records to find the plate appearances in prime seasons even though only some of the records belong to the prime-seasons subset. The irrelevant seasons show a zero value in the projected field and so don't contribute to the total:

```
career_epochs = FOREACH (GROUP age_seasons BY player_id) {
    PA_all    = SUM(age_seasons.PA_all  );
    PA_young  = SUM(age_seasons.PA_young);
    PA_prime  = SUM(age_seasons.PA_prime);
    PA_older  = SUM(age_seasons.PA_older);
    -- OBP = (H + BB + HBP) / PA
    OBP_all   = 1.0f*SUM(age_seasons.OB_all)   / PA_all  ;
    OBP_young = 1.0f*SUM(age_seasons.OB_young) / PA_young;
    OBP_prime = 1.0f*SUM(age_seasons.OB_prime) / PA_prime;
    OBP_older = 1.0f*SUM(age_seasons.OB_older) / PA_older;
    -- SLG = TB / AB
    SLG_all   = 1.0f*SUM(age_seasons.TB_all)   / SUM(age_seasons.AB_all);
    SLG_prime = 1.0f*SUM(age_seasons.TB_prime) / SUM(age_seasons.AB_prime);
    SLG_older = 1.0f*SUM(age_seasons.TB_older) / SUM(age_seasons.AB_older);
    SLG_young = 1.0f*SUM(age_seasons.TB_young) / SUM(age_seasons.AB_young);
    --
    GENERATE
        group AS player_id,
        MIN(age_seasons.year_id) AS beg_year,
        MAX(age_seasons.year_id) AS end_year,
        --
        OBP_all   + SLG_all        AS OPS_all:float,
        (PA_young >= 700 ? OBP_young + SLG_young : null) AS OPS_young:float,
        (PA_prime >= 700 ? OBP_prime + SLG_prime : null) AS OPS_prime:float,
        (PA_older >= 700 ? OBP_older + SLG_older : null) AS OPS_older:float,
        --
        COUNT_STAR(age_seasons)   AS n_seasons,
        SUM(age_seasons.is_young) AS n_young,
        SUM(age_seasons.is_prime) AS n_prime,
        SUM(age_seasons.is_older) AS n_older
    ;
};
```

If you do a sort on the different OPS fields, you'll spot Ted Williams (player ID wil lite01) as one of the top three young players, top three prime players, and top three old players. He's pretty awesome.

Pattern in use

Where You'll Use It

Summarizing the whole and a small number of discrete subsets: all/true/false, country/region/region/region/.., all visitors/cohort A/cohort B.

Project dummy fields for each subset you'll track, having an ignorable value for records not in that subset—aggregating over the whole then aggregates only over that subset.

Hello, SQL Users
This is a common trick in SQL cookbooks. Thanks y'all!

Important to Know
You have to manufacture one field per subset. At some point, you should use finer-grained grouping instead.

Output Count
As many records as the cardinality of its key (i.e., the number of distinct values); data size should decrease greatly.

Dataflow
Similar to any group-and-aggregate. Combiners become highly effective, as most of the values will be ignorable.

Testing for Absence of a Value Within a Group

We don't need a trick to answer "Which players have ever played for the Red Sox?"— just select seasons with BOS as the team ID and eliminate duplicate player IDs:

```
-- Players who were on the Red Sox at some time
onetime_sox_ids = FOREACH (FILTER bat_seasons BY (team_id == 'BOS'))
    GENERATE player_id;
onetime_sox     = DISTINCT onetime_sox_ids;
```

The summing trick is useful for the complementary question "Which players have *never* played for the Red Sox?" You might think to repeat the preceding code but filter for team_id != 'BOS' instead, but what that gives you is "Which players have ever played for a non–Red Sox team?" The right approach is to generate a field with the value 1 for a Red Sox season and the irrelevant value 0 otherwise. The never-Sox are those with zeros for every year:

```
player_soxness = FOREACH bat_seasons GENERATE
    player_id,
    (team_id == 'BOS' ? 1 : 0) AS is_soxy;

player_soxness_g = FILTER
    (GROUP player_soxness BY player_id)
    BY MAX(player_soxness.is_soxy) == 0;

never_sox = FOREACH player_soxness_g GENERATE
    group AS player_id;
```

Pattern in use

Where You'll Use It

Security (e.g., badges that have "entered reactor core" but no "signed in at front desk" events); users that clicked on three or more pages but never bought an item; devices that missed QA screening.

Standard Snippet

Create indicator field: `mt_f = FOREACH recs GENERATE ..., (test_of_foo ness ? 1 : 0) is_foo;`. Find the non-foos: `non_foos = FILTER (GROUP mt_f BY mykey) BY MAX(is_foo) == 0;`. Then project just the keys: `non_foos = FOREACH non_foos GENERATE group AS mykey.`

Hello, SQL Users

Another classic pattern from the lore.

Important to Know

If you're thinking, "Gosh, once I've got that indicator field, I could not only test its non-zeroness but sum it and average it and ...", then you're thinking along the right lines.

Output Count

As many records as the cardinality of its key (i.e., the number of distinct values); data size should decrease dramatically.

Records

List of keys.

Dataflow

Map, combiner, and reducer; combiners should be extremely effective.

Wrapping Up

In this chapter, we introduced grouping operations. We started with the basic Pig `GROUP BY` syntax, and worked through several baseball problems to explain how to group in practice. In addition to learning how to calculate statistics about grouped data, we learned how to print and format these statistical summaries. We summarized records, groups, fields, and entire relations using aggregate functions such as `MIN`, `MAX`, `COUNT_STAR`, and `SUM`. We used these aggregate functions to summarize the careers of every baseball player in the modern era!

The operations in this chapter on grouping data are foundational, and help to put data in context. Putting data in context is the *trick* to MapReduce. If we touched on some operations we didn't cover in detail, worry not! We'll get to operations like `DISTINCT` in Chapter 9.

Now that we can group data, we can COGROUP, or group between data relations. In Chapter 7, we'll look at a powerful extension of grouping techniques: JOINs. Inspired by SQL joins, Pig has extremely powerful joining capabilities that can pull additional data into the context of your analysis. We'll take this opportunity to once again dive into MapReduce and learn how joins work!

References

- Robert O. Deaner, Aaron Lowen, and Stephen Cobley, "Born at the Wrong Time: Selection Bias in the NHL Draft" (*http://bit.ly/selection_bias_nhl*), PLoS ONE 8:2 (2009).
- Steve Lombardi, "The Impact of Baseball Age-Cutoff Date Rules" (*http://bit.ly/baseball_age-cutoff*), WasWatching.com, May 23, 2013.
- Greg Spira, "The Boys of Late Summer" (*http://bit.ly/late_summer_boys*), Slate, April 16, 2008.

## CHAPTER 7

Joining Tables

In this chapter, we'll cover JOIN operations in Pig. A join is used to *join* multiple datasets or relations into a single relation based on the presence of a common key or keys. Pig supports several types of JOIN operations, including INNER, OUTER, and FULL joins. We'll learn how to perform different kinds of joins in Pig, and we'll also walk through how a join works at a low level, in Python/MrJob. By the end of the chapter, you'll understand how to join like a pro.

To understand this chapter, it helps if you're familiar with joining data from a SQL or related background. If you're new to joins, a more thorough introduction will help. Check out Jeff Atwood's post "A Visual Explanation of SQL Joins" (*http://bit.ly/ sql_joins_explanation*).

In database terminology, a *join* combines the rows of two or more tables based on some matching information, known as a *key*. For example, you could join a table of names and a table of mailing addresses, so long as both tables had a common field for the user ID. You could also join a table of prices to a table of items, given an item ID column in both tables. Joins are useful because they permit people to *normalize* data (that is to say, eliminate redundant content between multiple tables) yet still bring several tables' content to a single view on the fly.

Joins are pedestrian fare in relational databases. Far less so for Hadoop, as MapReduce wasn't really created with joins in mind, and you have to go through acrobatics to make it work.[1] Pig's JOIN operator provides the syntactical ease of a SQL query. While Pig will shield you from handcoding joins in MapReduce, it's still all MapReduce behind the scenes, so your joins are still subject to certain performance

---

1 Hence why you may see Hadoop joins on data scientist tech interviews.

considerations. This section will dig into the basics of Pig joins and then explain how to avoid certain mishaps.

Matching Records Between Tables (Inner Join)

Inner joins are used to find the set of records having matching join keys in *both* tables. If a record's join key in table A doesn't have a match in any record's join key in table B, it will be filtered from the output. If there is a match, the records with matched keys will be crossed to produce as many records as the number of records in table A times the number of records in table B, for that join key.

In other words, an *inner join* drops records that don't have matching keys in both tables. This means that the result of an inner join may have fewer rows than either of the original tables, or it may have more records than either of the original tables—up to an upper limit of A * B.

Joining Records in a Table with Directly Matching Records from Another Table (Direct Inner Join)

There is a stereotypical picture in baseball of a "slugger": a big fat man who comes to the plate challenging your notion of what an athlete looks like, and challenging the pitcher to prevent him from knocking the ball for multiple bases (or at least far enough away to lumber up to first base). To examine the correspondence from body type to ability to hit for power (i.e., high SLG), we will need to join the people table (listing height and weight) with each player's hitting stats:

```
fatness = FOREACH people GENERATE
    player_id, name_first, name_last,
    height_in, weight_lb;

slugging_stats = FOREACH (FILTER bat_careers BY (PA > 1000))
    GENERATE
        player_id,
        SLG;
```

The syntax of the JOIN statement itself shouldn't be much of a surprise:

```
slugging_fatness_join = JOIN
    fatness        BY player_id,
    slugging_stats BY player_id;

just_20 = LIMIT slugging_fatness_join 20; DUMP @;

DESCRIBE just_20

/*
{
    fatness::player_id: chararray,
```

```
            fatness::name_first: chararray,
            fatness::name_last: chararray,
            fatness::height_in: int,
            fatness::weight_lb: int,
            slugging_stats::player_id: chararray,
            slugging_stats::SLG: double
    }
    */
```

Disambiguating field names with ::

As a consequence of flattening records from the `fatness` table next to records from the `slugging_stats` table, the two tables each contribute a field named `player_id`. Although *we* privately know that both fields have the same value, Pig is right to insist on an unambiguous reference. The schema helpfully prefixes the field names with a slug, separated by `::`, to make it unambiguous.

You'll need to run a `FOREACH` across the joined data, specifying the qualified names of the fields you want to keep. One thing to keep in mind is that it is easy to get confused as to whether you should reference a field via `x::y` or `x.y`.

 Try to remember: `x::y` is used to disambiguate joined records, and `x.y` is used to reference values in bags when you are calling aggregate functions.

Body type versus slugging average

So having done the join, we finish by preparing the output:

```
bmis = FOREACH (JOIN fatness BY player_id, slugging_stats BY player_id) {

    BMI = 703.0*weight_lb/(double)(height_in*height_in);

    GENERATE
        fatness::player_id,
        name_first,
        name_last,
        SLG,
        height_in,
        weight_lb,
        BMI;
};
```

We added a field for BMI (body mass index), a simple measure of body type. We find it by dividing a person's weight by their height squared, and, since we're stuck with English units, multiplying by 703 to convert to metric.

Though BMI can't distinguish between 180 pounds of muscle and 180 pounds of flab, it reasonably controls for weight-due-to-tallness versus weight-due-to-bulkiness: beanpole Randy Johnson (6′10″2.1m, 225lb/102kg) and pocket rocket Tim Raines (5′8″1.7m, 160lb/73kg) both have a low BMI of 23; Babe Ruth (who in his later days was 6′2″1.88m 260lb/118kg) and Cecil Fielder (of whom Bill James wrote "…his reported weight of 261 leaves unanswered the question of what he might weigh if he put his other foot on the scale") both have high BMIs well above 30.[2]

How a Join Works

So that you can effectively reason about the behavior of a JOIN, it's important that you think about its operation in the following two ways: (a) as the equivalent of a COGROUP +FLATTEN, and (b) as the underlying MapReduce job it produces. Understanding how a JOIN works in MapReduce goes a long way to understanding MapReduce itself.

A Join Is a COGROUP+FLATTEN

A JOIN in Pig is just shorthand for the equivalent COGROUP operation. Applying the COGROUP operation with a FLATTEN in place of the JOIN gives us the equivalent command:

```
-- Original JOIN
slugging_fatness_join = JOIN fatness BY player_id,
                             slugging_stats BY player_id;

-- Equivalent COGROUP/FLATTEN
slugging_fatness_join = FOREACH
  (COGROUP fatness BY player_id, slugging_stats BY player_id)
  GENERATE
    FLATTEN(fatness),
    FLATTEN(slugging_stats);

DESCRIBE slugging_fatness_join;

slugging_fatness_join: {
  fatness::player_id: chararray,
  fatness::name_first: chararray,
  fatness::name_last: chararray,
  fatness::height_in: int,
  fatness::weight_lb: int,
  slugging_stats::player_id: chararray,
  slugging_stats::SLG: double
}
```

---

2 The dataset we're using unfortunately only records players' weights at the start of their career, so you will see different values listed for Mr. Fielder and Mr. Ruth.

In this sense, a JOIN is just a convenience—shorthand for a COGROUP+FLATTEN. We haven't introduced COGROUP before, but it is a fundamental operation in Pig. A COGROUP is direct shorthand for a *reduce* operation on more than one table. Used on one table, it is equivalent to GROUP BY. Used on two tables, it causes a joint reduce on the join keys between the tables.

A Join Is a MapReduce Job with a Secondary Sort on the Table Name

The way to perform a join in MapReduce is similarly a particular application of the COGROUP we stepped through before. In the next example, we'll walk through it on its own in Python/MrJob. We'll be joining an example customers table (created by Joe Stein):

```
Alice Bob|not bad|US
Sam Sneed|valued|CA
Jon Sneed|valued|CA
Arnold Wesise|not so good|UK
Henry Bob|not bad|US
Yo Yo Ma|not so good|CA
Jon York|valued|CA
Alex Ball|valued|UK
Jim Davis|not so bad|JA
```

to an example countries table:

```
United States|US
Canada|CA
United Kingdom|UK
Italy|IT
```

The mapper receives its set of input splits either from the customers table or from the countries table and makes the appropriate transformations: splitting the line into fields, and emitting a key/value pair. The key is the join key—in this case, the country code field of both sets of records. The mapper knows which file and type of record it is receiving based on the length of the fields (in Pig, the JOIN code would have the schema). The records it emits follow the COGROUP pattern: the join field as the key, which acts as the partitioning key. We use the SORT_VALUES option, which ensures the values are sorted as well. Then, we employ a trick to ensure that for each join key, country records are seen always before customer records. We achieve this by adding an arbitrary key to the front of the value: *A* for countries, *B* for customers. This makes countries sort before customers for each and every join/partition key. After that trick, the join is simply a matter of storing countries (*A* records) and crossing this array with each customer record:

```
# Adapted for MrJob from Joe Stein's example at:
# http://bit.ly/python_joins_keys

import sys, os, re
from mrjob.job import MRJob

class MRJoin(MRJob):

  # Performs secondary sort
  SORT_VALUES = True

  def mapper(self, _, line):
    splits = line.rstrip("\n").split("|")

    if len(splits) == 2: # country data
      symbol = 'A' # make country sort before person data
      country2digit = splits[1]
      yield country2digit, [symbol, splits]
    else: # person data
      symbol = 'B'
      country2digit = splits[2]
      yield country2digit, [symbol, splits]

  def reducer(self, key, values):
    countries = [] # should come first, as they are sorted on artificial key 'A'
    for value in values:
      if value[0] == 'A':
        countries.append(value)
      if value[0] == 'B':
        for country in countries:
          yield key, country[1:] + value[1:]

if __name__ == '__main__':
  MRJoin.run()
```

To run our join locally using MrJob:

```
cd examples/ch_07
python ./join.py countries.dat customers.dat
```

Our output is as expected for an inner join. The key is the join key, and the value is the pair of records joined:

```
"CA"  [["Canada", "CA"], ["Jon Sneed", "valued", "CA"]]
"CA"  [["Canada", "CA"], ["Jon York", "valued", "CA"]]
"CA"  [["Canada", "CA"], ["Sam Sneed", "valued", "CA"]]
"CA"  [["Canada", "CA"], ["Yo Yo Ma", "not so good", "CA"]]
"UK"  [["United Kingdom", "UK"], ["Alex Ball", "valued", "UK"]]
"UK"  [["United Kingdom", "UK"], ["Arnold Wesise", "not so good", "UK"]]
"US"  [["United States", "US"], ["Alice Bob", "not bad", "US"]]
"US"  [["United States", "US"], ["Henry Bob", "not bad", "US"]]
```

The output of this join has one record for each discrete combination of the keys in A (countries) and B (customers). As you will notice in our Python/MrJob version of the join, the secondary sort ensures that for each key the reducer receives all the records for table A strictly followed by all records for table B. We gather all the A records into an array, then on each B record emit the A records stapled to the B records. All the A records have to be held in memory at the same time, while all the B records simply flutter by; this means that if you have two datasets of wildly different sizes or distribution, it is worth ensuring the reducer receives the smaller group first. In MapReduce, the table with the largest number of records per key should be assigned the last-occurring field group label; in Pig, that table should be named last in the JOIN statement.

Note that there is no requirement that we store relation A in memory in an array. We could, if there were too many records for one key in both sides of a join, write it to disk and then stream it through for every record in relation B. Storing it in RAM is much more convenient whenever possible.

For more on MapReduce algorithms, *Data-Intensive Text Processing with MapReduce* (*http://bit.ly/mapreduce_algs*), by Jimmy Lin and Chris Dyer, is an excellent read and helped a great deal in crafting this example.

Pattern in use

Exercise
> Explore the correspondence of weight, height, and BMI to SLG using a medium-data tool such as R, Pandas, or Excel. Spoiler alert: the stereotype of the big fat slugger is quite true.

Handling nulls and Nonmatches in Joins and Groups

It's important to understand how null keys are handled in JOIN and GROUP operations. Briefly:

- In MapReduce, nulls are respected as keys.
- In a single-table Pig GROUP, nulls are also respected as keys.
- In a multitable COGROUP, nulls are respected as keys, *but not grouped together*.
- In a JOIN operation, rows with nulls *do not take place in the join* at all, but are *processed anyway*.
- If you have a lot of null keys, watch out: it is somewhere between costly and foolish.

When we say *null key*, we mean that if the group or join key is a scalar expression, that it has a null result; and if the key is a tuple, that all elements of the tuple are null. So these are null keys: Null, (Null,Null,Null), ("hi",Null,"howareyou") (even one non-null field). And these are not: "" (empty string), 0 (zero); {} (an empty bag) and {()} (a bag with a tuple holding null) are both not-null, but a bag cannot be used as a join or group key.

In the base Hadoop infrastructure, there's not much to understand: a key is a key, and Hadoop doesn't treat nulls specially in any way. Anything different is up to your program, and Pig does in fact supply something different.

A single-table GROUP statement does treat nulls as keys. It's pretty easy to come up with a table having many nulls values for the key you're grouping on; and if you do, all of them will be sent to the same reducer. If you actually need those keys, well, whaddayagonnado? Sounds like one of the reducers will have to endure a bad day at work. But if you don't need the groups having nulls keys, get rid of them as early as possible.

A COGROUP statement with multiple tables also treats nulls as keys (so get rid of them if unwanted). But take note! Multitable groups treat *each table's nulls as distinct*. That is, if table A had four records with null keys, and table B had two records with null keys, COGROUP A by key, B by key would produce:

- A row whose three fields are the null key; a bag holding the four associated records from A, and an empty bag; and
- A row whose three fields are the null key; an empty bag; and a bag holding the two associated records from B.

What do you do if you want null keys treated like any other tuple? Add an indicator field saying whether the value is null, and coalesce the actual key to non-null value. So instead of JOIN aa BY has_nulls, bb BY has_nulls, write this:

```
JOIN
  aa BY ( (has_nulls IS NULL ? 'x' : 'Y'),
    (has_nulls IS NULL ? -999 : has_nulls) ),
  bb BY ( (has_nulls IS NULL ? 'x' : 'Y'),
    (has_nulls IS NULL ? -999 : has_nulls) );
```

Even if there are records whose value is –999, they will have 'Y' for the indicator, while the null-keyed records will have 'x', and so they will not meet up. (For your sanity, if it's possible to choose a replacement value that can't occur in the dataset, do so.) The file j-important_notes_about_joins.pig in the sample code repo has a bunch more demonstrations of edge cases in groups and joins.

Pattern in use: inner join

Where You'll Use It

Any time you need to match records among tables—reattaching metadata about a record to the record; combining incidences of defective products with the manufacturing devices that made them; and so on.

Standard Snippet

```
JOIN aa BY key, bb BY key;.
```

Hello, SQL Users

The only join that Hadoop admits is the "equi-join"—equality of values. Much more on this follows in Chapter 7.

Important to Know

- List the tables in the statement from smallest to largest (largest table last)
- You can do a multiway join; see the documentation
- The key does not appear in the output
- :: is for disambiguation, . is for projecting tuples in a bag; JOIN doesn't create new bags, so :: is probably what you want

Output Count

For each key that matches, the number of pairings among keys. This can be anywhere from much smaller to explosively bigger.

Records

Schema of the result is the schema from each table stapled end-to-end. Values are unchanged from their input.

Dataflow

Pipelinable: it's composed onto the end of the preceding map or reduce, and if it stands alone becomes a map-only job.

See Also

- DataFu's bag left outer join
- Left outer join on three tables: *http://bit.ly/datafu_tips*
- Range query using cross
- Range query using prefix and UDFs (the ip-to-geo example)
- Self-join for successive row differences
- Sparse joins for filtering, with a HashMap (replicated)
- The Internet, for information on bitmap index or Bloom filter joins

Enumerating a Many-to-Many Relationship

In the previous examples, there has been a direct pairing of each line in the main table with the unique line from the other table that decorates it. Therefore, the output had exactly the same number of rows as the larger input table. When there are multiple records per key, however, the output will have one row for each *pairing* of records from each table. A key with two records from the left table and three records from the right table yields six output records.

Using the GROUP ALL trick we discussed in Chapter 6, we can count the total records before and after a many-to-many JOIN:

```
-- Count the number of bat_seasons records
total_bat_seasons = FOREACH (GROUP bat_seasons ALL) GENERATE
    'bat_seasons' AS label,
    COUNT_STAR(bat_seasons) AS total;

-- Count the number of park_team_years
total_park_team_years = FOREACH (GROUP park_team_years ALL) GENERATE
    'park_team_years' AS label,
    COUNT_STAR(park_team_years) AS total;

-- Always trim the fields we don't need
player_team_years = FOREACH bat_seasons GENERATE year_id, team_id, player_id;
park_team_years   = FOREACH park_team_years GENERATE year_id, team_id, park_id;

player_stadia = FOREACH (JOIN
    player_team_years BY (year_id, team_id),
    park_team_years   BY (year_id, team_id)
    ) GENERATE
        player_team_years::year_id AS year_id,
        player_team_years::team_id AS team_id,
        player_id,
        park_id;
total_player_stadia = FOREACH (GROUP player_stadia ALL) GENERATE
    'player_stadium' AS label,
    COUNT_STAR(player_stadia) AS total;

-- Finally, UNION our label/totals and dump them together
answer = UNION total_bat_seasons, total_park_team_years, total_player_stadia;
  DUMP @;
```

which results in:

```
(park_team_years,2911)
(bat_seasons,77939)
(player_stadio,80565)
```

You'll see that the 77,939 bat_seasons became 80,565 home stadium–player pairings. The cross-product behavior didn't cause a big explosion in counts—as opposed to our next example, which will generate much more data.

Joining a Table with Itself (Self-Join)

Joining a table with itself is very common when you are analyzing relationships of elements within the table (when you're analyzing graphs or working with datasets represented as attribute-value lists, it becomes predominant). Our example here will be to identify all teammate pairs: players listed as having played for the same team in the same year. The only annoying part about doing a self-join in Pig is that you can't, at least not directly. Pig won't let you list the same table in multiple slots of a JOIN statement, and also won't let you just write something like `"mytable_dup = myta ble;"` to assign a new alias.[3] Instead, you have to use a FOREACH to create a duplicate representative. If you don't have any other excuse, use a project-star expression: `p2 = FOREACH p1 GENERATE *;`. In this case, we already need to do a projection; we feel the most readable choice is to repeat the statement twice.

```
-- Pig disallows self-joins so this won't work:
wont_work = JOIN bat_seasons BY (team_id, year_id),
                bat_seasons BY (team_id, year_id);

"ERROR ... Pig does not accept same alias as input for JOIN operation :
                bat_seasons"
```

That's OK, we didn't want all those stupid fields anyway; we'll just make two copies and then join the table copies to find all teammate pairs. We're going to say a player isn't his own teammate, and so we also reject the self-pairs:

```
p1 = FOREACH bat_seasons GENERATE player_id, team_id, year_id;
p2 = FOREACH bat_seasons GENERATE player_id, team_id, year_id;

teammate_pairs = FOREACH (JOIN
    p1 BY (team_id, year_id),
    p2 by (team_id, year_id)
  ) GENERATE
    p1::player_id AS pl1,
    p2::player_id AS pl2;

teammate_pairs = FILTER teammate_pairs BY (pl1 != pl2);
```

Let's get to know our data a little better, before we proceed. How big is a baseball team, anyway?

```
-- Get the total players per team per year
players_per_team = FOREACH (
    GROUP bat_seasons BY (team_id, year_id))
    GENERATE
        FLATTEN(group) AS (team_id, year_id),
        COUNT_STAR(bat_seasons) AS total_players;
```

---

3 If it didn't cause such a surprisingly hairy set of internal complications, it would have long ago been fixed.

```
-- Then get the average of that total
avg_players = FOREACH (GROUP players_per_team ALL) GENERATE
    ROUND(AVG(players_per_team.total_players)) AS avg_players;

DUMP @;

(29)
```

As opposed to the slight many-to-many expansion of the previous section, there are on average about 29 players per roster to be paired:

```
-- Finally: how big is our join?
total_teammate_pairs = FOREACH (group teammate_pairs ALL) GENERATE
  COUNT_STAR(teammate_pairs) AS total;
DUMP @;

(2292658)
```

The result set here is explosively larger: 2,292,658 pairings from the original 77,939 player seasons, an expansion of almost 30x. You might have reasonably expected the expansion factor to be very close to the average number of players per team, thinking "29 average players per team, so 29 times as many pairings as players." But a join creates as many rows as the product of the records in each tables' bag—the square of the roster size in this case—and the sum of the squares necessarily exceeds the direct sum.

Our bat_seasons table ignores mid-season trades and only lists a single team the player played the most games for, so in infrequent cases, this will identify some teammate pairs that didn't actually overlap. There's no simple option that lets you join on players' intervals of service on a team: joins must be based on testing key equality, and we would need an "overlaps" test. There are tools for handling such cases, but it's a big jump in complexity for a small number of renegades. You'd be better off handling it by first listing every stint on a team for each player in a season, with separate fields for the year and for the start/end dates. Doing the self-join on the season (just as we have here) would then give you every *possible* teammate pair, with some fraction of false pairings. Lastly, use a FILTER to reject the cases where they don't overlap. Any time you're looking at a situation where 5% of records are causing 150% of complexity, look to see whether this approach of "handle the regular case, then fix up the edge cases" can apply.

It's worth noting that the equivalent SQL would be:

```
SELECT DISTINCT b1.player_id, b2.player_id
  FROM bat_season b1, bat_season b2
  WHERE b1.team_id = b2.team_id        -- same team
    AND b1.year_id = b2.year_id        -- same season
    AND b1.player_id != b2.player_id   -- reject self-teammates
```

```
    GROUP BY b1.player_id
;
```

Joining Records Without Discarding Nonmatches (Outer Join)

The Baseball Hall of Fame is meant to honor the very best in the game, and each year a very small number of players are added to its rolls. It's a significantly subjective indicator, which is its cardinal virtue and its cardinal flaw—it represents the consensus judgment of experts, but colored to some small extent by emotion, nostalgia, and imperfect quantitative measures. But as you'll see over and over again, the best basis for decisions is the judgment of human experts backed by data-driven analysis. What we're assembling as we go along this tour of analytic patterns isn't a mathematical answer to who the highest performers are, it's a basis for centering discussion on the right mixture of objective measures based on evidence and human judgment where the data is imperfect.

So we'd like to augment the `career_stats` table we assembled earlier with columns showing, for Hall of Famers, the year they were admitted, and a null value for the rest. (This allows that column to also serve as a Boolean indicator of whether the players were inducted.) If you tried to use the `JOIN` operator in the form we have been, you'll find that it doesn't work. A plain `JOIN` operation keeps only rows that have a match in all tables, and so all of the non–Hall of Famers will be excluded from the result. (This differs from COGROUP, which retains rows even when some of its inputs lack a match for a key.) The answer is to use an *outer join*:

```
career_stats = FOREACH (JOIN
    bat_careers BY player_id LEFT OUTER,
    hof_bat BY player_id) GENERATE
        bat_careers::player_id,
        bat_careers::n_seasons,
        hof_bat::year_inducted AS hof_year;

DUMP @;
```

Because the `batting_hof` table has exactly one row per player, the output has exactly as many rows as the `career_stats` table, and exactly as many non-null rows as the Hall of Fame table:[4]

```
...
(foxja01,1,)
```

---

[4] Note that the `hof_bat` table excludes players admitted to the Hall of Fame based on their pitching record. With the exception of Babe Ruth—who would likely have made the Hall of Fame as a pitcher if he hadn't been the most dominant hitter of all time—most pitchers have very poor offensive skills and so are relegated back with the rest of the crowd.

```
(foxja02,4,)
(foxjo01,4,)
(foxne01,19,1997)
...
```

Now we'll look at another example: let's JOIN ballpark/team locations and generic geographic data from GeoNames (*http://geonames.org*):

```
geonames = FILTER geonames BY feature_code == 'STDM';

parks_geonames = JOIN parks BY (park_name, state, country) LEFT OUTER,
                      geonames BY (name, admin1_code, country_code);

DUMP @;
```

which gets us some records with matched place names, and some without:

```
(STP01,Tropicana Field,1998-03-31,2013-09-23,1,1286,-82.65,27.77,
    St. Petersburg,FL,US,4175752,Tropicana Field,Tropicana Field,Tropikana-fild,
    teulopikana pildeu,Тропикана-филд,トロピカーナ・フィールド,트로피카나 필드,
    27.76781,-82.6526,S,STDM,US,,FL,103,,,0,8,27,America/New_York,2013-01-09)
(CHI02,23rd Street Park,1872-05-29,1877-10-06,0,129,-87.63,41.85,
    Chicago,IL,US,,,,,,,,,,,,,,,,,,,,,)
(KAN02,Association Park,1886-04-30,1888-09-29,0,114,-94.56,39.11,
    Kansas City,MO,US,,,,,,,,,,,,,,,,,,,,,)
(CLE04,Brotherhood Park,1890-04-30,1890-10-04,0,62,-81.65,41.48,
    Cleveland,OH,US,,,,,,,,,,,,,,,,,,,,,)
(STL09,Busch Stadium II,1966-05-12,2005-10-02,0,3174,-90.19,38.62,
    St. Louis,MO,US,,,,,,,,,,,,,,,,,,,,,)
(SFO02,Candlestick Park,1960-04-12,1999-09-30,0,3173,-122.39,37.71,
    San Francisco,CA,US,7521373,Candlestick Park,Candlestick Park,
    kaendeulseutig pakeu,kaindalastika parka,باراك كانديلستيك,ملعب,
    कैन्डलस्टिक पार्क,キャンドルスティック・パーク,캔들스틱 파크,37.7135,-122.38443,
    S,STDM,US,,CA,075,,,0,,4,America/Los_Angeles,2010-08-16)
```

In this example, there will be some parks that have no direct match to location names and, of course, there will be many, many places that do not match a park. The first two JOINs we did were "inner" JOINs—the output contains only rows that found a match. In this case, we want to keep all the parks, even if no places matched, but we do not want to keep any places that lack a park. Because all rows from the left (first dataset) will be retained, this is called a LEFT OUTER JOIN. If, instead, we were trying to annotate all places with such parks as could be matched—producing exactly one output row per place—we would use a RIGHT OUTER JOIN instead. If we wanted to do the latter but (somewhat inefficiently) flag parks that failed to find a match, you would use a "full outer" JOIN. (Full JOINs are pretty rare.)

In a Pig JOIN, it is important to order the tables by size — putting the smallest table first and the largest table last (refer back to Chapter 2 if you need a refresher on this topic). So while a RIGHT JOIN is not terribly common in traditional SQL, it's quite valuable in Pig. If you look back at the previous examples, you will see we took care to always put the smaller table first. For small tables or tables of similar size, it is not a big deal—but in some cases, it can have a huge impact, so get in the habit of always following this best practice.

 A Pig JOIN is outwardly similar to the JOIN portion of a SQL SELECT statement, but notice that although you can place simple expressions in the JOIN expression, you can make no further manipulations to the data whatsoever in that statement. Pig's design philosophy is that each statement corresponds to a specific data transformation, making it very easy to reason about how the script will run; this makes the typical Pig script more long-winded than corresponding SQL statements but clearer for both human and robot to understand.

Pattern in Use

Where You'll Use It

Any time only some records have matches but you want to preserve the whole; all products from the manufacturing line paired with each incident report about a product (keeping products with no incident report); all customers that took a test drive matched with the past cars they bought from you (but not discarding the new customer records).

Standard Snippet

```
FOREACH (JOIN aa BY key LEFT OUTER, bb BY key) GENERATE
a::key..a::last_field,b::second_field...;.
```

Hello, SQL Users

RIGHT JOINs are much more common in Pig, because you want the table size to determine the order they're listed in.

Important to Know

Records with null keys are dropped even in an OUTER JOIN.

Output Count

At least as many records as the OUTER table has, expanded by the number of ways to pair records from each table for a key; like any join, output size can be explosively higher.

DataFlow

Pipelinable: it's composed onto the end of the preceding map or reduce, and if it stands alone becomes a map-only job.

Joining Tables That Do Not Have a Foreign-Key Relationship

With the exception of the last one, all of the joins we've done so far have been on nice clean values designed in advance to match records among tables. In SQL parlance, the `career_stats` and `hof_bat` tables both had `player_id` as a primary key (a column of unique, non-null values tied to each record's identity). The `team_id` field in the `bat_seasons` and `park_team_years` tables points into the teams table as a foreign key: an indexable column whose only values are primary keys in another table, and that may have `null`s or duplicates. But sometimes you must match records among tables that do not have a polished mapping of values. In that case, it can be useful to use an `OUTER JOIN` as the first pass to unify what records you can before you bring out the brass knuckles or big guns for what remains.

Suppose we wanted to plot where each Major League player grew up—perhaps as an answer in itself as a browsable map, or to allocate territories for talent scouts, or to see whether the quiet wide spaces of country living or the fast competition of growing up in the city better fosters the future career of a high performer. While the people table lists the city, state, and country of birth for most players, we must geolocate those place names (i.e., determine their longitude and latitude) in order to plot or analyze them.

There are geolocation services on the Web, but they are imperfect, rate limited, and costly for commercial use.[5] Meanwhile, the freely available geonames database gives geocoordinates and other information on more than 7 million points of interest across the globe, so for informal work it can make a lot of sense to opportunistically decorate whatever records match and then decide what to do with the rest:

```
-- Filter to only populated places in the US,
-- see http://www.geonames.org/export/codes.html
geonames = FILTER geonames BY feature_code matches 'PPL.*'
  AND country_code == 'US';
geonames = FOREACH geonames GENERATE
  geonameid, latitude, longitude, name, admin1_code;

-- Trim extra fields from players, and limit to those born in the USA
players = FILTER players BY birth_country == 'USA';
players = FOREACH players GENERATE player_id, name_first, name_last, birth_city,
  birth_state, birth_country;

-- Now make our 'approximate' JOIN
geolocated_somewhat = JOIN LEFT OUTER
    players BY (birth_city, birth_state),
    geonames BY (name, admin1_code)
;
```

---

5 Put another way, "accurate, cheap, fast: choose any two."

```
DESCRIBE geolocated_somewhat;

/*
geolocated_somewhat: {
    players::player_id: chararray,
    players::name_first: chararray,
    players::name_last: chararray,
    players::birth_city: chararray,
    players::birth_state: chararray,
    players::birth_country: chararray,
    geonames::geonameid: chararray,
    geonames::latitude: float,
    geonames::longitude: float,
    geonames::name: chararray,
    geonames::admin1_code: chararray}
*/

geolocated_trimmed = FOREACH geolocated_somewhat GENERATE
  player_id, name_first, name_last, latitude, longitude;

DUMP @;
```

Let's take a look at a metric behind the JOIN:

```
total = FOREACH (GROUP geolocated_trimmed ALL) GENERATE
  'total' AS label, COUNT_STAR(geolocated_trimmed) AS total;

with_lat = FILTER geolocated_trimmed BY latitude IS NOT NULL;
with_lat_total = FOREACH (GROUP with_lat ALL) GENERATE
  'with_lat' AS label, COUNT_STAR(with_lat) AS total;

without_lat = FILTER geolocated_trimmed BY latitude IS NULL;
without_lat_total = FOREACH (GROUP without_lat ALL) GENERATE
  'without_lat' AS label, COUNT_STAR(without_lat) AS total;

report = UNION total, with_lat_total, without_lat_total;

DUMP @;
```

In the important sense, this JOIN worked quite well—76.7% of records found a match:

```
(without_lat,3893)
(with_lat,12868)
(total,16761)
```

Experienced database hands might now suggest doing a join using some sort of fuzzy-match or some sort of other fuzzy equality. However, in MapReduce, the only kind of join you can do is an "equi-join"—one that uses key equality to match records. Unless an operation is *transitive* (i.e., unless a `joinsto` b and b `joinsto` c guarantees a `joinsto` c), a plain join won't work, which rules out approximate string matches; joins on range criteria (where keys are related through inequalities $(x < y)$);

graph distance; geographic nearness; and edit distance. You also can't use a plain join on an OR condition: "match stadiums and places if the place name and state are equal or the city and state are equal," "match records if the postal code from table A matches any of the component zip codes of place B." Much of the latter part of this book centers on what to do when there *is* a clear way to group related records in context, but it is more complicated than key equality.

Pattern in use

Where You'll Use It
> Any time you're geolocating records, sure, but the lessons here hold any time you're combining messy data with canonical records.

Hello, SQL Users
> No fuzzy matches, no string distance, no inequalities; there's no built-in SOUNDEX UDF, but that would be legal as it produces a scalar value to test with equality.

Important to Know
> Watch out for an embarrassment of riches—there are many towns named "Springfield."

Joining on an Integer Table to Fill Holes in a List

In some cases, you want to ensure that there is an output row for each potential value of a key. For example, a histogram of career hits will show that Pete Rose (4,256 hits) and Ty Cobb (4,189 hits) have so many more hits than the third-most player (Hank Aaron, 3,771 hits) that there are gaps in the output bins.

To fill the gaps, generate a list of all the potential keys, then generate your (possibly hole-y) result table, and do a join of the keys list (LEFT OUTER) with results. In some cases, this requires one job to enumerate the keys and a separate job to calculate the results. For our purposes here, we can simply use the integer table. (We told you it was surprisingly useful!)

If we prepare a histogram of career hits, similar to the one above for seasons, you'll find that Pete Rose (4,256 hits) and Ty Cobb (4,189 hits) have so many more hits than the third-most player (Hank Aaron, 3771 hits) there are gaps in the output bins. To make it so that every bin has an entry, do an outer join on the integer table:

```
-- SQL Equivalent:
SET @H_binsize = 10;
SELECT bin, H, IFNULL(n_H,0)
  FROM      (SELECT @H_binsize * idx AS bin FROM numbers WHERE idx <= 430) nums
  LEFT JOIN (SELECT @H_binsize*CEIL(H/@H_binsize) AS H, COUNT(*) AS n_H
    FROM bat_career bat GROUP BY H) hist
  ON hist.H = nums.bin
```

```
    ORDER BY bin DESC
  ;
```

Regular old histogram of career hits, bin size 100:

```
player_hits = FOREACH (GROUP bat_seasons BY player_id) GENERATE
    100 * ROUND(SUM(bat_seasons.H)/100.0) AS bin;
histogram = FOREACH (GROUP player_hits BY bin) GENERATE
    group AS bin,
    COUNT_STAR(player_hits) AS total;
```

Generate a list of all the bins we want to keep, then perform a LEFT JOIN of bins with histogram counts. Missing rows will have a null ct value, which we can convert to zero:

```
-- Numbers, from 0 to 9999
numbers = LOAD '/data/gold/numbers10k.txt' AS (number:int);

-- Get a count of hits per player, across all player seasons
player_hits = FOREACH (GROUP bat_seasons BY player_id) GENERATE
    100 * ROUND(SUM(bat_seasons.H)/100.0) AS bin;

-- Get the maximum player hits bin to filter the numbers relation
max_hits = FOREACH (GROUP player_hits ALL) GENERATE
  MAX(player_hits.bin) AS max_bin;

-- Count the number of occurrences for each bin
histogram = FOREACH (GROUP player_hits BY bin) GENERATE
    group AS bin,
    COUNT_STAR(player_hits) AS total;

-- Calculate the complete set of histogram bins up to our limit
histogram_bins = FOREACH (FILTER numbers BY 100 * number <= max_hits.max_bin)
  GENERATE 100 * number AS bin;

-- Finally, join the histogram bins with the histogram data
-- to get our gap-less histogram
joined_histogram_bins = JOIN histogram_bins BY bin LEFT OUTER, histogram BY bin;
filled_histogram = FOREACH joined_histogram_bins GENERATE
    histogram_bins::bin,
    (total IS NULL ? 0 : total)
  ;

DUMP @;
```

You can see Pete Rose, Ty Cobb, and Hank Aaron:

```
...
(3800,1)
(3900,0)
(4000,0)
(4100,0)
(4200,1)
(4300,1)
```

Pattern in use

Where You'll Use It

Whenever you know the values you want (whether they're integers, model numbers, dates, etc.) and always want a corresponding row in the output table.

Selecting Only Records That Lack a Match in Another Table (Anti-Join)

In the case of an anti-join, we want to remove records from one table that do not have a match in the other table. We can achieve this with an OUTER JOIN followed by a FILTER on those records lacking the *required* fields from the join:

```
-- Always trim fields we don't need
all_stars_p  = FOREACH all_stars GENERATE player_id, year_id;

-- An outer join of the two will leave both matches and non-matches.
scrub_seasons_join = JOIN
    bat_seasons BY (player_id, year_id) LEFT OUTER,
    all_stars_p BY (player_id, year_id);

-- ...and the non-matches will have Nulls in all the all-stars slots
anti_join = FILTER scrub_seasons_join
    BY all_stars_p::player_id IS NULL;
```

Once the matches have been eliminated, pick off the first table's fields. The double-colon in `all_stars_p::` makes clear which table's field we mean.

Selecting Only Records That Possess a Match in Another Table (Semi-Join)

A semi-join is the counterpart to an anti-join: you want to find records that *do* have a match in another table, but not keep the fields from that table around.

Let's use the same example—player seasons where they made the All-Star team—but only look for seasons that *were* All-Stars. You might think you could do this with a join:

```
-- Don't do this... produces duplicates!
bats_g  = JOIN all_stars BY (player_id, year_id),
              bat_seasons BY (player_id, year_id);
badness = FOREACH bats_g GENERATE bat_seasons::player_id .. bat_seasons::HR;
```

The result is wrong, and even a diligent spot-check will probably fail to notice. You see, from 1959–1962 there were multiple `all_stars` games (!), and so players who appeared in both have two rows in the All-Star table. In turn, each singular row in the bat_season table became two rows in the result for players in those years. We've broken the contract of leaving the original table unchanged.

This is the biggest thing people coming from a SQL background need to change about their thinking. In SQL, the JOIN rules all. In Pig, GROUP and COGROUP rule the land, and nearly every other structural operation is some piece of syntactic sugar on top of those. So when the going gets rough with a JOIN, remember that it's just a convenience and ask yourself whether a COGROUP would work better. In this case, it does:

```
-- Players with no entry in the all_stars_p table have an empty all_stars_p bag
allstar_seasons_cg = COGROUP
    bat_seasons BY (player_id, year_id),
    all_stars_p  BY (player_id, year_id);
```

Now select all cogrouped rows where there was an All-Star record, and project just the records from the original table:

```
-- One row in the batting table => One row in the result
all_star_seasons = FOREACH
    (FILTER all_star_seasons_cg BY (COUNT_STAR(all_stars_p) > 0L))
    GENERATE FLATTEN(bat_seasons);
```

The JOIN version was equivent to flattening both bags (GENERATE FLATTEN(bat_sea
sons), FLATTEN(all_stars_p)) and then removing the fields we had just flattened. In the COGROUP version, neither the incorrect duplicate rows nor the unnecessary columns are created.

An Alternative to Anti-Join: Using a COGROUP

As a lesson on the virtues of JOINs and COGROUPs, let's examine an alternative version of the anti-join we introduced earlier:

```
-- Players with no entry in the all_stars_p table have an empty all_stars_p bag
bats_ast_cg = COGROUP
    bat_seasons BY (player_id, year_id),
    all_stars_p BY (player_id, year_id);
```

Select all cogrouped rows where there were no All-Star records, and project the batting table fields:

```
anti_join = FOREACH
    (FILTER bats_ast_cg BY (COUNT_STAR(all_stars_p) == 0L))
    GENERATE FLATTEN(bat_seasons);
```

There are three opportunities for optimization here. Though these tables are far too small to warrant optimization, it's a good teachable moment for when to (not) optimize:

- You'll notice that we projected off the extraneous fields from the `all_stars` table before the map. Pig is sometimes smart enough to eliminate fields we don't need early. There's two ways to see if it did so. The surest way is to consult the tree that `EXPLAIN` produces. If you make the program use `all_stars` and not `all_stars_p`, you'll see that the extra fields are present. The other way is to look at how much data comes to the reducer with and without the projection. If there is less data using `all_stars_p` than `all_stars`, the explicit projection is required.

- The `EXPLAIN` output also shows that the `COGROUP` version has a simpler MapReduce plan, raising the question of whether it's more performant.

- Usually we put the smaller table (`all_stars`) on the right in a `JOIN` or `COGROUP`. However, although the `all_stars` table is smaller, it has larger cardinality (barely): (`player_id, team_id`) is a primary key for the `bat_seasons` table. So the order is likely to be irrelevant.

But "more performant" or "possibly more performant" doesn't mean "use it instead."

Eliminating extra fields is almost always worth it, but the explicit projection means extra lines of code and it means an extra alias for the reader to understand. On the other hand, the explicit projection reassures the experienced reader that the projection is for-sure-no-doubt-about-it taking place. That's actually why we chose to be explicit here: we find that the more complicated script gives the reader less to think about.

In contrast, any SQL user will immediately recognize the join formulation of this as an anti-join. Introducing a `RIGHT OUTER JOIN` or choosing the `COGROUP` version disrupts that familiarity. Choose the version you find most readable, and then find out if you care whether it's more performant; the simpler `EXPLAIN` graph or the smaller `LEFT JOIN` table *does not* necessarily imply a faster dataflow. For this particular shape of data, even at much larger scale we'd be surprised to learn that either of the latter two optimizations mattered.

Wrapping Up

In this chapter, we've learned how to `JOIN` and `COGROUP`. These operations allow us to bring additional data sources into our analysis. The `INNER JOIN` lets us combine records from multiple datasets with common join keys. The `OUTER JOIN` or semi-join decorates one relation with matches from another relation. An anti-join filters records with a match in another table, leaving only those that don't match. The self-join showed us how to explore groupings within a given relation. Taken together, these techniques constitute a powerful toolset for working with one or more sources of data.

Joins are a fundamental data operation, and by adding them to our toolkit we've broadened our capabilities dramatically. Now we can look at hitting records in combination with player records, or ballpark records in combination with city data. We've seen how to join relational data that is meant to be joined, and also how to join disparate data sources to bring in related data from the Web. We've even learned how to join data to itself, to analyze pairs within groups.

In the next chapter, we'll learn about sorting, or ordering data. We'll be able to manipulate records individually with map-only patterns, group and join data using MapReduce, and sort data within and without groups. Our data vocabulary is nearly complete!

CHAPTER 8

Ordering Operations

In this chapter, we will cover ordering operations, or operations that sort data according to some criteria. Pig has two concepts of order: entire datasets can be sorted, as can the contents of a bag. We'll learn how to sort relations and bags, and also how to calculate the top records of a relation by combining ORDER with LIMIT. With these skills in hand, we'll be one step closer to being able to solve any arbitrary data-processing task using the set of patterns we've learned.

Ordering operations are a fundamental part of storytelling. A big part of telling stories with data is coming up with examples that prove a point. This means diving into the data to produce the most exceptional records. When data is big, this invariably means you need to sort the data to pick up the highest or lowest value(s) of some metric.

So far we've mostly limited ourselves to the ordering inherently provided by the shuffle/sort phase of MapReduce, which does provide a sorted list on the reduce key for each file. If we're running a small job with a single reducer, that does provide a total sort. However, if we want an overall sort using multiple reducers (as we must, if we're working with big data), we must employ Pig's ORDER command. Let's begin!

Preparing Career Epochs

In order to demonstrate ordering records, we're going to prepare a dataset detailing the performance of players at three phases of their career: young, prime, and older. To do so, we'll be making use of familiar patterns. We use the map-only patterns we covered in "Selecting Records That Satisfy a Condition: FILTER and Friends" on page 67 and "Selecting Records That Satisfy Multiple Conditions" on page 68 with an initial FILTER, to include only seasons in the National or American leagues in our analysis. The map-only patterns we covered in "Transforming Records Individually Using

FOREACH" on page 79 and "A Nested FOREACH Allows Intermediate Expressions" on page 80 assist in calculating the properties of player seasons. Finally, we employ the pattern covered in "Summarizing Multiple Subsets of a Group Simultaneously" on page 139 to compute career metrics across different age categories:

```
mod_seasons = FILTER bat_seasons BY ((year_id >= 1900) AND
  (lg_id == 'NL' OR lg_id == 'AL'));

-- Create a season marked with the period of career it was in: young/prime/older
age_seasons = FOREACH mod_seasons {
    young = (age <= 21              ? true : false);
    prime = (age >= 22 AND age <= 29 ? true : false);
    older = (age >= 30              ? true : false);
    OB = H + BB + HBP;
    TB = h1B + 2*h2B + 3*h3B + 4*HR;
    GENERATE
        player_id,
        year_id,
        PA AS PA_all,
                AB AS AB_all,
                OB AS OB_all,
                TB AS TB_all,
        (young ? 1 : 0) AS is_young,
        (young ? PA : 0) AS PA_young, (young ? AB : 0) AS AB_young,
        (young ? OB : 0) AS OB_young, (young ? TB : 0) AS TB_young,
        (prime ? 1 : 0) AS is_prime,
        (prime ? PA : 0) AS PA_prime, (prime ? AB : 0) AS AB_prime,
        (prime ? OB : 0) AS OB_prime, (prime ? TB : 0) AS TB_prime,
        (older ? 1 : 0) AS is_older,
        (older ? PA : 0) AS PA_older, (older ? AB : 0) AS AB_older,
        (older ? OB : 0) AS OB_older, (older ? TB : 0) AS TB_older
    ;
};

-- Calculate metrics by career epoch: young/prime/older
career_epochs = FOREACH (GROUP age_seasons BY player_id) {
    PA_all    = SUM(age_seasons.PA_all  );
    PA_young  = SUM(age_seasons.PA_young);
    PA_prime  = SUM(age_seasons.PA_prime);
    PA_older  = SUM(age_seasons.PA_older);
    -- OBP = (H + BB + HBP) / PA
    OBP_all   = 1.0f*SUM(age_seasons.OB_all)   / PA_all  ;
    OBP_young = 1.0f*SUM(age_seasons.OB_young) / PA_young;
    OBP_prime = 1.0f*SUM(age_seasons.OB_prime) / PA_prime;
    OBP_older = 1.0f*SUM(age_seasons.OB_older) / PA_older;
    -- SLG = TB / AB
    SLG_all   = 1.0f*SUM(age_seasons.TB_all)   / SUM(age_seasons.AB_all);
    SLG_prime = 1.0f*SUM(age_seasons.TB_prime) / SUM(age_seasons.AB_prime);
    SLG_older = 1.0f*SUM(age_seasons.TB_older) / SUM(age_seasons.AB_older);
    SLG_young = 1.0f*SUM(age_seasons.TB_young) / SUM(age_seasons.AB_young);
    --
    GENERATE
```

```
        group AS player_id,
        A_all   AS PA_all,
        PA_young AS PA_young,
        PA_prime AS PA_prime,
        PA_older AS PA_older,
        --
        MIN(age_seasons.year_id)  AS beg_year,
        MAX(age_seasons.year_id)  AS end_year,
        --
        OBP_all   + SLG_all       AS OPS_all:float,
        (PA_young >= 700 ? OBP_young + SLG_young : Null) AS OPS_young:float,
        (PA_prime >= 700 ? OBP_prime + SLG_prime : Null) AS OPS_prime:float,
        (PA_older >= 700 ? OBP_older + SLG_older : Null) AS OPS_older:float,
        --
        COUNT_STAR(age_seasons)   AS n_seasons,
        SUM(age_seasons.is_young) AS n_young,
        SUM(age_seasons.is_prime) AS n_prime,
        SUM(age_seasons.is_older) AS n_older
      ;
};

    STORE career_epochs INTO 'career_epochs';
```

We'll be using this epoch data throughout the chapter to demonstrate different ordering techniques, so don't delete the data in the `career_epochs` directory!

Sorting All Records in Total Order

Anyone who has performed a SQL `ORDER BY` query has prepared a dataset and then sorted it for human consumption. Indeed, creating metrics and then sorting records based on them is at the heart of any data analysis. For this reason, `ORDER` is a one-line command in Pig:

```
sorted_records = ORDER records BY field1;
```

For this analysis, we're only going to look at players who were able to make solid contributions over several years. We'll define this as playing for five or more seasons and 2000 or more plate appearances (enough to show statistical significance), and achieving an OPS of 0.650 (an acceptable-but-not-All-Star level) or better. This means we must `FILTER`, and then `ORDER` and finally `LIMIT` to a data size we, as humans (as opposed to Mentats), can read:

```
career_epochs = FILTER career_epochs BY
    ((PA_all >= 2000) AND (n_seasons >= 5) AND (OPS_all >= 0.650));

career_young = ORDER career_epochs BY OPS_young DESC;
top_10_young = LIMIT career_young 10;

career_prime = ORDER career_epochs BY OPS_prime DESC;
top_10_prime = LIMIT career_prime 10;
```

```
career_older = ORDER career_epochs BY OPS_older DESC;
top_10_older = LIMIT career_older 10;
```

You'll spot Ted Williams (`willite01`) as one of the top three young players, top three prime players, and top three old players (Ted Williams was pretty awesome):

```
(willite01,9788,1336,3279,5173,1939,1960,1.115402,1.0398661,1.1660492,1.103679,
    19,2,5,12)
(foxxji01,9676,1302,5306,3068,1925,1945,1.0341599,1.0045433,1.0723403,0.98065215,
    20,5,8,7)
(troskha01,5749,732,4122,895,1933,1946,0.890712,0.9756794,0.919405,0.6866708,
    11,2,7,2)
```

To put all records in a table in order, it's not sufficient to use the sorting that each reducer applies to its input. If you sorted names from a phonebook, file `part-00000` will have names that start with A, then B, up to Z; `part-00001` will also have names from A to Z; and so on. The collection has a *partial* order, but we want the *total order* that Pig's ORDER BY operation provides. In a total sort, each record in `part-00000` is in order and precedes every record in `part-00001`; records in `part-00001` are in order and precede every record in `part-00002`; and so forth. For this reason, Pig's ORDER command is necessary whenever we have more than one reducer.

Sorting by Multiple Fields

Sorting by one field is great, but sometimes our data is a little more complex than that. For instance, we might want to sort by one metric but use another as a tie-breaker. In Pig, sorting on multiple fields is as easy as adding them in order with commas. For instance, to sort by number of older seasons, breaking ties by number of prime seasons:

```
career_older = ORDER career_epochs
    BY n_older DESC, n_prime DESC;
```

Wherever reasonable, "stabilize" your sorts by adding enough columns to make the ordering unique, which will ensure the output remains the same from run to run (a best practice for testing and maintainability that we introduced in Chapter 5):

```
-- makes sure that ties are always broken the same way.
career_older = ORDER career_epochs
    BY n_older DESC, n_prime DESC, player_id ASC;
```

Sorting on an Expression (You Can't)

Which players have aged the best—made the biggest leap in performance from their prime years to their older years? You might think the following would work to determine that, but you cannot use an expression in an ORDER..BY statement:

```
by_diff_older = ORDER career_epochs BY (OPS_older-OPS_prime) DESC; -- fails!
```

Instead, generate a new field, sort on it, then project it away. Though it's cumbersome to type, there's no significant performance impact:

```
by_diff_older = FOREACH career_epochs GENERATE
    OPS_older - OPS_prime AS diff,
    player_id..;
by_diff_older = FOREACH (ORDER by_diff_older BY diff DESC, player_id) GENERATE
    player_id..;
```

If you browse through that table, you'll get a sense that current-era players seem to be overrepresented. This is just a simple whiff of a question, but more nuanced analyses (*http://bit.ly/baseball_age*) do show an increase in longevity of peak performance. Part of that is due to better training, nutrition, and medical care—and part of that is likely due to systemic abuse of performance-enhancing drugs.

Sorting Case-Insensitive Strings

Pig's ORDER command will sort capitalized words and lowercase words independently. There's no intrinsic way to sort case-insensitive; instead, just force a lowercase field to sort on. We don't have an interesting table with mixed-case records in the baseball dataset, but most UNIX-based computers come with a dictionary in the /usr/share directory tree. Here's how to sort that ignoring case:

```
dict        = LOAD '/usr/share/dict/words' AS (word:chararray);
sortable    = FOREACH dict GENERATE LOWER(word) AS l_word, *;
dict_nocase = FOREACH (ORDER sortable BY l_word, word) GENERATE word;
dict_case   = ORDER dict BY word DESC;
```

 You'll want to use Pig 'local mode' to run the preceding command:

```
pig -x local
```

Note that we sorted on l_word *and* word: this stabilizes the sort, ensuring that even though Polish and polish tie in case-insensitivity those ties will always be resolved the same way.

Dealing with nulls When Sorting

Real data has nulls (missing data), and creating sane, rational, and consistent dataflows in Pig requires careful thought about how to handle them. The default behavior of Pig is thus: when the sort field has nulls, Pig sorts them as least–most by default. That is, they will appear as the first rows for DESC order and as the last rows for ASC order. If you want to alter that behavior, you can project a dummy field having the *favoritism* or artificial sort order you want to impose. Name this column first in your

ORDER..BY clause, and you can achieve whatever *null behavior* you desire. We call this the *dummy field trick*.

For example, in the following, we sort players' careers with nulls first, and then in another way with nulls last:

```
nulls_sort_demo = FOREACH career_epochs GENERATE
    (OPS_older IS NULL ? 0 : 1) AS has_older_epoch,
    player_id..;
nulls_then_vals = FOREACH (ORDER nulls_sort_demo BY
    has_older_epoch ASC,
    OPS_all DESC,
    player_id)
    GENERATE
        player_id..;
vals_then_nulls = FOREACH (ORDER nulls_sort_demo BY
    has_older_epoch DESC,
    OPS_all DESC,
    player_id)
    GENERATE
        player_id..;
```

Floating Values to the Top or Bottom of the Sort Order

Use the *dummy field trick* any time you want to float records to the top or bottom of the sort order based on a criterion. The following example moves all players whose careers start in 1985 or later to the top, but otherwise sorts on number of older seasons:

```
post1985_vs_earlier = FOREACH career_epochs GENERATE
    (beg_year >= 1985 ? 1 : 0) AS is_1985,
    player_id..;
post1985_vs_earlier = FOREACH (ORDER post1985_vs_earlier BY
    is_1985 DESC,
    n_older DESC,
    player_id)
    GENERATE
        player_id..;
```

Note that again we add a tie-breaker, player_id, to the sort.

Pattern in use

Standard Snippet
    ORDER tbl BY mykey;.

Hello, SQL Users
    • Usually this is part of a SELECT statement; in Pig it stands alone.
    • You can't put an expression in the BY clause.

Important to Know

Pound-for-pound, unless followed by a `LIMIT` statement this is one of the most expensive operations you can perform, requiring two to three jobs and a full reduce.

Output Count

Unchanged.

Records

Unchanged.

Dataflow

Map-only on a sample of the data; map and reduce to perform the sort. In some cases, if Pig isn't confident that it will sample correctly, an extra map-only to perform the map-only/pipelinable operations before the sample.

Sorting Records Within a Group

Sorting an entire relation is powerful, but more often we want to sort data that has been partitioned by some key, as within a `GROUP..BY` operation. This operation is straightforward enough and so useful we've been applying it all this chapter, but it's time to be properly introduced and clarify a couple of points.

We can sort records within a group using `ORDER BY` within a nested `FOREACH` (which we introduced in Chapter 5). Rather than sorting all players, we'll try sorting the players on each team in a given season. Here's a snippet to list the top four players for each team season, in decreasing order by plate appearances:

```
players_PA = FOREACH bat_seasons GENERATE
    team_id,
    year_id,
    player_id,
    name_first,
    name_last,
    PA;

team_playerslist_by_PA = FOREACH (GROUP players_PA BY (team_id, year_id)) {
    players_o_1 = ORDER players_PA BY PA DESC, player_id;
    players_o   = LIMIT players_o_1 4;
    GENERATE
        group.team_id,
        group.year_id,
        players_o.(player_id, name_first, name_last, PA) AS players_o;
};
```

Ordering a group in the nested block immediately following a structural operation does not require extra operations, as Pig is able to simply specify those fields as secondary sort keys. Basically, as long as it happens first in the reduce operation it's free (though if you're nervous, look for the line Secondary sort: true in the output of EXPLAIN). Messing with a bag before the ORDER..BY causes Pig to instead sort it in-memory using quicksort, but will not cause another MapReduce job. That's good news unless some bags are so huge they challenge available RAM or CPU, which won't be subtle.

If you depend on having a certain sorting, specify it explicitly, even when you notice that a GROUP..BY or some other operation seems to leave it in that desired order. It gives a valuable signal to anyone reading your code, and a necessary defense against some future optimization deranging that order.[1]

Once sorted, the bag's order is preserved by projections, by most functions that iterate over a bag, and by the nested pipeline operations FILTER, FOREACH, and LIMIT. The return values of nested structural operations CROSS, ORDER BY, and DISTINCT do not follow the same order as their input; neither do structural functions such as CountEach (in-bag histogram) or the set operations Chapter 9 described at the end of the chapter. (Note that though their outputs are disarranged these of course don't mess with the order of their inputs: everything in Pig is immutable once created.) The following is an example of creating ordered and unordered bags within a FOREACH:

```
team_playerslist_by_PA_2 = FOREACH team_playerslist_by_PA {
    -- will not have same order, even though contents will be identical
    disordered    = DISTINCT players_o;
    -- this ORDER BY does _not_ come for free, though it's not terribly costly
    alt_order     = ORDER players_o BY player_id;
    -- these are all iterative and so will share the same order of descending PA
    still_ordered = FILTER players_o BY PA > 10;
    pa_only       = players_o.PA;
    pretty        = FOREACH players_o GENERATE
        StringConcat((chararray)PA, ':', name_first, ' ', name_last);
    GENERATE
        team_id,
        year_id,
        disordered,
        alt_order,
        still_ordered,
        pa_only,
        BagToString(pretty, '|');
};
```

---

1 That's not too hypothetical: there are cases where you could more efficiently group by binning the items directly in a map rather than sorting.

Pattern in Use

Where You'll Use It

Extracting top records from a group (see "Selecting Rows with the Top-K Values for a Field" on page 177; preceding many UDFs that depend on ordering; to make your output readable; to stabilize results.

Hello, SQL Users

This is not directly analogous to the ORDER BY part of a SELECT statement, as it is done to the inner bag; for users of Oracle and other databases, this is similar to a sort within a windowed query.

Important to Know

If it can be applied to the records coming from the mapper, it's free; verify by looking for Secondary sort: true in the output of EXPLAIN.

Output Count

Unchanged.

Records

Unchanged.

Selecting Rows with the Top-K Values for a Field

On its own, LIMIT will return the first records it finds. What if you want to *rank* the records—sort by some criteria—so you don't just return the first ones, but the *top* ones?

Use the ORDER operator before a LIMIT to guarantee this "top K" ordering. This technique also applies a clever optimization (reservoir sampling) that sharply limits the amount of data sent to the reducers.

Let's say you wanted to select the top 20 seasons by number of hits:

```
sorted_seasons = ORDER (FILTER bat_seasons BY PA > 60 AND year_id > 1900)
  BY H DESC;
top_20_seasons = LIMIT sorted_seasons 20;
```

In SQL, this would be:

```
SELECT * FROM bat_season WHERE PA > 60 AND year_id > 1900
  ORDER BY H DESC LIMIT 20;
```

There are two useful optimizations to make when the number of records you will keep (K) is much smaller than the number of records in the table (N). The first one, which Pig does for you, is to only retain the top K records at each mapper; this is a great demonstration of where a combiner is useful. After each intermediate merge/sort on the map side and the reduce side, the combiner discards all but the top K records.

Top K Within a Group

Pig's top function accepts a bag and returns a bag with its top *K* elements:

```
top_5_per_season = FOREACH (GROUP bat_seasons BY year_id) GENERATE
    group AS year_id,
    TOP(5,19,bat_seasons); -- 19th column is RBIs (start at 0)
```

You could achieve the same output with the more cumbersome:

```
top_5_per_season = FOREACH (GROUP bat_seasons BY year_id) {
    sorted = ORDER bat_seasons BY RBI DESC;
    top_5 = LIMIT sorted 5;
    ascending = ORDER top_5 BY RBI;
    GENERATE
        group AS year_id,
        ascending AS top_5;
};
```

Numbering Records in Rank Order

The RANK command prepends a ranked label for each record in a relation. You can RANK an entire record, or one of more fields in a record:

```
ranked_seasons = RANK bat_seasons;
ranked_rbi_seasons = RANK bat_seasons BY
    RBI DESC,
    H DESC,
    player_id;
ranked_hit_dense = RANK bat_seasons BY
    H DESC DENSE;
```

If you supply only the name of the table, RANK acts as a pipeline operation, introducing no extra MapReduce stage. Each split is numbered as a unit: the third line of chunk `part-00000` gets rank 2, the third line of chunk `part-00001` gets rank 2, and so on.

It's important to know that in current versions of Pig, the RANK operator sets parallelism to one, forcing all data to a single reducer:

gift_id gift	RANK	RANK gift_id	RANK gift DENSE
1 partridge	1	1	1
4a calling birds	2	4	7
4b calling birds	3	4	7
2a turtle dove	4	2	2
4d calling birds	5	4	7
5 golden rings	6	5	11
2b turtle dove	7	2	2
3a french hen	8	3	4
3b french hen	9	3	4
3c french hen	10	3	4
4c calling birds	11	4	7

Finding Records Associated with Maximum Values

Sometimes we want to find the record with the maximum value and preserve it. In Pig, we can do this with a nested ORDER BY/LIMIT inside a FOREACH. For example, for each player, find his best season by RBI:

```
-- For each season by a player, select the team they played the most games for.
-- In SQL, this is fairly clumsy (involving a self-join and then elimination of
-- ties) In Pig, we can ORDER BY within a foreach and then pluck the first
-- element of the bag.

top_stint_per_player_year = FOREACH (GROUP bat_seasons BY (player_id, year_id)) {
    sorted = ORDER bat_seasons BY RBI DESC;
    top_stint = LIMIT sorted 1;
        stints = COUNT_STAR(bat_seasons);
    GENERATE
        group.player_id,
        group.year_id,
                stints,
        FLATTEN(top_stint.(team_id, RBI)) AS (team_id, RBI);
};

DUMP @;
```

It turns out this dataset has no stints; only the most significant stint is listed in the bat_seasons data.

Shuffling a Set of Records

One common use of Hadoop is to run simulations at scale. When you are doing this, it is often handy to prepare multiple unique sorts of a single dataset—in other words, multiple *shuffles* of the same data. To shuffle a set of records, we're going to apply a unique ID pattern to generate an arbitrary key (one that is decoupled from the records' content), and then use that to order the records:

```
DEFINE Hasher datafu.pig.hash.Hasher('sip24', 'rand');

people_hashed = FOREACH people GENERATE Hasher(player_id) AS hash, *;

people_ranked = RANK people_hashed;

-- Back to the original records by skipping the first, hash field
people_shuffled = FOREACH people_ranked GENERATE $2..;

STORE people_shuffled INTO 'people_shuffled/1/';
```

You can run this script multiple times with different output paths to get different shuffles of the same data.

We use a randomized hash function UDF for each record, then number each line within the split. The important difference here is that the hash function we generated accepts a seed that we can mix in to each record. If you supply a constant to the constructor (see the documentation) then the records will be put into an effectively random order, but the same random order each time. By supplying the string `'rand'` as the argument, we tell the UDF to use a different seed on each run. What's nice about this approach is that although the ordering is different from run to run, it does not exhibit the anti-pattern of changing from task attempt to task attempt. The seed is generated once and then used everywhere. Rather than creating a new random number for each row, you use the hash to define an effectively random ordering, and the seed to choose which random ordering to apply.

Wrapping Up

In this chapter, we've learned to sort, rank, and order data. We learned how to sort entire relations by one or more fields, how to prioritize certain records when sorting, and how to deal with sorting `nulls` and mixed-case strings. We showed how to sort within a group with `TOP` and a nested `ORDER BY`. Finally, we learned how to shuffle, or sort randomly using a hash.

Our bag of tricks is getting larger and larger. Soon there will be no data-processing problem for which you can't come up with a solution for using the patterns in this book. Your applied knowledge of Pig and Hadoop will constitute a working knowledge of analytics in general, and you'll be able to arbitrarily process data at scale and implement algorithms on big data. When you become as comfortable processing big data as you are small, there are boundless opportunities to work with the ever-increasing onslaught of new, big data to create new insights, build new products, and make better decisions.

In the next chapter, we'll learn about creating unique values and relations, and working with sets. This will complete our analytic toolkit.

## CHAPTER 9

Duplicate and Unique Records

This chapter will cover the data processing of duplicate and unique records. We define duplicate records as those with the same value in the same field across two or more records. Unique records are those for which, for the value of a given field, no other records have the same value. Note that in each case we must describe which field(s) we mean when we say *unique* or *duplicate*. Pig is no different: by default, the DISTINCT command uses all fields, but we can trim fields from data relations to evaluate uniqueness in different ways, in terms of different fields.

We often find ourselves dealing with multiple records for a given concept or entity. At those times, we may want to reduce our data to just one, unique instance of each key. We'll introduce the operations UNION and DISTINCT, and various DataFu user-defined functions (UDFs) that achieve this operation.

We'll also introduce set operations among relations using Pig, and set operations between data bags using DataFu UDFs.

Handling Duplicates

It is often the case that you want to determine the unique set of values in a table or relation (i.e., you want to remove duplicate values and retain only unique records). For instance, if you were creating a set of labels that describe items in an inventory, you would only want to see each label once in the final output, which you might use for a web page's autocomplete form.

The DISTINCT operator in Pig performs this operation.

Eliminating Duplicate Records from a Table

We'll begin with a familiar example: the `park_team_years` table. It contains a row for every team for every season and every park in which the team played. Let's say we wanted to find what ballparks each team played in at least once. To find every distinct pair of team and home ballpark, we use Pig's `DISTINCT` operator:

```
many_team_park_pairs = FOREACH park_team_years GENERATE
    team_id,
    park_id;
team_park_pairs = DISTINCT many_team_park_pairs;

DUMP @;


...
(WS8,WAS05)
(WS8,WOR02)
(WS9,WAS06)
(WSN,WAS06)
(WSU,WAS03)
```

This is equivalent to the SQL statement `SELECT DISTINCT player_id, team_id from batting;`. Don't fall in the trap of using a `GROUP` statement to find distinct values:

```
dont_do_this = FOREACH (GROUP park_team_years BY (team_id, park_id)) GENERATE
    group.team_id,
    group.park_id;
```

The `DISTINCT` operation is able to use a combiner, eliminating duplicates at the mapper before shipping them to the reducer. This is a big win when there are frequent duplicates, especially if duplicates are likely to occur near each other. For example, duplicates in web logs (from refreshes, callbacks, etc.) will be sparse globally, but found often in the same logfile.

The combiner may impose a minor penalty when there are very few or very sparse duplicates. In that case, you should still use `DISTINCT`, but disable combiners with the `pig.exec.nocombiner=true` setting.

Eliminating Duplicate Records from a Group

We've seen how to eliminate duplicate records in relations, but what about within groups? For instance, what if we want to find what parks a team played in each year as a single record?

This can be done with the `DISTINCT` operator inside a nested `FOREACH`. Instead of finding every distinct team/home ballpark pair in a relation as we just did, let's find the list of distinct home ballparks for each team, having performed a `GROUP..BY` on `team_id`:

```
-- Eliminating Duplicate Records from a Group
team_park_list = FOREACH (GROUP park_team_years BY team_id) {
    parks = DISTINCT park_team_years.park_id;
    GENERATE
        group AS team_id,
        BagToString(parks, '|');
};

DUMP @;


...
(SLN,KAN03|STL03|STL05|STL07|STL09|STL10)
(SLU,STL04)
(SR1,SYR01)
(SR2,SYR02|SYR03|THR01)
(TBA,LBV01|STP01|TOK01)
```

You may be familiar with the equivalent SQL:

```
SELECT team_id, GROUP_CONCAT(DISTINCT park_id ORDER BY park_id) AS park_ids
  FROM park_team_years
  GROUP BY team_id
  ORDER BY team_id, park_id DESC
  ;
```

Eliminating All But One Duplicate Based on a Key

The DataFu DistinctBy UDF selects a single record for each key in a bag: the first record of each key it encounters.

It has the nice feature of being order-preserving: only the first record for a key is output, and all records that make it to the output follow the same relative ordering they had in the input bag.

What if we want to look at what teams a player played in, as well as where he began and ended his career? DistinctBy gives us a clean way to retrieve the distinct teams a player served in, along with the first and last year of his tenure:

```
-- Find distinct tuples based on the 0th (first) key
DEFINE DistinctByYear datafu.pig.bags.DistinctBy('1');

bat_seasons = FOREACH bat_seasons GENERATE
    player_id,
    year_id,
    team_id;

player_teams = FOREACH (GROUP bat_seasons BY player_id) {
    sorted = ORDER bat_seasons.(team_id, year_id) BY year_id;
    distinct_by_year = DistinctByYear(sorted);
    GENERATE
        group AS player_id,
        BagToString(distinct_by_year, '|');
```

```
};

dump @;

...
(zupcibo01,BOS|1991|BOS|1992|BOS|1993|CHA|1994)
(zuvelpa01,ATL|1982|ATL|1983|ATL|1984|ATL|1985|NYA|1986|NYA|1987|CLE|1988|
    CLE|1989)
(zuverge01,DET|1954|BAL|1955|BAL|1956|BAL|1957|BAL|1958)
(zwilldu01,CHA|1910|CHF|1914|CHF|1915|CHN|1916)
```

The key is specified with a string argument in the DEFINE statement, naming the positional index(es) of the key's fields as a comma-separated list.

Selecting Records with Unique (or with Duplicate) Values for a Key

The DISTINCT operation is useful when you want to eliminate duplicates based on the whole record. But to instead find only rows having a unique record for its key, or to find only rows having multiple records for its key, do a GROUP BY and then filter on the size of the resulting bag using COUNT_STAR().

On a broadcast a couple of years ago, announcer Tim McCarver paused from his regular delivery of the obvious and the officious to note that second baseman Asdrubal Cabrera "is the only player in the majors with that first name." This raises the question: How many other people in the history of baseball similarly are uniquely yclept?[1] Let's create a table for the biography site awarding players the "Asdrubal" badge if they are the only one in possession of their first name:

```
people = FOREACH people
  GENERATE name_first, name_last, player_id, beg_date, end_date;

by_first_name      = GROUP   people BY name_first;
unique_first_names = FILTER  by_first_name BY COUNT_STAR(people) == 1;
unique_players     = FOREACH unique_first_names GENERATE
    group AS name_first,
    FLATTEN(people.(name_last, player_id, beg_date, end_date));
```

which results in some interesting names:

```
...
(Kristopher,Negron,negrokr01,2012-06-07,\N)
(La Schelle,Tarver,tarvela01,1986-07-12,1986-10-05)
(Mysterious,Walker,walkemy01,1910-06-28,1915-09-29)
(Peek-A-Boo,Veach,veachpe01,1884-08-24,1890-07-25)
(Phenomenal,Smith,smithph01,1884-04-18,1891-06-15)
```

---

1 *yclept* /i ˈklept/: by the name of; called.

Our approach should be getting familiar. We group on the key (`name_first`) and eliminate all rows possessing more than one record for the key. Because there is only one element in the bag, the `FLATTEN` statement just acts to push the bag's fields up into the record itself.

There are some amazing names in this list. You might be familiar with some of the more famous players in the list: Honus Wagner, Eppa Rixey, Boog Powell, and Yogi Berra. But have you heard recounted the diamond exploits of Firpo Mayberry, Zoilo Versalles, Pi Schwert, or Bevo LeBourveau? Mul Holland, Sixto Lezcano, Welcome Gaston, and Mox McQuery are names that really should come attached to a film noir detective; the villains could choose among Mysterious Walker, The Only Nolan, or Phenomenal Smith for their name. For a good night's sleep on the couch, tell your spouse that your next child must be named for Urban Shocker, Twink Twining, Pussy Tebeau, Bris Lord, Boob Fowler, Crazy Schmit, Creepy Crespi, Cuddles Marshall, Vinegar Bend Mizell, or Buttercup Dickerson.

Set Operations

Set operations (intersection, union, set difference, etc.) are a valuable strategic formulation for the structural operations we've been learning. In terms of set operations, "Which users both clicked an ad for shirts and bought a shirt?" becomes "Find the intersection of shirt-ad-clickers set with the shirt-buyers set." "What patients either were ill but did not test positive, or tested positive but were not ill?" becomes "Find the symmetric difference of the actually ill patients and the tested-positive patients." The relational logic that powers traditional database engines is, at its core, the algebra of sets. We've actually met many of the set operations in certain alternative guises, but set operations are so important it's worth calling them out specifically.

When we say *set*, we mean an unordered collection of distinct elements. Those elements could be full records, or they could be key fields in a record—allowing us to intersect the shirt-ad-clickers and the shirt-buyers while carrying along information about the ad they clicked on and the shirt they bought.

In the next several sections, you'll learn how to combine sets in the following ways:

*Distinct union (*A ∪ B*)*
   All distinct elements that are in *A* or in *B*

*Set intersection (*A ∩ B*)*
   All distinct elements that are in *A* and also in *B*

*Set difference (*A - B*)*
   All distinct elements that are in *A* but are *not* in *B*

Symmetric difference (a ^ b)

> All distinct elements that are in *A* or in *B* but not both (put another way, it's all distinct elements that are in *A* but not *B* as well as all distinct elements that are in *B* but not *A*)

Set equality (A == B)

> Every element in *A* is also in *B*; the result of the set equality operation is a Boolean true or false, as opposed to a set as in the preceding operations

The following table may help. The rows correspond to the kind of elements that are in both *A* and *B*; *A* but not *B*; and *B* but not *A*. Under the column for each operator, only the kinds of elements marked *T* will be present in the result:

	A	B	Union A∪B	Inters A∩B	Diff a-b	Diff b-a	Sym.Diff a^b
A B	T	T	T	T	-	-	-
A -	T	-	T	-	T	-	T
- B	-	T	T	-	-	T	T

The mechanics of working with sets depends on whether the set elements are represented as records in a bag or as rows in a full table. Set operations on bags are particularly straightforward thanks to the purpose-built UDFs in the DataFu package. We perform set operations on tables using a certain COGROUP-and-FILTER combination— wordier, but no more difficult. Let's start with the patterns that implement set operations on full tables.

Set Operations on Full Tables

To demonstrate full-table set operations, we can relate the set of major U.S. cities[2] with the set of U.S. cities that have hosted a significant number (more than 50) of Major League games. To prove a point about set operations with duplicates, we will leave in the duplicates from the team cities (the Mets and Yankees both claim New York):

```
main_parks = FILTER parks BY n_games >= 50 AND country_id == 'US';

major_cities = FILTER geonames BY
    (feature_class == 'P') AND
    (feature_code matches 'PPL.*') AND
    (country_code == 'US') AND
    (population > 10000);

bball_city_names = FOREACH main_parks   GENERATE city;
major_city_names = FOREACH major_cities GENERATE name;
```

---

2 We'll take "major city" to mean one of the top 60 incorporated places in the United States or Puerto Rico.

Distinct Union

If the only contents of the tables are the set membership keys, finding the distinct union is done how it sounds: apply UNION, then DISTINCT:

```
major_or_baseball = DISTINCT (UNION bball_city_names, major_city_names);
```

Distinct Union (Alternative Method)

For all the other set operations, or when the elements are keys within a record (rather than the full record), we will use some variation on a COGROUP to generate the result:

```
combined     = COGROUP major_cities BY city, main_parks BY city;

major_or_parks   = FOREACH combined GENERATE
  group AS city,
  FLATTEN(
    FirstTupleFromBag(
      major_cities.(state, pop_2011), ((chararray)NULL,(int)NULL))),
  main_parks.park_id AS park_ids;
```

The DataFu FirstTupleFromBag UDF is immensely simplifying. Because the city value is a unique key for the major_cities table, we know that the major_cities bag has only a single element. Applying FirstTupleFromBag turns the bag-of-one-tuple into a tuple-of-two-fields, and applying FLATTEN lifts the tuple-of-two-fields into top-level fields for state and for population. When the city key has no match in the major_cities table, the second argument to FirstTupleFromBag forces those fields to have NULL values.

Our output looks like this:

```
...
(Seaford,Seaford,15294,{})
(Seaside,Seaside,33025,{})
(Seattle,Seattle,608660,{(SEA03),(SEA01),(SEA02)})
...
```

As we mentioned, there are potentially many park records for each city, and so the main_parks bag can have zero, one, or many records. Here, we keep the list of parks around as a single field.

Set Intersection

Having used COGROUP on the two datasets, set intersection means that records lie in the set intersection when neither bag is empty:

```
combined = COGROUP major_cities BY name, main_parks BY city;

major_and_parks_f = FILTER combined BY
    (COUNT_STAR(major_cities) > 0L) AND
```

```
      (COUNT_STAR(main_parks) > 0L);

   major_and_parks = FOREACH major_and_parks_f GENERATE
       group AS city,
       FLATTEN(
         FirstTupleFromBag(
           major_cities.(state, pop_2011), ((chararray)NULL,(int)NULL))),
       main_parks.park_id AS park_ids;
```

Two notes. First, we test against COUNT_STAR(bag), and not SIZE(bag) or IsEmpty(bag). Those latter two require actually materializing the bag—all the data is sent to the reducer, and no combiners can be used. Second, because COUNT_STAR returns a value of type long, it's best to do the comparison against 0L (a long) and not 0 (an int).

Set Difference

Having used COGROUP on the two datasets, set difference means that records lie in A - B when the second bag is empty, and they lie in B - A when the first bag is empty:

```
   combined = COGROUP major_cities BY name, main_parks BY city;

   major_minus_parks_f = FILTER combined BY (COUNT_STAR(main_parks) == 0L);
   major_minus_parks   = FOREACH major_minus_parks_f GENERATE
       group AS city,
       FLATTEN(
         FirstTupleFromBag(major_cities.(
           name, population), ((chararray)NULL,(int)NULL))),
       main_parks.park_id AS park_ids;

   parks_minus_major_f = FILTER combined BY (COUNT_STAR(major_cities) == 0L);
   parks_minus_major   = FOREACH parks_minus_major_f GENERATE
       group AS city,
       FLATTEN(FirstTupleFromBag(major_cities.(name, population),
         ((chararray)NULL,(int)NULL))),
       main_parks.park_id AS park_ids;

   difference = UNION major_minus_parks, parks_minus_major;
```

Symmetric Set Difference: (A–B)+(B–A)

Having used COGROUP on the two datasets, records lie in the symmetric difference when one or the other bag is empty (we don't have to test for them both being empty—there wouldn't be a row if that were the case):

```
   combined = COGROUP major_cities BY name, main_parks BY city;

   major_xor_parks_f = FILTER combined BY
       (COUNT_STAR(major_cities) == 0L) OR (COUNT_STAR(main_parks) == 0L);
```

```
major_xor_parks = FOREACH major_xor_parks_f GENERATE
    group AS city,
    FLATTEN(
      FirstTupleFromBag(
        major_cities.(name, population), ((chararray)NULL,(int)NULL))),
    main_parks.park_id AS park_ids;
```

Set Equality

Set equality indicates whether the elements of each set are identical—here, it would tell us whether the set of keys in the `major_cities` table and the set of keys in the `main_parks` table were identical.

There are several ways to determine full-table set equality, but likely the most efficient is to see whether the two sets' symmetric difference is empty. An empty symmetric difference implies that every element of A is in B, and that every element of B is in A (which is exactly what it means for two sets to be equal).

Properly testing whether a table is empty is a bit more fiddly than you'd think. To illustrate the problem, first whip up a set that should compare as equal to the `major_cities` table, run the symmetric difference stanza from above, and then test whether the table is empty:

```
major_cities_also = FOREACH major_cities GENERATE name;
major_xor_major = FILTER
    (COGROUP major_cities BY name, major_cities_also BY name)
    BY ((COUNT_STAR(major_cities) == 0L) OR
      (COUNT_STAR(major_cities_also) == 0L));

-- Does not work
major_equals_major_fail = FOREACH (GROUP major_xor_major ALL) GENERATE
    (COUNT_STAR(major_xor_major) == 0L ? 1 : 0) AS is_equal;
```

The last statement of the code block attempts to measure whether the count of records in `major_xor_major` is zero. And if the two tables were unequal, this would have worked. But `major_xor_major` is empty and so the `FOREACH` has no lines to operate on. The output file is not a 1 as you'd expect; it's an empty file.

Our integer table to the rescue! Actually, we'll use her baby brother `one_line.tsv`: it has one record, with fields uno (value 1) and zilch (value 0). Instead of a `GROUP..ALL`, do a `COGROUP` of `one_line` on a constant value 1. Because there is exactly one possible value for the group key, there will be exactly one row in the output:

```
-- Does work, using "1\t0" table
one_line = LOAD '/data/gold/one_line.tsv' AS (uno:int, zilch:int);

-- will be `1` (true)
major_equals_major = FOREACH (COGROUP one_line BY 1, major_xor_major BY 1)
    GENERATE (COUNT_STAR(major_xor_major) == 0L ? 1 : 0) AS is_equal;
```

```
-- will be `0` (false)
major_equals_parks = FOREACH (COGROUP one_line BY 1, major_xor_parks BY 1)
    GENERATE (COUNT_STAR(major_xor_parks) == 0L ? 1 : 0) AS is_equal;
```

Set Operations Within Groups

To demonstrate set operations on grouped records, let's look at the year-to-year churn of mainstay players on each team.

Other applications of the procedure we follow here would include analyzing how the top-10 products on a website change over time, or identifying sensors that report values over threshold in N consecutive hours (by using an N-way COGROUP).

Constructing a Sequence of Sets

To construct a sequence of sets, perform a self-COGROUP that collects the elements from each sequence key into one bag and the elements from the next key into another bag. Here, we group together the roster of players for a team's season (i.e., players with a particular team_id and year_id) together with the roster of players from the following season (players with the same team_id and the subsequent year_id).

Because it's a self-COGROUP, we must do a dummy projection to make new aliases (see the earlier section on self-join for details):

```
sig_seasons = FILTER bat_seasons BY
    ((year_id >= 1900) AND
    (lg_id == 'NL' OR lg_id == 'AL') AND
    (PA >= 450));

y1 = FOREACH sig_seasons GENERATE player_id, team_id, year_id;
y2 = FOREACH sig_seasons GENERATE player_id, team_id, year_id;

-- Put each team of players in context with the next year's team of players
year_to_year_players = COGROUP
    y1 BY (team_id, year_id),
    y2 BY (team_id, year_id-1)
;

-- Clear away the grouped-on fields
rosters = FOREACH year_to_year_players GENERATE
    group.team_id AS team_id,
    group.year_id AS year_id,
    y1.player_id  AS pl1,
    y2.player_id  AS pl2
;

-- The 1st & last years of existence don't have anything interesting to compare
rosters = FILTER rosters BY (COUNT_STAR(pl1) == 0L OR COUNT_STAR(pl2) == 0L);
```

Set Operations Within a Group

The content of `rosters` is a table with two key columns (team and year), and two bags (the set of players from that year and the set of players from the following year).

Applying the set operations lets us describe the evolution of the team from year to year:

```
DEFINE SetUnion datafu.pig.sets.SetUnion();
DEFINE SetIntersect datafu.pig.sets.SetIntersect();
DEFINE SetDifference datafu.pig.sets.SetDifference();

roster_changes_y2y = FOREACH rosters {
    -- Distinct Union (doesn't need pre-sorting)
    either_year  = SetUnion(pl1, pl2);
    -- The other operations require sorted bags.
    pl1_o = ORDER pl1 BY player_id;
    pl2_o = ORDER pl2 BY player_id;

    -- Set Intersection
    stayed       = SetIntersect(pl1_o, pl2_o);
    -- Set Difference
    y1_departed = SetDifference(pl1_o, pl2_o);
    y2_arrived  = SetDifference(pl2_o, pl1_o);
    -- Symmetric Difference
    non_stayed = SetUnion(y1_departed, y2_arrived);
    -- Set Equality
    is_equal     = ( (COUNT_STAR(non_stayed) == 0L) ? 1 : 0);

    GENERATE
        year_id,
        team_id,
        either_year,
        stayed,
        y1_departed,
        y2_arrived,
        non_stayed,
        is_equal;
};
```

The distinct union, A ∪ B, describes players on the roster in either year of our two-year span. We'll find it using the DataFu SetUnion UDF:

```
either_year = SetUnion(pl1, pl2);
```

All the DataFu set operations here tolerate inputs containing duplicates, and all of them return bags that contain no duplicates. They also each accept two or more bags, enabling you to track sequences longer than two adjacent elements.

As opposed to SetUnion, the other set operations require sorted inputs. That's not as big a deal as if we were operating on a full table, because a nested ORDER BY makes use of Hadoop's secondary sort. As long as the input and output bags fit efficiently in memory, these operations are efficient:

```
pl1_o = ORDER pl1 BY player_id;
pl2_o = ORDER pl2 BY player_id;
```

The set intersection A ∩ B describes the players that played in the first year and also stayed to play in the second year. We'll find the set intersection using the DataFu SetIntersect UDF:

```
stayed = SetIntersect(pl1_o, pl2_o);
```

The set difference A - B contains the elements in the first bag that are not present in the remaining bags. The first line therefore describes players that did *not* stay for the next year, and the second describes players that newly arrived in the next year. The DataFu SetDifference UDF comes in handy:

```
y1_departed = SetDifference(pl1_o, pl2_o);
y2_arrived  = SetDifference(pl2_o, pl1_o);
```

The symmetric difference contains all elements that are in one set or the other but not both. You can find this using either (A - B) union (B - A) (players who either departed after the first year or newly arrived in the next year) or ((A ∪ B) minus (A ∩ B)) (players who were present in either season but not both seasons):

```
non_stayed = SetUnion(y1_departed, y2_arrived);
```

Set equality indicates whether the elements of each set are identical—here, it selects seasons where the core set of players remained the same. There's no direct function for set equality, but you can repurpose any of the set operations to serve.

If *A* and *B* each have no duplicate records, then *A* and *B* are equal if and only if:

- size(A) == size(B) AND size(A ∪ B) == size(A)
- size(A) == size(B) AND size(A ∩ B) == size(A)
- size(A) == size(B) AND size(A - B) == 0
- size(symmetric difference(A,B)) == 0

For multiple sets of distinct elements, A, B, C... are equal if and only if all the sets and their intersection have the same size: size(intersect(A,B,C,...)) == size(A) == size(B) == size(C) == ...

If you're already calculating one of the functions, use the test that reuses its result. Otherwise, prefer the A - B test if most rows will have equal sets, and the A ∩ B test if most will not or if there are multiple sets:

```
is_equal = ( (COUNT_STAR(non_stayed) == 0L) ? 1 : 0);
```

Wrapping Up

That wraps up our chapter on duplicate and unique records. We started with simple definitions of unique and distinct, showed you how to make relations and then groups unique, explained how to find unique records, and finally took a tour of set operations for both relations and between groups. With these tools in hand, you can work with unique sets of values to create ontologies, tags, and curated datasets. You can also use the set operations to combine different datasets with complex semantics—beyond the simple joins we covered in Chapter 6.

We started with the basics: LOAD, STORE, LIMIT, and DESCRIBE. We then showed you map-only operations where you learned to FILTER, SPLIT, and FOREACH/GENERATE. Then we introduced grouping via the GROUP BY operation. Next, we showed you how to JOIN and COGROUP, and we covered sorting and introduced ORDER BY. Finally, we taught you DISTINCT and set operations.

This completes our presentation of analytic patterns in Pig. Congratulations! By now, you should have a strong toolkit of techniques fit for attacking any data-processing problem you encounter. You may use this book as a reference as you go forth and process data at scale.

Index

About the Authors

Philip Kromer is the founder and CTO of Infochimps, a data marketplace to find any dataset in the world. He holds a B.S. in physics and computer science from Cornell University, and attended graduate school in physics at the University of Texas at Austin. Philip enjoys riding his bicycle around Austin, eating homemade soup, and playing extreme *Scrabble*. The idea for Infochimps was inspired by Philip's abhorrence of redundancy and desire to make the world a happier place for data lovers of all kinds.

Russell Jurney is founder and CEO of Relato, a startup that maps the markets that make up the global economy. He is the author of another O'Reilly book, *Agile Data Science* (2013). He was previously a data scientist in product analytics at LinkedIn and a Hadoop evangelist at Hortonworks, before launching startup E8 Security as data scientist-in-residence at the Hive incubator. He lives in Pacifica, California, with Bella the data dog.

Colophon

The animal on the cover of *Big Data for Chimps* is a chimpanzee. In casual usage, the name "chimpanzee" now more often designates only the common chimpanzee, or *Pan troglodytes*, rather than the entire *Pan* genus, to which the bonobo, or *Pan paniscus*, also belongs. Chimps, as their name is often shortened, are the human species's closest living relative, having diverged from the evolutionary line along which *Homo sapiens* developed between 4 and 6 million years ago. Indeed, the remarkable sophistication of the chimpanzee, according to the standard of those same *Homo sapiens*, extends to the chimp's capacity for making and using tools, for interacting with other members of its species in complex social and political formations, and for displaying emotions, among other things. On January 31, 1961, a common chimp later named "Ham" even preceded his human counterparts into space by a full 10 weeks.

Chimpanzees can associate in stable groups of up to 100, a number that comprises smaller groups of a handful or more that may separate from the main group for periods of time. Male chimps may hunt together, and the distribution of meat from such expeditions may be used to establish and maintain social alliances. Well-documented accounts of sustained aggression between groups of chimpanzees have made them less attractive analogs for human potential, in recent years, than the chimp's more promiscuous, frugivorous, and possibly more matriarchal bonobo cousins.

Many of the animals on O'Reilly covers are endangered; all of them are important to the world. To learn more about how you can help, go to *animals.oreilly.com*.

The cover image is from Lydekker's *Royal Natural History*. The cover fonts are URW Typewriter and Guardian Sans. The text font is Adobe Minion Pro; the heading font is Adobe Myriad Condensed; and the code font is Dalton Maag's Ubuntu Mono.

Have it your way.

Get even more for your money.

Join the O'Reilly Community, and register the O'Reilly books you own. It's free, and you'll get:

- $4.99 ebook upgrade offer
- 40% upgrade offer on O'Reilly print books
- Membership discounts on books and events
- Free lifetime updates to ebooks and videos
- Multiple ebook formats, DRM FREE
- Participation in the O'Reilly community
- Newsletters
- Account management
- 100% Satisfaction Guarantee

Signing up is easy:

1. Go to: oreilly.com/go/register
2. Create an O'Reilly login.
3. Provide your address.
4. Register your books.

Note: English-language books only

To order books online:
oreilly.com/store

For questions about products or an order:
orders@oreilly.com

To sign up to get topic-specific email announcements and/or news about upcoming books, conferences, special offers, and new technologies:
elists@oreilly.com

For technical questions about book content:
booktech@oreilly.com

To submit new book proposals to our editors:
proposals@oreilly.com

O'Reilly books are available in multiple DRM-free ebook formats. For more information:
oreilly.com/ebooks

O'REILLY®

CPSIA information can be obtained at www.ICGtesting.com
Printed in the USA
BVOW07s0602071015

421185BV00004B/7/P